THE DEMANDS OF LIBERAL EDUCATION

The Demands of Liberal Education

MEIRA LEVINSON

OXFORD

UNIVERSITY PRESS

OXFORD
UNIVERSITY PRESS

Great Clarendon Street, Oxford ox2 6DP

Oxford University Press is a department of the University of Oxford.
It furthers the University's objective of excellence in research, scholarship,
and education by publishing worldwide in

Oxford New York

Athens Auckland Bangkok Bogotá Buenos Aires Calcutta
Cape Town Chennai Dar es Salaam Delhi Florence Hong Kong Istanbul
Karachi Kuala Lumpur Madrid Melbourne Mexico City Mumbai
Nairobi Paris São Paulo Singapore Taipei Tokyo Toronto Warsaw

and associated companies in Berlin Ibadan

Oxford is a registered trade mark of Oxford University Press
in the UK and in certain other countries

Published in the United States
by Oxford University Press Inc., New York

British Library Cataloguing in Publication Data

Data available

Library of Congress Cataloging in Publication Data
Levinson, Meira.
The demands of liberal education/Meira Levinson.
Includes bibliographical references (p.) and index.
1. Citizenship—Study and teaching. 2. Liberalism. 3. Autonomy
(Psychology). 4. Education—Aims and objectives. 5. Education and
state. I. title.
LC1091.L38 1999 370.11'2—dc21 99–24528

ISBN 0–19–829544–8

1 3 5 7 9 10 8 6 4 2

Typeset by
Cambrian Typesetters, Frimley, Surrey
Printed in Great Britain
on acid-free paper by
Bookcraft Limited,
Midsomer Norton, Somerset

To my parents, Cynthia and Sanford Levinson,
and in memory of Oded Shur,
all liberal teachers in the truest sense

ACKNOWLEDGEMENTS

A great number of people and institutions have helped me with this book. It is my pleasure to thank them here.

I start with Nuffield College, Oxford, which provided unsurpassed academic, financial, and social support for three crucial years. I thank the College for the Funded Studentship in Politics, as well as for the private office space that should be the right of all graduate students everywhere. Within Nuffield, the Political Theory Workshop proved a challenging testing ground for early drafts of Chapters 1, 2, and 3. Many thanks especially to Marc Stears, Stuart White, Christopher Lake, Daniel Attas, Selina Chen, Robert van der Veen, and Cécile Fabre, as well as the other members of the Workshop, for their comments and criticisms. Marc Stears and Stuart White deserve particular thanks for hashing out many of the ideas in this book virtually *ad nauseum*; I hope they recognize in these pages the influence they have had, and will forgive me for those sections where I have unwisely ignored their advice. I also wish to thank Byron Shafer, John Darwin, Randall Hansen, Kurt Strovink, Antonia Taddei, Heather Bell, and Matthew Clayton for productive conversations about individual chapters or ideas.

Three people at Nuffield were especially influential in the development of this book. Andrew Hurrell provided invaluable advice about Chapters 1–4 and helped to shape my thinking about education in general. Robert Bickers was astoundingly generous with his time and friendship, serving as a sounding board for initial ideas, reading and commenting on each chapter as it was written, and in some cases overseeing the transformation of chapters into final drafts and conference presentations. David Miller earns my enduring gratitude for being an ideal D.Phil. supervisor, as well as now a good friend. Depending on my progress, he was at different times cajoling, firm, encouraging, stern, indulgent, pragmatic, sympathetic—and always supportive. I never doubted that he expected me to write something worthwhile, even when I didn't feel up to the task. He was also a thoughtful and extremely careful critic; this book would be far poorer without his insights.

Outside of Nuffield, my critics and interlocutors have been similarly numerous. Jerry Cohen, Terry McLaughlin, Tamar Barkay, Daniel

viii   *Acknowledgements*

Markovits, Stephen Macedo, Eamonn Callan, Harry Brighouse, Jim Sleeper, Jill Rothenberg, and two anonymous reviewers all read the entire manuscript at least once, and in some cases multiple times. Their comments and criticisms were unfailingly helpful. To thank each one properly here would require an Acknowledgements section longer than the Introduction; I hope simply that they can see their influence throughout the book. David Lyons also read the manuscript and helpfully introduced me to the publishing world. Dominic Byatt has been a thoughtful and responsive editor, and Amanda Watkins, his assistant editor has been unfailingly efficient and helpful. I look forward to continuing to work with both of them. Amy Gutmann, Marnie Hughes-Warrington, Geraint Perry, Kevin Stack, Ajume Hassan Wingo, John White, Patricia White, Andrew Weale, and three anonymous reviewers for the *British Journal of Political Science* provided helpful discussions of or comments on drafts of earlier chapters of this book. I am grateful to Cambridge University Press for permission to reprint material from 'Liberalism versus Democracy? Schooling Private Citizens in the Public Square', *British Journal of Political Science*, 27, (1997): 333-60, which appears here in revised form as Chapter 4. Many thanks to the editors of the *Oxford Review of Education*, as well, for permission to reprint sections of 'Liberalism, Pluralism, and Political Education: Paradox or Paradigm?' *Oxford Review of Education*, 25/1 & 2 (March–June 1999), 39–58. Jan Anderson, librarian for the Texas Education Agency, flooded me with information on educational policy whenever I asked—including while the library was in the midst of moving. The Nuffield College Library provided further crucial sources. In addition, I benefited from having the opportunity to present my work in seminars and conferences at the American Political Science Association Annual Meeting, Manchester University, Cambridge University, the University of London, Wolfson College (Oxford), All Souls College, University College (Oxford), the Political Studies Association Annual Meeting, ECPR Joint Sessions of Workshops, and the Annual Conference of the Philosophy of Education Society of Great Britain (PESGB). The PESGB also provided ongoing support for my induction into the philosophy of education, as well as providing financial support for my travel to conferences. I am also grateful to the Overseas Research Scheme and the Henry Fellowship for substantial financial support while I was working on this manuscript. Given all the help that I have received, it should go without saying that I alone am culpable for the errors that remain.

For the past three years, I have taught in the Atlanta Public Schools in Atlanta, Georgia. I would like to thank my principal, Alicia Oden, and the rest of the faculty and staff at Walden Middle School for keeping me focused on the more practical aspects of education provision even while I was trying to revise this book. Shirley Smith has been especially supportive of my efforts to finish this book while teaching. Although my students certainly did not help me complete this book in a timely manner, they did continually remind me about why children's education is so important, and they continue to give a fulfilling purpose to both my writing and my teaching.

Finally, I owe an immeasurable debt of gratitude to four people who have been in my life for a long time, and who have shaped my thinking beyond compare. I have laughed with my parents, Cynthia and Sanford Levinson, many times about the extent to which my work represents the marriage of their two vocations, educational planning and legal theory. It is possible that I ended up adopting their interests so strongly because I have never been sufficiently rebellious—an irony, as Jim Sleeper has pointed out, that becomes especially apparent in Chapter 2. I suspect, however, that I have done so far more because of the incomparable example they have set of the value of living one's life via learning, teaching, helping others, and taking responsibility for reflecting on one's beliefs and for realizing one's principles. My parents pursue these ideals through different means but both have guided me unswervingly and with love, for which I am profoundly grateful. Both of my parents have also read every word of this book—often multiple times in multiple drafts—as well as supported its completion in many other ways essential for my intellectual, psychological, and physical well-being. Without their searching comments and unwavering support this would be a profoundly different and far worse book. I am pleased to be able to dedicate this book to them.

I further delight in following family tradition by acknowledging my sister, Rachel Levinson, as an altogether splendid human being. She has always been ready with words of encouragement when I have been frustrated by teaching or writing or both, and she continues to model the autonomous yet grounded life to which I think we should all aspire. I look forward to acknowledging Rachel and her husband, Aaron Campbell, again in the years to come.

Last but certainly not least, my husband, Marc Lipsitch, has had to live with me and this book more closely than anyone else, and has provided encouragement and help at every turn. Although he has never read the manuscript straight through (I think because of fear of what he might find), his influence can be felt in every chapter, and especially on every page of the Introduction. The fact that this book exists at all is also in large part due to his ongoing support. In deference to his taste for short acknowledgements, I will say no more than that he has been central to making my time in New Haven, Oxford, and Atlanta a joy; I look forward to many more years of joy with him to come.

M. L. L.

CONTENTS

Introduction

'The more control a state acquires and exercises over education, the greater the potential for tyranny in that state.'

'Respecting diversity in a liberal society in part means valuing parents' freedom to educate their children as they wish.'

'Schools provide a service or product to parent and student consumers. As with any business, therefore, schools should be responsive to their consumers' preferences and directly accountable to them.'

These statements all have some intuitive appeal. They all exercise substantial sway over education policy and provision in many countries around the world: the United States and Great Britain in particular; Canada, the Netherlands, Denmark, Australia, and New Zealand (among other countries) to a lesser but still significant extent. They are so influential, in part, because they apparently stem from a commitment to individual liberty, which is one of the foundational commitments that hold together each of the above countries and their citizens. Whether consciously or not, citizens of liberal states (such as those mentioned above) favor educational policies that seem to protect individual liberty.

From the perspective of liberalism, however, the above statements are wrong. Furthermore, they are wrong in ways that are harmful to the maintenance of liberty itself, and thus also to the maintenance of liberal states. Although these claims do support some individuals' liberty— namely, parents' liberty to control their children's education—they do not value individual liberty as such. Instead, they disvalue the liberty of most future citizens: namely, the liberty of all children and of the adults they will grow into. As a result, as I shall argue in this book, they are illiberal. Although these claims may appeal to our common sense as educators, political theorists, policy makers, policy analysts, philosophers, parents, and/or citizens, none of these common-sense claims holds up under careful scrutiny. Each derives from some combination of unexamined cultural and historical biases, fuzzy thinking, careless policy analysis, political theorizing that ignores children, and/or indifference to the influence of certain forms of political, educational, and familial structures on children's development. This book aims to counter these sources of 'common sense', and to substitute in their place a carefully reasoned, theoretically and empirically sensitive liberal political policy of children's education provision.

Such a book is necessary for a number of reasons. To begin with, education theory, policy, and praxis are all undergoing increasing scrutiny and criticism in North America, Western Europe, Australia, and New Zealand. Schools and educators are being challenged to justify their aims and effectiveness, to reorient to a market-driven conception of education, to address and implement new or revised national curricula, to set higher standards, to reconceive in some cases the relationship between state and private schools, and so forth. Insofar as the states in which these debates are taking place are (or believe themselves to be) liberal democracies, citizens' conceptions of the nature and practice of liberalism play an important role in shaping the political and educational debate. It is thus important that both liberalism itself and liberalism's relationship to education be understood correctly.

The statements that opened this introduction exemplify how liberal politics currently influence education reform. Consider the third statement: 'Schools provide a service or product to parent and student consumers. As with any business, therefore, schools should be responsive to their consumers' preferences and directly accountable to them.' As I mentioned above, this claim makes some intuitive sense. It also exercises enormous influence over education reform initiatives in the United States, Britain, and elsewhere. State schools are being actively encouraged, if not forced, to market themselves to parents, students, business leaders, and other community members in order to get sufficient 'business' to stay open. Schools must develop mission statements and publish informational brochures, submit to widely publicized rankings (league tables in the UK; newspaper reports which fashion themselves as the *Consumer Reports* of the education business in the US), and in some cases even advertise on billboards in order to attract students and maintain funding. The provision of education is thus becoming increasingly market-oriented. This growing influence of market-based ideas in education results, I suggest, from the growing importance of the market in liberal thought more generally. In many countries, especially (again) the United States and Britain, the association between liberalism and capitalism has been embraced with renewed vigor in recent years. The fall of the Iron Curtain, for example, has generally been taken to symbolize the triumph of free markets over centralized planning, rather than the triumph of political freedom over political repression. Liberalism's ascendancy is thus also identified with market values rather than political or social values. Likewise, many liberal freedoms and institutions are defended these days on economic grounds ('good for business') rather than on civic or social grounds. As liberal politics goes, I suggest, so goes education reform. As a result of liberalism's new market–oriented status, schools have also been remade in a capitalist, market–oriented image.

A second example of the influence of liberal political reform on education can be found in the relatively recent politics of diversity and multiculturalism. Diversity politics have both challenged and taken root within liberal thought and practice in the past two decades. As a result, substantial changes have taken place in liberal democracies. Protection of, support for, and accommodation of diversity and pluralism have overshadowed old goals of assimilation; the assertion and realization of sectarian identities (racial, religious, ethnic, socio–economic, gendered, or otherwise) play an ever–increasing role in civic and social discourse. Again as a result, citizens' conceptions about who should provide what kind of education to whose children have taken on increasingly diversity–oriented and sectarian overtones. For instance, although local control over schools has always been substantial in America, state and federal control were also acknowledged to have their place. Now, more and more parents are coming to see *any* state-sponsored regulation over education as discredited because of the newly elevated demands of pluralism and diversity. This is true even among parents who self-consciously reject 'liberalism' or 'liberal ideology' as such: for example, some homeschoolers and Afrocentrists. In liberal states, even illiberal citizens base their claims about education on liberal values.

These two examples demonstrate that citizens (parents, academics, policy makers, voters, etc.) are already deciding education policy on the basis of their beliefs about liberal principles. Because they (and we) are relying on 'common sense' intuitions about liberalism rather than on a coherent, well-articulated theory of liberal education provision, however, many of the policies that are being established and implemented (such as the ones described above) are actually illiberal. It is therefore essential to develop a carefully conceived, coherent liberal political theory of children's education. And although a few political theorists and philosophers of education have written thoughtfully about liberalism and education in recent years,[1] there has been no full, book–length treatment that goes beyond civic education into the broader range of questions about both the theoretical and the practical relationship between liberalism and education. There is thus an urgent practical need to examine and explain how liberal principles should be applied to educational practice.

There are also strong theoretical reasons to examine the interplay between liberal political theory and education. To begin with, contrary to the assertions made by the philosopher of education R. S. Peters,[2] the aims of education are not internal to or given by the concept of 'education' itself. In other words, to know that one's aim is 'to educate' is not enough to give purpose to one's actions; rather, one must also know *to what end(s)* one is educating, and these ends cannot be given by the concept of education itself. Thus, education can function as a substantive, directed practice only if it is embedded within a broader practice or set of goals—one such set of goals being the liberal political principles that already (more or less) guide (more or less) liberal states. Second, within liberal states, liberal political theory is properly applied not only to the aims but also to the structure and administration of educational institutions. This is because all such decisions have political aspects. For example, independent of education's particular curricular aims, many egalitarian political theories would forbid the existence of elite private schools on grounds of equality of opportunity or resources. Libertarians, on the other hand, presumably would not forbid such disparities between elite private and common state schools; if anything, libertarians view state schools themselves as illegitimate. Opposing political theories and principles would also resolve in very different ways questions about optimal distribution of scarce educational resources, school desegregation measures, school choice, and the ideal composition and power of school governing bodies. Since political principles are inevitably relevant to determining the aims, structure, and administration of education provision, the politics of education provision in a liberal state should be guided by liberal principles.

Just as liberal political theory has important ramifications for the aims, structure, and content of education, so education has important ramifications for liberalism in both theory and practice. Liberal theory requires that adult citizens have a wide range of capacities and opportunities, many of which can be achieved primarily by means of education during childhood. While there is disagreement about exactly which abilities citizens should possess—examples include the capacity for democratic citizenship (embraced most explicitly by John Rawls and almost all liberals), the capacity for respecting people who are very different from oneself (embraced by many liberal theorists but rejected by some[3]), and the capacity for autonomy (embraced by Joseph Raz and a few other theorists)—all contemporary liberal theories require that adults have some opportunities and capacities provided for by education. Thus, liberals must integrate a conception of education into their political theory in order to ensure that liberal educational aims can be achieved in a manner that is theoretically consonant with liberal political aims as a whole. Furthermore, on an even more practical level, citizens' possession and exhibition of these capacities are essential to the very preservation of the liberal state. As I will discuss in Chapters 3 and 4, a liberal state can thrive (indeed, can survive) only if a large portion of its members are tolerant of each other, value the preservation of liberal freedoms, and exhibit liberal democratic civic virtues. Individuals most reliably develop these characteristics, I will argue throughout the book, by participating as children in a particular system of state-regulated education. As a result, liberal institutions can be maintained and liberal goals achieved in practice only if certain defined educational aims and practices can be achieved. In this respect, education is not simply one more public policy issue (like health care or environmentalism) to which to apply liberal principles. Rather, education lies at the heart of the liberal project; it is upon the realization of liberal educational goals that the success of liberalism itself depends.

There are thus two reasons that it is important for liberalism to address head-on the problem of educating future citizens. First, insofar as liberal political principles have implications for how education should be structured and what its aims should be, these implications should be spelled out. From a liberal perspective, modern education policy should be led by liberal theory, not vice versa. Thus, liberals should be deeply engaged in asking (and answering) such questions as: What should the aim(s) of education be? Do parents have the right to determine the content of their children's education? Is liberal education coterminous with education in civic virtues? Or finally, is there a liberal case for or against re-establishing a market in education? Second, it is important for liberals to come to terms with the constraints that education can impose on the achievement of liberal aims. Liberalism must become aware of and responsive to the pedagogical and political boundaries within which the liberal educational project can operate, for they have implications for liberalism's success in general. As I will discuss in the following chapters, children's education reveals a number of internal tensions within liberalism that are either hidden or seemingly irrelevant in relation to adults. Although liberal theory has a fairly clear vision of the relationship between the state and the adult individual (which I address in Chapter 1), this vision will be thrown into question when we consider in greater depth the relation between the state and the *formation* of the individual. It is therefore important to develop a theory of contemporary liberal education, both to guide liberal thinkers and citizens in their responses to various educational proposals (such as school choice or parent control), and to guide the future development of liberal theory so that it better takes into account educational issues and concerns.

Having sketched out in a preliminary fashion the reasons that a liberal theory of education is needed, I must now make clear exactly the ways in which this book does and does not satisfy this need: i.e., I must delineate the scope and aims of this book. As I said above, my aim is to develop a theory of children's education provision in line with contemporary liberal political principles—or in other words, to apply contemporary liberal political theory

to the problem of determining the aims, content, and institutional structures of children's education. All of these terms require definition and clari-
fication.

To begin with, my aim is not to justify liberalism itself. Although I
discuss various justifications for liberal principles and policies in Chapter
1, and settle on the value of autonomy as motivating liberal concerns, I do
not try to argue that all readers should be liberals, or that all readers value
autonomy in the way that liberalism does. Contemporary liberalism does
see its own legitimacy as depending upon the unanimous consent of potential citizens, usually under a variety of hypothetical conditions. I thus must
(and do) argue that when understood in a certain way, state valuation of
autonomy will draw the greatest possible number and range of people to
affirm liberal principles and institutions. I do not believe or argue, however,
that *all* people will affirm liberal principles based on the value of autonomy.
Nor do I present any independent argument for the value of autonomy.
Rather, I simply argue that liberal principles depend for their justification
on an appeal to the value of individual autonomy, and that this justification
must also therefore guide the development of a liberal theory of education.
This project takes liberalism's value or significance as a given, and works to
construct and justify a theory of education within that context. It does not
try to provide an independent justification for liberal theory or principles.

In order to take liberalism as a given, I must clarify what I take 'liberalism' itself to refer to. When I use the terms 'liberalism', 'contemporary
liberalism', or 'contemporary liberal theory', I mean to refer to Anglo-
American liberal thought of the past 150, and especially the past thirty,
years. I emphasize the past three decades because it was in 1971 that John
Rawls published his magisterial *A Theory of Justice* and fundamentally
transformed the face of subsequent political theory, especially liberal political theory. I am most interested in (and inspired by) liberal thought that
follows this transformation. In practice, this means that the liberalism I
describe has a more 'human' face than some readers might expect.
Liberalism is not solely about rights, according to this analysis; it is also
about obligations, and about ensuring that as many individuals as possible
have the ability to determine and make use of the freedoms provided them
by a liberal state. To place this in historical context, I focus upon the tradition of liberal thought represented by J. S. Mill, Rawls, and Joseph Raz,
rather than that of Thomas Hobbes, F. A. Hayek, or Herbert Spencer.
Chapter 1 further clarifies the characteristics of contemporary liberalism
that I believe to be significant and definitive of contemporary liberal
thought.

One common characteristic of most contemporary liberal theories is that
they are limited to modern, Western, industrialized democracies. Liberals

are often wary of 'imposing' liberalism on illiberal countries, and especially upon cultures which exhibit traditional but non-tyrannical ways of life. For the purposes of this book, I remain agnostic about whether liberalism's application *should* be limited in this way, but I do follow precedent in limiting my own theory to the context of modern, industrialized, democratic countries which are predominantly, although imperfectly, liberal. This is not to say that I exempt illiberal *cultures* within the liberal state from the conclusions of my book. I explain in Chapters 2, 3, and 4 why children who are raised in illiberal cultures within liberal states must none the less be subject to a liberal education. But I do not address the application of these principles to non-liberal, non-industrialized, or anti-democratic countries.

Next, by 'children', I mean people who are still legally minors—people, in other words, who are under 16 or 18 years old. Insofar as this book is about the application of liberal theory to children's education in particular, therefore, it has nothing to say about higher education. Despite the undeniable importance of political questions about university-level education, technical training programs, and adult education, I do not address them here.

One might ask, of course, why I focus on schooling at all. There is a profound difference between *education* in general and *schooling* in particular, in that the latter represents only one small part of the former. Children learn from their parents, their relatives, their peers, television, other forms of mass media, their coaches, billboards, magazine advertisements, their experiences of caring for a pet; in other words, they learn from and are educated by life. Thus, a book that aims at clarifying the relationship between liberal principles and children's education must justify focusing on formal education's (i.e. schooling's) role in particular. I do this in Chapter 2, in which I argue that the institutional and particularly communal structure of a school is ideally suited to realizing liberalism's goals for and obligations toward children: namely, to help them develop their capacities for autonomy. Thus in this book, the institution of the school is *derived from* the liberal political theory developed in Chapters 1 and 2, rather than being taken as a given, or as being tantamount to the process of education itself. When I use the term 'education' in this book, therefore, I will primarily mean to refer to formal schooling, because I will have shown that a liberal theory of children's education requires the construction of liberal schools. But I also acknowledge the important role of informal education, such as that mediated by families, peers, communities, and cultures, at various points in Chapters 2, 3, and 5. Ultimately, therefore, I attempt a balancing act in this book. Informal and non-school-based education play a significant role in my theory. But I argue even more strongly that to apply contemporary liberal political theory to the problem of determining the

aims, content, and institutional structures of children's education is in
large part to apply liberal political theory to the problem of determining the
aims, content, and structures of children's schooling. This is what I try to
accomplish in this book.

As I mentioned above, although there are a number of articles (and a few
good books) about liberal *civic* education, there is a tremendous gap in the
literature regarding the relationship between contemporary liberal political
theory and education policy more generally. This is less true for the
concept of democratic education. In addition to John Dewey's classic
Democracy and Education and Amy Gutmann's influential *Democratic
Education*, other books include James Tarrant's *Democracy and Education*
and David Steiner's *Rethinking Democratic Education*.[4] These works are
significant in their own right, but they cannot and should not be read as
proxies for works on liberal education. Just as democratic and liberal theory
are not the same, although they are related, neither are democratic and
liberal education equivalent enterprises. Therefore, as I discuss at points in
Chapters 4 and 5, a theory of democratic education, cannot and should not
stand in for a theory of liberal education.

Finally, one can construct only so much in a single work, especially if
one tries seriously, as I do, to integrate empirical data into one's educational
and liberal theory. As I argued above, liberal theory must be responsive to
practical, empirical educational concerns and outcomes if it is to be
tenable—just as educational theory and goals must be responsive to practical political concerns and outcomes. In order to construct an intelligent
conception of liberal education, therefore, it is necessary to ground philosophical claims about education's ideal aims, distributions of control, and
institutional structures within a practical framework of political and educational research. In this book, I focus on questions concerning the aims of
liberal education, the structure of liberal education provision, levels of
parent involvement, and the character of the school as a community, rather
than on the more microscopic level of teaching techniques, classroom practice, the administrative structure of a particular school, and so forth. I take
this approach because it makes sense to figure out the broad structures of
education provision before one addresses the specific techniques and practices that should be used within the school itself. I intend that the book
itself will justify these observations.

1

Autonomy and the foundations of contemporary liberalism

The first task in developing a theory of liberal education is to clarify the meaning of liberalism itself. What distinguishes liberalism from other political theories? What are the justifications upon which liberal principles rest? What characteristics of the individual does the liberal state see as important and worthy of encouragement? Finally, can one give a coherent account of the principle(s) that motivate both liberal theory and liberal policy? Chapter 1 addresses these questions.

1.1 LIBERALISM'S THREE COMMITMENTS

I suggest that contemporary liberal theory has three constitutive elements. These are:

(A) An acceptance—and more rarely, an embracing—of the fact of deep and irremediable pluralism in modern society. People subscribe to a huge range of values, sources of identity, and conceptions of the good that often conflict with each other and are as often incommensurable. Few if any values are shared by all members of a society. Furthermore, because of the incommensurability of value and the enormous range of 'reasonable' ways of life, there is no reason to think that individuals will come to settle on a shared conception of value in the future. I shall call this condition the *fact of pluralism*.

(B) A concern that there exist a (theoretical) public legitimation process for the establishment of the state and/or the principles of justice by which the state operates. This legitimation process must display the following five characteristics: it must be (1) a public or transparent process in which (2) all (potential) citizens participate (3) equally and (4) freely (i.e. without fear of coercion or intimidation) in order to generate a set of foundational principles and basic institutional structures that are (in theory) (5) agreeable to all. I will term these the *legitimation conditions*, and this process the *legitimation process* or *project*.

(C) A judgement that the outcome of the legitimation project entails constitutional democracy accompanied by a broad range of specified individual liberties and accompanying governmental duties. I will refer to these as the *substantive liberal institutions*.

Let me expand on each in turn. First, I suggest that (A), the fact of pluralism, provides the context in which (B) and (C) are to be realized or met. The fact of pluralism has enormous implications for what principles and institutional structures will be agreeable to all potential citizens of a state. Principles that appeal to non-pluralistic values, or that reject the existence of pluralism entirely, are unlikely to gain widespread support from individuals in a position of deliberative equality and freedom. The same is true for the kinds of reasons that individuals can offer during the legitimation process for adopting one principle of justice over another. Arguments such as 'The Bible tells us that we must . . .' do not sufficiently respond to the fact of pluralism, because only believers can take them seriously as reasons for action—although, as I will suggest below, to *prevent* people from using biblically based arguments may be equally non-responsive to pluralism, since some people believe that the Bible provides the *only* fundamental moral reasons for action.

Applying the fact of pluralism to the legitimation project, then, (B) is meant to provide a principled means through which a state can be justified given (A). Liberals intend that (B), the legitimation project, will provide the means for a plural citizenry to establish and live within a principle-governed state whose legitimacy all individuals acknowledge. This is the reason that liberals insist that the principles upon which the state is founded must be justified by good reasons that are publicly acknowledged and in theory agreeable to all citizens of the state, given a set of conditions that always includes deliberative equality and the acknowledgement of irremediable pluralism. By establishing these hypothetical procedural conditions, liberals hope to achieve the development of public political principles to which all citizens would knowledgeably and freely offer their allegiance, given the fact of pluralism.

It is an admirable effort. A state whose existence depends on a 'noble lie' (such as Plato's Kalipolis), for example, would be immediately rejected by (B) because its structure and institutions depend on reasons that not all citizens could (or would be permitted to) understand. It violates the conditions of both publicity and equal participation. Likewise, a state whose existence depends on the subjugation of one group by another would be illegitimate, because the subjugated individuals could reasonably object to its governing principles. Neither deliberative equality nor deliberative freedom is satisfied by an enslaving state. Finally, a state founded on principles that some citizens accept only because they are fearful of recriminations by others is also illegitimate, as these principles, too, violate the terms of deliberative equality and freedom.

The conditions specified by (B) are stronger, then, than they might first appear. Liberal theories are constrained to a limited number of patterns they can offer for the legitimation process. As a means of responding to these requirements, liberalism often surfaces as a contractarian theory. John Locke may be credited as the 'founding father' of this liberal contractarian approach:[1] 'Men being, as has been said, by nature all free, equal, and independent, no one can be put out of this estate [of natural equality and freedom] and subjected to the political power of another without his own consent, which is done by agreeing with other men, to join and unite into a community.'[2] We can see here Locke's explicit fulfillment of four of the legitimacy conditions as he insists on non-coercive, equal participation leading to unanimous agreement. He also fulfills the fifth condition, that of publicity, by declaring that individuals can be considered subjects of the state only if they have 'actually entered into it by positive engagement and express promise and compact'.[3] While the efficacy and possibility of this approach might trouble some modern-day liberals,[4] they often seem to agree with Locke that as an ideal 'this is that, and that only, which did or could give beginning to any lawful government in the world'.[5]

This is not to say that contractarianism is the only way to satisfy the liberal legitimation conditions. In *Social Justice in the Liberal State*, Bruce Ackerman shies away from the contractual form per se, but he does similarly embrace the liberal focus on equal, public deliberation by individuals as the primary condition of state legitimacy. He imagines a hypothetical conversation among all potential citizens, in which the participants may put forth any and all claims that fulfill three constraining principles: rationality, consistency within the claims of each speaker, and neutrality, insofar as no one can assert one person's or group's intrinsic superiority over (or inferiority to) another.[6] A legitimate state is one founded on those principles that would be adopted in such a conversation.[7] This approach does avoid some of the Lockean pitfalls of non-hypothetical contractualism, in that it is the principles that result from the hypothetical conversation that are important, not the explicit agreement of present-day individuals. In this sense, Ackerman's solution recommends itself over Locke's (although some of Ackerman's ideas are far more loony otherwise!). But notwithstanding this difference, the process for grounding the liberal state is fairly much the same as for Locke. The same can be said of Ronald Dworkin. While he takes both a less science-fictional approach to the problem than Ackerman and a less contractarian approach than Locke, Dworkin grounds liberalism on an ideal of public equality in which any inequalities would have to be strongly and convincingly publicly justified to the world at large.[8] I suggest that other contemporary liberal theorists such as William Galston and David Gauthier also integrate the five legitimation conditions into their own theories of liberal justification.[9]

It is John Rawls, however, who takes the liberal legitimation project to its most fully developed contractarian conclusion,[10] and in order to understand his solution to the problem we must turn to the third condition of liberalism I suggested above. The institutional conditions specified by (C) are basically a touchstone that informs us when the legitimation process, (B), has succeeded—succeeded both in terms of generating a practical conclusion and in terms of that conclusion's remaining liberal. As I said above, it constitutes a judgement that the outcome of (A) plus (B) entails constitutional democracy accompanied by a broad range of individual liberties and governmental duties. In more detail, these liberties include freedom of speech; freedom of religion, association, and conscience; freedom to own a certain amount of private property; freedom over one's own body; freedom from undue coercion by the state or by others; and far more vaguely, freedom to do anything that does not violate some version of a Millian harm principle.[11] In addition to being obligated to provide these various liberties (which obligation is frequently interpreted, especially in modern political theory, to be a positive requirement for the state to provide citizens the means to exercise their liberties, as opposed to the state's simply safeguarding negative liberties), the state is also usually under an obligation in the liberal ideal to remain neutral among (or at the least equally tolerant of) citizens' competing conceptions of the good.[12] This ideal derives from the fact of pluralism combined with the final condition of (B), that all participants in the legitimation process agree on the principles governing the state and be shown equal respect. In combination with the legitimation conditions, these are the characteristics of a state (or a theory) that I argue are necessary for such a state's or theory's being liberal.

It might be thought unnecessary or even misleading to elaborate on the institutional and political outcomes of (B) as an equally important characteristic of liberal doctrine. Such an enumeration, it might be charged, implies that (C) may be achieved or judged independent of (B), whereas Rawls, Ackerman, and Dworkin (to continue with three emblematic contemporary liberals) all claim that if the procedure and conditions within (B) are just, the outcome will automatically be just, too. One need not look at the substance of the outcome itself, our critic would argue; one need only adhere to the original legitimation procedure. This argument echoes Rawls' notion of 'pure procedural justice', which 'obtains when there is no independent criterion for the right result: instead there is a correct or fair procedure such that the outcome is likewise correct or fair, *whatever it is*, provided that the procedure has been properly followed'.[13] In fact, following Rawls, one *could not* specify the institutional outcomes as I have in (C) in advance of going through the process of (B), because as Rawls points out, we have no independent criteria for what (C) should be: 'A distinctive feature of pure procedural justice is that the procedure for determining the just result must actually be carried out; for in these cases there is no independent criterion by reference to which a definitive outcome can be known to be just.'[14]

I adduce two reasons, however, to keep the conditions specified in (C) as an independent defining characteristic of liberalism. First, I believe that there exist theories which might adhere to the legitimation conditions in (B) but which would be counted as liberal neither by the theories' exponents themselves nor by 'fully fledged' liberals. Anarchism, I would claim, is one of these; utilitarianism might be another. Anarchism results when people claim that no agreement would (or should?) be reached that satisfies all of the legitimation conditions in (B); or that, while participants would reach an agreement, it would be the agreement that there should exist no state. In either case, the anarchist conclusion can be reached from (B) without prima facie inconsistency or illogic. The same is true for some versions of utilitarianism. In the utilitarian case, theorists do not believe that no state would result from deliberations about the state's legitimacy, but they do conclude that the state would take a radically different shape than that proposed by liberal theorists. Claiming to follow the formal conditions specified by (B), but motivated by less risk aversion and/or a sharply different conception of equality than that adopted by most liberal theorists, utilitarians reduce the primacy of individual rights and liberties and elevate welfarist considerations and the notion of the common good. Liberals would reject both the anarchist and utilitarian conclusions for a variety of reasons, which may all be very good. But if our aim is to determine the criteria that uniquely identify liberal theories, independent of our judgement of these theories' ultimate soundness, then we need a third criterion to distinguish a theory such as anarchism or utilitarianism from true liberalism. These criteria reveal themselves in (C), as they specify the broad institutional and structural outcomes of (B) that distinguish a theory as liberal.

The second reason we need (C), I believe, is that there exist theories that reject (B) as impossible yet still count as liberal because of their adherence to (A) and the institutions specified by (C). Joseph Raz's approach in *The Morality of Freedom* exemplifies this sort of liberalism.[15] Attuned to the tremendous plurality of incompatible views, Raz despairs of ever achieving a universally acceptable set of principles to which all individuals would willingly offer their adherence; thus, while he strongly supports liberalism's institutional commitments, he argues that liberals must acknowledge the partisan nature of their claims.[16] J. S. Mill's *On Liberty*[17] is related to this camp, although it has very different origins. His stirring invocation of individual liberties and state restraint attest to his liberal credentials in respect to (C), while his perfectionist adoption of individual autonomy as the basis for these liberties seems again to violate (B).[18] But Mill's partisanship expresses itself not because he despairs of bridging individuals' beliefs, as Raz does, but because he views (B) as almost trivially satisfiable insofar as he believes substantive arguments can be generated to convince all individuals to protect and defend liberty. Essentially, whereas Raz heightens the problem of irremediable pluralism to argue for (B)'s impossibility in modern society, Mill sees pluralism's scope as sufficiently restricted that (B) is not a matter of fundamental concern. I suggest that both thinkers, however, are and should be treated as liberals, and that therefore we must retain (C) as an important (albeit partial) characterization of the liberal project.

In sum, my intent in this section has been to demonstrate that despite their wide differences in many areas, contemporary liberal theories are characteristically composed of three commitments regarding state legitimacy: (A) that a liberal state (and its citizens) must recognize and accept the fact of deep and irremediable pluralism in modern society; (B) that a legitimate state (and its supporting theory) must be governed by a public notion of justice that would be unanimously agreed upon by all potential citizens in a process that respected participants' freedom and equality; and (C) that such a state (and its supporting institutions) will take the form of a constitutional democracy that supports a wide range of inalienable personal liberties and behaves tolerantly and in some fashion neutrally toward all conceptions of the good. Many contemporary theorists would add to (C) a state obligation to engage in some significant measure of economic redistribution. If it can truly achieve the aim of grounding the institutional conclusions of (C) in an argument that all people within a plural society could freely and equally accept, then liberalism would be able to claim credit for the incredible accomplishment of justifying a tolerant, liberal state in unassailable terms. This is a goal worth striving for.

1.2 POLITICAL LIBERALISM, COHERENCE, AND THE ROLE OF AUTONOMY

Uniting all three liberal commitments—the fact of pluralism, the legitimation project, and substantive liberal freedoms and institutions—within one coherent theory is difficult. As we saw above, liberal theorists have responded to the challenge in a variety of ways. Raz rejects the legitimation conditions as unattainable in light of the fact of pluralism, and thus makes a positive argument for the value of autonomy that attempts to bridge directly from pluralism to substantive liberal institutions. He rejects (B), in other words, in favor of linking (A) with (C) via an argument for the value of autonomy. Mill, on the other hand, attempts to take all three commitments seriously but misconstrues the depth of pluralism in modern society. He thus also makes a positive argument for the value of autonomy (or 'individuality'), but in contrast to Raz, he believes all participants in an ideal, hypothetical legitimation process would and should accept it. From a contemporary perspective, therefore, he rejects (or misunderstands) (A) in favour of linking (B) directly with (C) via an argument for the value of individuality.[19]

What links Raz and Mill is a belief in the value of autonomy both for itself and as a means of justifying substantive liberal freedoms, combined with a devaluation of one of liberalism's other two commitments (either to plurality or to the legitimation process). By positing autonomy as an important liberal value—where autonomy is understood for the purposes of this section to mean the capacity to form a conception of the good, to evaluate one's values and ends with the genuine possibility of revising them should they be found wanting, and then to realize one's revised ends—these theorists argue that substantive liberal institutions can be justified and perpetuated, even though the three liberal commitments identified above can never be fully and coherently unified. This strand of liberalism has come to be called in recent years 'comprehensive' or 'perfectionist' liberalism.

In self-conscious contrast to this approach stand the self-appointed 'political liberals'—theorists who argue that all three commitments can be coherently unified within a single, non-autonomy-valuing (and otherwise 'non-metaphysical'[20]) political theory. Rawls, again, offers the most thoroughly worked-out version of political liberalism,[21] and it is his theory that I propose to examine as the best representative of political liberalism as a whole.[22] In contrast to 'comprehensive' or 'perfectionist' liberals such as Raz and Mill, Rawls suggests that liberals *can* 'have it all'—that liberalism's three commitments are compatible with one another precisely because they need not rely on the value of autonomy for their justification. Rather, Rawls argues, the legitimation project can succeed even in a deeply plural society, and can give rise to the right kinds of substantive rights and freedoms, because all potential liberal citizens must (and will) accept and display the 'two moral powers' of human beings: (1) a capacity for a sense of justice, and (2) the capacity for a conception of the good.[23] Let us examine each capacity in turn.

Of the three liberal commitments listed in section 1, acceptance of the

fact of pluralism creates the greatest number of difficulties for liberal justification. If society is truly as deeply divided as the fact of pluralism
suggests, then it is nearly impossible to see how individuals could come to
agree, within the context of the five legitimation conditions, on what principles of justice should govern the basic structure of a state. Rawls tries to
overcome this problem by reinterpreting the fact of pluralism in the
context of what he calls the 'burdens of judgement', the acceptance of
which is one element of the first moral capacity for a sense of justice.[24] To
accept the burdens of judgement, Rawls writes, is to accept the fact that
reasonable people can reasonably and fundamentally disagree about what is
important and/or valuable in life. Reasonable disagreement derives from a
number of sources, including: the existence of conflicting evidence,
disagreement over the relative weight of different pieces of evidence, the
indeterminacy of 'hard cases', the effect of past experience on our interpretation of present experience, incommensurability of values, and the
circumscription of value within any particular society.[25] These six (and
many more besides) all serve as sources of reasonable disagreement
between reasonable people. To accept the existence of these sources is to
accept the burdens of judgement. Rawls thus reinterprets (A), the fact of
pluralism, as the fact of the burdens of judgement (which are themselves
the source of pluralism). To accept the fact of pluralism, therefore, is in
Rawls' terms to accept the burdens of judgement, which is in turn to realize (in combination with a commitment to moral reciprocity) one's capacity for a sense of justice.

What is distinctive about this move is that by recasting the fact of pluralism in terms of the burdens of judgement, Rawls reshapes the character of
political discourse and reason within the legitimation process. For if a
person accepts the burdens of judgement, he is led not only to acknowledge
the *existence* of deep and irremediable pluralism in modern society, but also
to accept a particular explanation of the *reasons* for its existence. As a result,
he responds to the fact of pluralism differently.[26] Rather than trying to
limit diversity within the new state, for example, a person who has accepted
the burdens of judgement will be willing to work with others to accommodate it. And rather than trying to convince others to base the principles of
justice on one particular conception of the good because it is the only
reasonable way to live, a person with a sense of justice will work with others
to find principles of justice that are compatible with every reasonable
person's conception of the good. Thus, to accept the burdens of judgement
is 'to accept their consequences for the use of public reason in directing the
legitimate exercise of political power in a constitutional regime',[27] and thus
to succeed at the legitimation project where others have failed.

I suggest, however, that by requiring participants in the legitimation process to alter their reasoning about the nature of pluralism, as opposed to asking that they merely accept its existence, Rawls violates the boundaries of pluralism itself and ends up with the same discontinuities of justification with which Mill and Raz were forced to grapple. For to claim that all 'reasonable' people accept the burdens of judgement is radically to underestimate (or willfully to redefine) the depth of pluralism and disagreement in modern society. According to Rawls, 'The evident consequence of the burdens of judgement is that reasonable persons ... recognize that all persons alike, including themselves, are subject to those burdens, and so many reasonable comprehensive doctrines are affirmed, not all of which can be true (indeed none of them may be true). The doctrine any reasonable person affirms is but one reasonable doctrine among others.'[28] For many individuals, especially although not only for many religious fundamentalists, accepting this would require that they fundamentally reconceive their relationship to their communities and churches, the character of their beliefs, the content of their values, and even their conception of their own identities. In this respect, to accept the burdens of judgement is to diminish the pluralism that the burdens of judgement claim to respect and explain.

To restrict liberal citizenship to those who take on the burdens of judgement, therefore, is either to exclude a number of people—many more people, I believe, than Rawls means to—or to reconstruct (through political re-education) the boundaries of pluralism itself. I do not mean to say that either of these is necessarily the wrong thing to do. As I argue in Chapter 4, liberal citizenship does require certain habits and virtues, and pluralism is rightly restricted to individuals holding conceptions of the good which are compatible with liberal citizenship. Political re-education can be justified. But it does undermine Rawls' attempt unproblematically to reconcile the legitimation project with the fact of deep pluralism. Rawls is no more successful at unifying liberalism's three commitments than either Mill or Raz is.

Furthermore, insofar as accepting the burdens of judgement requires individuals to gain sufficiently critical distance from their own conception of the good to realize that theirs is not the only reasonable way of life, Rawls' political liberalism seems to require that citizens exercise at least a rudimentary level of autonomy.[29] Rawls argues in his own defense that this critical distance need be achieved only in the political sphere and not in individuals' private lives. People must accept the burdens of judgement (and thus acknowledge the status of their values as representing merely one reasonable possibility among many) as citizens, but not as private individuals. Whether or not this mental compartmentalization is psychologically or empirically possible, however, it is, as Eamonn Callan notes, normatively distasteful: 'To retain a lively understanding of the burdens of judgement in political contexts while suppressing it everywhere else would require a feat of gross self-deception that cannot be squared with personal integrity.'[30] I shall say nothing more about this problem here, since my argument in this section does not depend on this point. I address the relationship between civic virtue and autonomy in detail in Chapter 4. Still, it is worth noting that it is a problem for political liberalism.

We now turn to the role of the second moral power in Rawls' justification of political liberalism. The claim that all potential liberal citizens must accept the burdens of judgement was intended to make the legitimation conditions tenable in light of the fact of pluralism. As we saw above, this attempt to reconcile (A) with (B) was at best a mixed success. Even if it had been fully successful, however, Rawls must still provide a transition from (B) to (C)—from the liberal legitimation process to the substantive institutions it is meant to generate. This he accomplishes through positing the second moral power: namely, 'the capacity to form, to revise, and rationally to pursue . . . a conception of what we regard for us as a worthwhile human life'.[31] In addition to accepting the burdens of judgement, Rawls argues, participants in the liberal legitimation project must accept the existence of individuals' capacities to form, revise, and pursue a conception of the good. As such, they must also ensure that state institutions enable individuals to exercise this capacity. These institutions (and the 'primary goods'[32] they protect), as it happens, are the traditional liberal freedoms and governmental duties represented by (C). In support of the freedoms of conscience and association, for example, Rawls states:

There is no guarantee that all aspects of our present way of life are the most rational for us and not in need of at least minor if not major revision. For these reasons the adequate and full exercise of the capacity for a conception of the good is a means to a person's good. Thus, on the assumption that liberty of conscience, and therefore the liberty to fall into error and to make mistakes, is among the social conditions necessary for the development and exercise of this power, the parties have another ground for adopting principles that guarantee this basic liberty. Here we should observe that freedom of association is required to give effect to liberty of conscience; for unless we are at liberty to associate with other like-minded citizens, the exercise of liberty of conscience is denied.[33]

Hence we see that humans' moral capacity to revise their conceptions of the good results in a powerful argument in favour of freedom of conscience and association.

In the interest of textual fidelity, it should be noted that these two freedoms can actually both be justified on the weaker grounds of individuals' interest in pursuing their conception of the good, as Rawls argues in an earlier passage. Given the fact of pluralism, individuals in society will have many, often conflicting, conceptions of what it means to live a worthwhile life. Freedoms of conscience and association are thus essential to permitting individuals to realize these conceptions without hindrance.[34]

Not all liberal freedoms and institutional structures, however, can be justified on the basis of the 'form and pursue' clauses alone. As Will Kymlicka persuasively argues, 'It is all too easy to reduce individual liberty to the freedom to pursue one's conception of the good. But in fact much of what is distinctive to a liberal state concerns the forming and revising of people's conceptions of the good, rather than the pursuit of those conceptions once chosen.'[35] He uses the example of religion to prove his point. While freedom of conscience is certainly necessary for people to be able to pursue their religious faith, he argues, many other traditional liberal freedoms are not; their justification relies on the importance of *revising* one's faith:

A liberal society not only allows individuals the freedom to pursue their existing faith, but it also allows them to seek new adherents for their faith (proselytization is allowed), or to question the doctrine of their church (heresy is allowed), or to renounce their faith entirely and convert to another faith or to atheism (apostasy is allowed). It is quite conceivable to have the freedom to pursue one's current faith without having any of these latter freedoms. . . . These aspects of a liberal society only make sense on the assumption that revising one's ends is possible, and sometimes desirable, because one's current ends are not always worthy of allegiance. A liberal society does not compel such questioning and revision, but it does make it a genuine possibility.[36]

Thus, Rawls does require all three elements of the second moral power— to form, to revise, and to pursue a conception of the good—in order to bridge successfully from the legitimation project to the liberal institutional conditions represented in (C).

The problem for political liberalism, however, is that the capacity 'to form, to revise, and rationally to pursue' one's conception of the good encompasses the capacity for autonomy—roughly defined above as the capacity to evaluate one's values and ends self-critically with the possibility of revising and then realizing them.[37] The justification of substantive liberal institutions and freedoms thus relies on the value of autonomy. Rawls attempts to circumvent this conclusion by emphasizing that it is the *existence* of the second moral power that is important and not its *value* or our interest in realizing it: 'Thus, from the start the conception of the person is regarded as part of a conception of political and social justice. That is, it characterizes how citizens are to think of themselves and of one another in their political and social relationships as specified by the basic structure. This conception is not to be mistaken for an ideal for personal life . . . much less as a moral ideal.'[38] Because this power exists, Rawls argues, the state (and individuals in their political capacities as citizens) must accommodate via liberal institutions and freedoms those people who wish to realize their moral capacities. But the state takes no stance on the moral value of revising (and forming and pursuing) a conception of the good.

I assert, however, that we must have a further reason beyond the mere presence of this capacity to regard it as an important part of even the political conception of the person. Human beings have many capacities, after all, not all of which deserve regard from the state or from ourselves as at all worthy of respect or aid—for example, humans' capacity for extreme cruelty. The only reason for the state to acknowledge one capacity over another is if the former is more worth realizing than the latter. But this is tantamount to asserting that the particular capacity has *worth* for all human beings (within the society in which the liberal debate is taking place)—i.e. that the capacity represents a substantive *good*. Ronald Dworkin asserts as much in his essay 'In Defense of Equality.' In response to Rawls' claim that '[s]ince citizens are regarded as having the two moral powers, we ascribe to them two corresponding higher-order interests in developing and exercising these powers',[39] Dworkin counters, 'Our higher-order interest is not an interest in exercising a capacity because we find we have it . . . but rather we develop and train capacities of the sort that [Rawls] describe[s] because we have a certain interest' in what they have to offer us.[40] I believe that Dworkin is clearly right here, and that one must conclude that if Rawls is committed to the participants in the original position recognizing and promoting individuals' fundamental capacity to form, revise, and pursue a conception of the good life, then he must admit he holds individual autonomy to be a political *good* (and not just an indifferent capacity). Rawls even admits almost as much (although not quite), in asserting that 'contained in the conception of a person' is the 'possibility' that 'in addition to our beliefs being true, our actions right, and our ends good, we may also strive to appreciate *why* our beliefs are true, our actions right, and our ends good and suitable for us'.[41] He must take the next step and acknowledge that this possibility is a good that the state should uphold; for if it is not, it is totally unclear why individuals should take it, as opposed to any other empirical 'possibility' of human life, into account in the legitimation process.

This is not to say that the state should or even can discriminate against individuals who do not fulfill their capacity for autonomous action. Just after making the above assertion, Rawls is quick to note that 'many persons may not examine their acquired beliefs and ends but take them on faith, or be satisfied that they are matters of custom and tradition. They are not to be criticized for this.'[42] If one replaces 'criticized' with 'discriminated against', this statement is perfectly true, and is fully compatible with the judgement that individual autonomy is a good that the state should foster. Rawlsian liberalism may move from (B) to (C) by adopting an ideal of individual moral autonomy, but it need not assert the ideal to be proper grounds for discriminating against those who do not live up to it. So long as people fulfill the basic requirements of citizenship, whatever those may be, they deserve to be treated equally as citizens. Furthermore, individuals are under no obligation to acknowledge that autonomy has value for their own lives, although as I noted above and discuss more fully in Chapter 4, it is true both that few individuals who do not themselves value autonomy will agree that the state should value and promote autonomy, and that individuals who have accepted the burdens of judgement are more likely in practice to value autonomy and behave autonomously. But within the structure of the legitimation project, they do need to agree as citizens that autonomy is a value which the state should uphold.

In this section, I have argued that in spite of itself, political liberalism implicitly invokes autonomy via the two moral powers in order to justify both the legitimation project and the protection of substantive liberal freedoms. These two powers work in slightly different ways in Rawls' argument, as the above analysis tried to make clear. In order for the legitimation process to succeed in the context of deep pluralism—i.e., in order to make (A) compatible with (B)—we saw that participants must actually *enact* the first moral power—i.e., they must *adopt* the burdens of judgement and modify their behavior and values accordingly. In order to derive (C) from (B), on the other hand, they must merely *acknowledge* the existence and importance of the second moral power; they need not develop or revise a conception of the good themselves. As we saw above, this asymmetry of application results in a somewhat unsettled system of liberal justification. In both cases, however, political liberalism (at least as represented by Rawls) is required to assert the value of autonomy in order to get its justification project off the ground. Furthermore, I suggested that the requirement that individuals *realize* their first moral power creates (or reveals) the same discontinuity or contradiction between (A) and (B) that Raz and Mill each highlight. In the end, therefore, 'political liberalism' is no more successful than 'comprehensive liberalism' at unifying liberalism's three commitments within a non-autonomy-valuing theory of justification. Autonomy, I conclude, is a necessary component of contemporary liberal theory.[43]

This does not mean, however, that liberalism is necessarily a strongly comprehensive theory. Rather, I suggest that liberalism is best understood as displaying *weak perfectionism*, which I define as follows: an autonomy-based weakly perfectionist state values citizens' exercise of autonomy, but does not discriminate against those who do not exercise autonomy in their own lives. This is in part because of the sheer impossibility of screening adults for their exercise of autonomy—and relatedly, the consequent potential tyranny of any state that did try to differentiate in its treatment of autonomous and non-autonomous adults on the basis of criteria easily susceptible to arbitrariness and abuse.[44] It also makes sense, however, because the exercise of autonomy is not required for equal citizenship. So long as individuals take responsibility for their actions, see themselves as 'self-authenticating sources of valid claims',[45] and are able to have a conception of the good, they are to be regarded as equal citizens and not discriminated against. Thus, a weakly perfectionist state: (1) values individual autonomy and provides citizens the means and freedoms to exercise it; (2) treats all responsible, self-authenticating individuals as equal citizens; and therefore (3) does not discriminate against non-autonomous citizens in protecting their rights or fulfilling its obligations toward them.

1.3 A CLOSER LOOK AT THE NATURE OF AUTONOMY

In the previous section, I proved that a weakly perfectionist commitment to individual autonomy is a necessary component of liberal theory. In this section, I argue that when autonomy is defined in the right way, weak perfectionism also provides a sufficient justification for contemporary liberalism. Section 3 thus takes on two, interrelated challenges: to develop a sophisticated and attractive conception of individual autonomy, and to prove that this conception provides a sufficient grounding for contemporary liberalism. If this section succeeds, it will complete the theoretical foundations on which the next four chapters are to be based, by proving that autonomy can be a necessary, sufficient, tenable, and desirable foundation for guiding the construction of the weakly perfectionist liberal state.

It is worth noting first, however, that I do not believe (A) and (B) can ever be fully reconciled, or at least not in a way that will also generate (C). All three commitments are important and liberalism is to be commended for taking them seriously. But I do not believe that any ideal can or will draw unanimous support within a deeply plural society, let alone give rise to fully mutually agreeable political institutions such as (C). In other words, liberalism is caught in a 'trilemma':[46] it embraces three important commitments but can fully satisfy only two at any one time. Since (A) correctly describes the world (or at least correctly describes the modern, Western societies in which liberal theory operates), and (C) is essential to liberalism's understanding of itself, I suggest that (B), the liberal legitimation condition, must be slightly relaxed. I relax it no more than Rawls does, or than any (political) liberal who insists that participants in the legitimation process accept something like the burdens of judgement. But either some limitations must be placed on the participants in the legitimation process (such as that they accept the burdens of judgement), or else unanimous agreement must cease to be required, if (B) is to succeed in generating (C) in the context of (A). Thus, while I do try in this section to make autonomy as attractive a notion as possible, the fact of pluralism means that not all adult participants in the legitimation process would agree to a weakly perfectionist liberal state. I shall argue that a weakly perfectionist commitment to autonomy provides the *best* grounding for liberal freedoms and institutions, and that it should also be acceptable to the vast majority of individuals— but it will not be acceptable to all. This will be especially true when we turn our attention from the implications of weak perfectionism for adults to its implications for children in Chapter 2. First, however, let us consider the nature of autonomy itself.

Having established the necessity of our taking liberal autonomy seriously, I must now clarify what 'autonomy' actually means in this context—i.e., what it is that the state should respect as a good. I will be pulled in two different directions by this investigation. On the one hand, my goal will be to generate a notion of autonomy that fulfills liberal purposes, that is to say, that is firm enough to provide a stable basis or justification for the institutional commitments specified by (C) yet thin enough to garner widespread support and provide a foundation for weakly perfectionist liberalism. In this respect, 'autonomy' functions as a placeholder for the idea I find most useful. On the other hand, the idea of 'autonomy' has independent existence and stature in its own right. I cannot attach to 'autonomy' any meaning I please. So I will have to make sure that I do not go too far adrift from autonomy's basic meaning of 'self-rule' or 'self-legislation'. Therefore, while this section will not function as a strict semantic investigation of the word 'autonomy', since it is driven by practical and partisan aims, neither will it concentrate solely on finding the most effective method of justifying (C) from (B). Rather, I will try to cut a sometimes schizophrenic path between these two loci of study, hoping by the end to emerge with a reasonable explication of autonomy that both does justice to our common-sense understanding of the term and provides a reasonable basis for liberal freedoms and state institutions.[47]

Before I enter into this fairly daunting exploration, however, I need to consider one question left dangling from the previous section. I claimed in my conclusion to section 2 that while the state must adopt autonomy as a political ideal for human beings as moral agents (in order to justify liberal institutions and freedoms), it must still treat non-autonomous citizens with equal respect and consideration. This is the essence of weak perfectionism. I did not sufficiently make clear in section 2, however, what moral or political qualities of persons should be preconditions for equal citizenship. I suggest here that this basis should be individuals' capacity for *autarchy*, which is a term appropriated for this purpose by Stanley Benn.[48] Benn characterizes an autarchic person as someone who has a sense of himself as an intentional source of cause-and-effect relationships.[49] He must be able both to see himself as causing changes in the world that he intends to take place, and to take responsibility for those changes (barring a mistake or bad luck). Part and parcel of this requirement is that the autarchic person sees his making choices about actions as an important part of that process: 'The agent's intention, not itself an event, gives a special character to the action, the causal event initiating the chain of events that follows.'[50] Linked to this emphasis on intention and responsibility, the autarchic person must also be able to make and act upon rational decisions about his interests. If a person knows that his aim is to eat ice cream, for example, he must be able to make rational decisions about how to secure that aim. He need not have the capacity to develop a complex plan of action (e.g. figure out how to take the bus to the ice cream shop), but he must be able at least to choose between two clearly presented options without having nervously to look to others to make the choice for him. Given a set of goals, an autarchic actor must be self-directed and rational in developing a plan to meet that goal. This does not mean, however, that autarchic individuals must themselves be able to generate their interests, or to choose their own aims. Autarchy is perfectly compatible with being told what one's interests are or what to look forward to. All it demands is that individuals recognize the causative role of their choice to act in the series of events that plays out, and to be able to make choices about realizing their goals (even if merely to fulfill other-imposed aims) on their own.

These seem like fairly minimal conditions for people, and so they are. But it is important to remember that not all human beings fulfill these conditions: psychopaths, infants, people who are severely retarded, autistic, comatose, or insane, and others, such as cult victims who are utterly dependent on the will of another for command and guidance, all fail these conditions in one form or another.[51] Thus, these conditions manage to distinguish agents who do have some level of causative responsibility from those who do not. They also make the distinction along lines that are reasonable for a state to recognize. The state does need to be given means to discriminate reasonably between autarchic people and those listed above, justifiably subjecting the latter to paternalistic or other restrictive measures that the former would rightly protest against. It would be a weak and short-lived state that could not discriminate between autarchic persons and the insane. Thus, the distinction between autarchic and heterarchic persons is a *necessary* one for developing a useful political theory.

In addition, autarchy is a *sufficient* condition of liberal citizenship, because while the demands of rationality, causative intentionality and responsibility, and deliberative independence are fairly minimal, they are strong enough to meet the minimum conditions that we intuitively demand of liberal democratic citizens, or of 'political agents', as Rawls terms them.[52] Although I cannot prove this claim, since it relies on unprovable intuitions about the basis of equal citizenship, I suggest that the following quotation from Benn helps to uphold these intuitions. Benn argues that we can derive a principle of equal respect from the responsibility and intentionality conditions of autarchy by taking note of the following:

[If we] resent . . . another person's lack of consideration [in interfering with our projects] . . ., we are already committed to the general principle that every natural person,[53] being conceptually equipped to grasp what it is to have and to value projects of his own, is thereby committed to respecting the standing of every other person as an originator of projects. . . . Claiming respect—the recognition of our moral personality—on the grounds of our natural personality, we are then committed to extending it to anyone else satisfying the same conditions.[54]

While Benn means this to be a moral argument, I believe that I can use it for our purposes as a political claim, one that supports the liberal legitimation conditions introduced in section 1. It is because the individual agents engaging in the hypothetical legitimation process are autarchic that they deserve equal respect and free and equal deliberative authority. Likewise, and more importantly, the state must respect this fundamental characteristic of its citizens beyond the legitimation stage, refraining from coercing them or otherwise treating them unequally as regards their power as rational, intentional, moral and political agents. I think that we can safely posit that all potential citizens would agree that these are valuable characteristics that rightly operate as necessary and sufficient conditions for equal political respect (although not necessarily for equal moral respect on an individual basis).

While they provide a compelling foundation for equal citizenship, however, the conditions of autarchy alone are not strong enough to secure the wide range of individual freedoms and government obligations specified by (C). As I pointed out via Kymlicka in section 2, many political liberties can be justified only with reference to individuals' interest in forming and revising their conceptions of the good, not merely in pursuing them. If autarchy is conceived as the sole basis for liberal institutions, and individuals can be autarchic while having their goals dictated by others, then the liberal state would have no obligation, for example, to provide education for the poor, to allow individuals to proselytize, or even to protect

certain forms of public speech. Thus, we need a stronger basis for the
liberal freedoms and state obligations articulated in (C) than merely a
recognition of autarchy—that basis being the value of human autonomy, as
I argued above.

Because the value of autonomy is contested within plural societies,
however, I will try to develop as minimal a notion of autonomy itself as
possible. Although I argued at the beginning of this section that liberalism
is unable to engineer a perfect fit among (A), (B), and (C), part of liberalism's appeal remains its inspiring (even if unrealizable) aim of establishing
principles through the legitimation process that all people would willingly
and comprehendingly support. Thus, I will attempt in this section to
develop a conception of autonomy whose adoption as a value will alienate
as few people as possible while still providing a sound foundation for liberal
freedoms and institutions (i.e. those of (C)) and remaining true to the
semantic connotations of autonomy in ordinary language.

In light of these aims, let us start by drawing upon the thinnest possible
notion of autonomy, which is Gerald Dworkin's theory of formal, as
opposed to substantive, autonomy. Dworkin characterizes autonomy as
follows:

> It is not the identification or lack of identification [with one's first-order motiva-
> tions] that is crucial to being autonomous, but the capacity to raise the question of
> whether I will identify with or reject the reasons for which I now act. . . . The idea
> of autonomy is not merely an evaluative or reflective notion, but includes as well
> some ability both to alter one's preferences and to make them effective in one's
> actions and, indeed, to make them effective because one has reflected on them and
> adopted them as one's own.[55]

Dworkin's description sounds reasonable. Autonomous individuals are
those who evaluate and revise their first-order desires and preferences—
which are desires of the form 'I want to X'—in order to make sure that they
act only upon those with which they identify. To identify with a desire is to
want it; in other words, it is to develop a second-order desire—'I want to
want to X'—that embraces the first-order desire.[56] According to Dworkin,
then, autonomous individuals are those people who are able to form and act
upon second-order desires and volitions (which are desires that one wishes
to act on), which in turn involves acting upon those first-order desires with
which they identify and revising or rejecting those first-order desires with
which they do not identify—which they do not 'adopt as their own'.

It is notable that this definition of autonomy does not place any restrictions on the *content* of autonomous individuals' second-order desires. Any
modification of first-order desires in line with the reflective generation of
second-order volitions will do to demonstrate that one is autonomous—even

if those second-order desires and volitions are themselves adopted within a context of heteronomy. As Dworkin himself points out, the very thinness of his characterization of autonomy prevents us from being able to distinguish between autonomous and heteronomous people on the basis of the content of either their first- or second-order desires. Under this formal (as opposed to substantive) notion of autonomy, someone can decide to adopt what we would usually consider to be a heteronomous lifestyle ('I will do whatever my mother or my buddies or my leader or my priest tells me to do'[57]), but by the mere act of raising and resolving the question of why she acts as she does, retain or even assert her autonomy.

This formal characterization of autonomy suffers, I assert, from two fatal weaknesses. First, it is unable to distinguish properly between heteronomous and autonomous individuals, and thus also fails to provide a stable justification for liberal freedoms and institutions. Consider two individuals, Harry and Abner. After a period of sustained reflection, Harry declares, 'I will do whatever my mother tells me to do, regardless of the consequences.' After a similar period of reflection, Abner announces, 'I will do whatever my mother tells me to do because she is wiser than I and will help me achieve my goal of X.' Both declarations are articulations of second-order desires that the speakers reached following a period of reflection on their first-order desires. For example, Harry might rightly have judged that he is psychologically deeply dependent on his mother's approval and therefore decided to follow his mother's advice no matter what the consequences. The actions resulting from this decision do not draw solely on first-order desires, nor are they enacted unthinkingly. Insofar as the same is true for Abner, Dworkin's theory of formal autonomy demands that we thus recognize both speakers as autonomous. This conclusion, however, seems inappropriate in Harry's case under any reasonable understanding of autonomy. Harry's second-order judgements are made within a context of heteronomy—i.e., as a result of an unalterable psychological dependence on his mother that he has not questioned or changed. If autonomy literally means 'self-legislation' or 'self-rule', then it cannot be enough that one legislates to oneself the path of least resistance (as Harry does), or more broadly, that one leaves heteronomous values untouched and legislates for oneself only in those areas that do not threaten those values (as Harry also does). Thus, I believe that a non-substantive notion of autonomy such as Dworkin's cannot sufficiently distinguish between autonomous and heteronomous people and also cannot ground the liberal freedoms demanded by (C).

Dworkin does introduce in a last-minute, rather haphazard fashion a condition of 'procedural independence', which tries to distinguish 'those influences such as hypnotic suggestion, manipulation, coercive persuasion, subliminal influence, and so forth'.[58] It is not clear, however, that this condition helps Dworkin's case. Dworkin himself admits that it is very difficult to make such distinctions in a non-*ad hoc* fashion. Furthermore, it does not appear that Harry's form of deep psychological dependence necessarily violates the condition of procedural independence as Dworkin defines it, since one can be psychologically dependent without having been indoctrinated or hypnotized into such dependence. Thus, Harry's second-order judgement may continue to be judged autonomous under Dworkin's theory. Even if procedural independence does distinguish Harry from Abner, however, the source of this condition is obscure, and its compatibility with the otherwise formalistic and non-substantive nature of Dworkin's theory is open to doubt.[59]

The second problem with Dworkin's formal conception of autonomy is that it allows the possibility that people may enslave themselves yet continue to be regarded as autonomous, which conclusion both seems patently absurd and could certainly have illiberal consequences. For example, by asserting that he will obey his mother 'regardless of the consequences', Harry abdicates control over the direction of his life, yet Dworkin still explicitly regards him as autonomous, since he has acted upon a second-order desire. The strangeness of this conclusion can be made clear if we consider our second speaker, Abner. Abner, remember, declares that 'I will do whatever my mother tells me to do because she is wiser than I and will help me achieve my goal of X' (where X is getting rich, say). We are willing to judge Abner as autonomous because obeying his mother in this scenario might be plausibly understood as a contingent good in service to a more fundamental good (getting rich) to which our speaker is autonomously committed. In this sense, obeying his mother would be a plausible means of enacting his autonomy.[60] But consider what would happen if Abner were to follow Harry's lead and add on 'no matter what the consequences'. Such an addition would vitiate the significance or seriousness of the reasons Abner gives for his action in the first place. 'I will do M to achieve X no matter what the consequences of M are' is simply a nonsensical, or at least self-deluded, declaration. As Dworkin himself declares, autonomy must allow for the re-examination of one's commitments in order again to 'raise the question of whether I will identify with or reject the reasons for which I now act'.[61] The commitment 'I will do M to achieve X no matter what the consequences of M are' does not leave space for such a re-evaluation.

The illogicality of this declaration also does much to clarify why we view Harry as heteronomous. First, it emphasizes again the way in which his actions are ultimately predicated on the unreflective aping of another, as opposed to on his own deliberate and rationally conceived ideals of the good. Second, even if Harry began with autonomously conceived ideals, he necessarily sacrifices them in subsuming his will to the will of another 'no matter what the consequences'. By abrogating his authority to pull out, he abrogates his authority over his own will—and thus abandons any further claim to 'self-rule' ever again. Irreversible self-enslavement necessarily brings with it heteronomy of the will.[62] The enslaved individual may well still be autarchic, and thus deserving of equal respect and concern. But he could not be self-legislating in even the minimal sense of the term. As Benn evocatively comments,

An absolute commitment . . . whether to the dice, to the priest, or to the total community, involves the distancing of oneself thereafter from the considerations that initially led to it. For if the commitment is to be absolute, the question whether there really were, and still are, good enough reasons for making it is not to be reopened. Though the rule is genetically one's own, in the sense that one originally prescribed it to oneself, both the rule and the prescriptions proceeding from it now confront one from the outside: the rule is now as much an alienation of the self as is the brute externality of a stone idol that one might carve to venerate.[63]

I conclude, therefore, that Dworkin's notion of autonomy is untenable as it currently stands, and furthermore that it cannot prove a fruitful foundation for liberal freedoms. Autonomy cannot and should not be understood in purely formal terms. We have already come to see one necessary substantive condition of autonomy, which is that individuals whose volitions involve enslaving themselves to another cannot be autonomous, no matter how many higher-order desires they can form. The substance of their volition to give up their will to the absolute control of another is itself sufficient to establish them as heteronomous, independent of the formal aspects of their actions and decision procedures. This means, therefore, that higher-order desires and volitions cannot provide the sole criterion for autonomy. While they represent a powerful idea that is well worth incorporating into a full understanding of autonomy—it does seem evident, after all, that individuals who *cannot* make second-order decisions and act upon them also cannot be autonomous—they are not the sum total of autonomy.

Before I try to construct a new, more substantive (although still minimal) theory of autonomy, however, there is one more thing to learn from Dworkin. As we have seen, for autonomy to incorporate, or at least to accommodate, self-enslavement and heteronomous choice-making is an odd characterization of a term that literally means 'self-rule'. It is worth asking, then, why Dworkin permits—even welcomes—this outcome, as it may reveal an aspect of autonomy that we have so far ignored. Dworkin argues that if one takes substantive autonomy seriously, meaning that one evaluates the content as well as the form of individuals' decisions and rejects as heteronomous those decisions which transfer effective power over one's own will to someone else, then one could not recognize as autonomous a person who commits himself to a cause or to another person: 'the conception of autonomy that insists upon substantive independence is not one that has claim to our respect as an ideal'; it is 'inconsistent with loyalty, objectivity, commitment, benevolence, and love'.[64] Such a notion of autonomy, if truly inconsistent with these virtues, is highly unappealing. If one does not have the ability to commit oneself wholeheartedly to a loved one or to a worthy cause while retaining one's autonomy, Dworkin suggests, then we shouldn't value autonomy in the first place. By building a formal conception of autonomy, Dworkin hopes to retain autonomy as a worthwhile ideal in its own right—in part because it permits the foundation of natural and desirable human commitments.

It is worth seeing if there is another solution to the problem of squaring autonomy with deep human commitments, since it seems to bastardize autonomy to claim that one can act autonomously while devoted to following unthinkingly the commands of another person. It is true that we have not fully adopted a cause (or belief or purpose or goal) if we are able *at any time* to re-evaluate our aim with the possibility of giving it up. I wonder, though, if this might not reveal instead a necessary characteristic of a compelling notion of autonomy—that one be able to be autonomous while making strong, apparently permanent commitments—rather than revealing a limitation of autonomy itself. Autonomy becomes far less attractive a notion if it cannot accommodate the personality-shaping and -identifying commitments we make throughout our lives to causes, beliefs, and other people. As Joel Feinberg points out in his discussion of 'autonomy-hoarders':

if we so desire, we can minimize our commitments and thus achieve a greater amount of de facto moral independence. We may, if we wish, go through life unmarried, or forgo having children, or near neighbors. . . . If we think of autonomy as de facto independence simply, then the uncommitted person is an autonomy-hoarder, who scores high on our scale. But if we think of autonomy as the name of a condition which is itself admirable, a kind of ideal condition, then the uncommitted person is subject to demerits on his score. He is clearly no paragon.[65]

Thus, we are faced with the task of constructing a minimal but substantive notion of autonomy that, on the one hand, effectively distinguishes between autonomous and heteronomous people and does not permit self-enslavement, but, on the other hand, does permit the adoption of deep commitments, including love, loyalty, religion, and patriotism.

I suggest that a conceptual point about the relationship between autonomy and agency helps to bridge this potential normative gap between wholehearted commitment self-rule. Regardless of how *valuable* we believe individuals' commitments to various ideals, ways of life, and other people to be, we must recognize that these commitments are simply *necessary* for the construction and maintenance of the self, and thus must be fostered and protected. 'Atomistic' individuals who are completely abstracted from their surroundings, preferences, values, and relationships are not perfectly autonomous selves; rather, they have no self at all. As Benn comments, 'Someone who had escaped such a socialization process would not be free, unconstrained, able to make *anything* of himself that he chose; he would be able to make nothing of himself, being hardly a person at all.'[66] We need limits in order to give shape to our explorations; in Cartesian terms, both position and direction can be designated only in reference to an origin. Otherwise we wander through space, never gaining anything, never in fact moving anywhere, insofar as there is nothing to look back upon, nothing by which to measure how far we have come, nothing to tell us when we have unexpectedly returned to where we started. To be a choosing person (i.e., to be autonomous), therefore, one first has to be a person: 'a person must already possess at least a rudimentary character before he can hope to *choose* a "new one." '[67]

Thus, a coherent, attractive conception of autonomy must incorporate not just the traditionally recognized conditions for specifically *autonomous* action (critical thinking skills, self-knowledge, etc.) but the conditions for *agency* or personality itself (and therefore also for autonomous agency). This fact has two implications. First, it means that our conception of autonomy must incorporate a commitment to the development and preservation of cultural coherence. Individuals must be able to feel embedded within a culture or set of cultures, and to mediate their choices via the norms and social forms constitutive of their culture(s).[68] Cultural coherence of this kind both aids individuals' senses of identity and hence agency, and helps to limit individuals' range of choices to a manageable level so as to prevent their development of anomie—paralysis as a result of massive anxiety and indecision about the choices one should make in the absence of binding commitments.[69] Second, the association between autonomy and personality means that people need to have developed and exercised a wide range of faculties within their personality in order to be able to exercise autonomy. For example, someone cannot make a truly autonomous choice about the relevance of spirituality or the importance of intellectual study to his life without having first developed his capacities to appreciate and engage in (even if he ultimately rejects) these enterprises:

giving a religious upbringing is in fact giving the child an experience which will enable him to evaluate religion for himself in a significant way. This could be linked to the point that it is impossible to develop an adequate understanding of religion *in abstractio*, but that this can only be achieved through a particular religion. So it might be argued, far from hindering the child's capacity for autonomy in this field, the provision of an appropriate form of religious upbringing is in fact facilitating it.[70]

I do not mean to suggest that individuals need to experience anything and everything they want to understand and therefore to choose (or reject) autonomously. Rather, individuals simply must have developed broad facets of their personality—emotional, intellectual, spiritual and aesthetic (which I regard as two aspects of the same experience), and moral—in order to make autonomous choices both about specific pursuits and about the broad direction of their lives. In this respect, too, the adoption and development of deep commitments to one's friends or spouse, one's religion, one's country, to music or dance, to teaching and research, or to the virtue of honesty are important elements in the construction of an autonomous personality, and not, as Dworkin suggests would occur with a more demanding notion of autonomy, inconsistent with it. For one can best judge the role one wishes love or intellectual excitement or musical understanding to play in one's life if one has experienced them already. Finally, it is worth noting that these two preconditions of autonomy (the possession of a well-developed personality and cultural coherence) are connected, insofar as membership in a complex and wide-ranging culture will help individuals develop a strong and varied personality—a fact which will be especially important in Chapters 2 and 3 when I analyze the complementary educative roles played by the family, the community, and the state.

By incorporating cultural coherence and the development of personality into my conception of autonomy, I have responded to Dworkin's concern that autonomy be compatible with the adoption of deep commitments. This is important if autonomy is to be a desirable ideal. But we are still faced with the problem of constructing a substantive conception of autonomy that avoids the other traps into which formal autonomy falls. As noted above, Dworkin had trouble distinguishing between autonomous and heteronomous people because he regarded the generation of any second-order volitions, possibly in the context of procedural independence, as sufficient for autonomy, even if they are developed within a context of heteronomy. As the case of Harry exemplifies, it is not enough to recognize or even accept the preferences one has. Certain conditions, such as extreme neediness or dependence, can never be compatible with autonomous action, because their substance precludes the process of agent choice and identification.

We must therefore demand a further capacity from the autonomous agent: namely, that the individual be able to challenge and reflect upon every first-order desire, including desires that are constitutive of the self, as with Harry's neediness. Although one obviously anticipates that some lower-order desires will be easier to change or even critically to question than others, the agent must be able to base every higher-order preference on reasons and lower-order desires with which she identifies. The mere fact of *having* certain preferences is not enough to justify their serving as foundations for one's higher-order volitions. This is especially true in reference to extreme neediness such as that demonstrated by Harry. (This implies, incidentally, that the achievement of autonomy requires that individuals' basic needs be fulfilled, including the provision of food, shelter, clothing, affection, and self-esteem, to give a partial but representative list. Physical deprivation can be just as inimical to autonomy as psychological neediness.) It is the process of reflecting upon our beliefs and desires, attempting to resolve such incoherences as are troubling, and *revising* our preferences in light of self-critical reflection that makes one's beliefs and desires our own—that permits us to claim that we truly are 'self-legislating'.

In order for this process to take place, however, individuals must have a *plurality* of constitutive desires and values. Plurality permits the development of autonomy in three ways. First, it enables individuals to question any particular value without suffering a wholesale loss of identity, insofar as their identities are not constituted on the basis of the affirmation of a single value, desire, or belief. If someone is committed to a single overriding value upon which her entire identity is based, then she cannot question it, let alone reject it, without questioning or rejecting herself in a way that would seem impossible for most people to endure without undergoing a nervous breakdown or worse. Consider Sister Susan, for example, a nun in a silent Carmelite sect. She has devoted her entire life to the service of God, shunning the establishment of an earthly family or close friends in favor of a singular focus on serving God. I believe that under these conditions it is virtually impossible for Sister Susan to be thoroughly autonomous, since the exercise of autonomy would require her to be able substantially to question her commitment to God, which would in turn put the very grounds of her selfhood into jeopardy. This is not to say that she cannot modify her belief gradually over time. Of course she can. But she cannot self-consciously challenge the foundations of her belief without challenging—and potentially destroying—the linchpins of her selfhood.[71] A construction of selfhood resting on a plurality of constitutive values, on the other hand, permits an individual to revise or reject one of her values in light of the knowledge that her other values remain (even if only temporarily) to preserve her identity.

Second, plurality is necessary for autonomy because one must have a standpoint from which to critique (i.e. to form higher-order desires about) one's values and desires, with the standpoint not grounded in those values or desires themselves under review. If I wish to question the validity of value *A*, for example, I will do so from the standpoint of (some subset of) values *B-Z*. I certainly could not do so from a grounding of no values whatsoever (and thus I reject the 'atomistic individual' argument so commonly and naively thrown at liberalism[72]), but nor could I do so if, like Sister Susan, I did not possess a range of constitutive values and desires. In the latter case, I would have to reflect upon my identification with *A* from the perspective of *A* (since it constitutes my sole defining normative commitment), which seems difficult and intellectually suspect, to say the least. This is not at all to say that there is no give and take among values or desires. We often come to reflect autonomously when we discover that two of our (perhaps heteronomously adopted) preferences conflict. In such a situation, we may attempt to resolve the conflict by adopting the standpoint of desire *B* in evaluating desire *A*, and adopting *A* as a context in which to evaluate *B*. By flipping back and forth between the two standpoints, we may come to reach a compromise between the two, or we may decide to abandon or revise one in favor of the other. Thus we come to legislate a new set of defining values and preferences for ourselves (and thereby enact our autonomy).[73] In any case, no matter how we decide in the end to resolve the conflict, we need a plurality of values and desires in order to establish alternative standpoints from which to make higher-order judgements about lower-order preferences.[74]

Finally, plurality of personal beliefs and values is necessary in order to understand the criticisms that others make of us. It is an often-ignored fact that we cannot be personally autonomous unless we have the capacity to comprehend and even to take seriously other people's criticisms of ourselves and our conceptions of the good. We must be able to take other people's evaluations of us into account on at least a minimal level, and furthermore, we must be able to discriminate among those evaluations. Gabrielle Taylor astutely makes this point about people of integrity, but I think it is equally applicable to those who claim to possess autonomy: 'The suppression of or turning away from such evidence [others' comments and criticisms] about herself and her values would be a threat to her integrity. Unless she is open to such evidence her pattern of reasoning is likely to remain unexamined and static, and is unlikely to reflect as it should the wider and more varied experiences of a person capable of change and development.'[75] There are, of course, problems with this reliance on the judgement of others, since if the community itself is hidebound and static, then one's autonomy might well be reduced rather than strengthened. But so long as individuals can distinguish between insightful and restrictive criticism, their autonomy can be significantly advanced by their attention to others' evaluations of their beliefs, values, and actions.[76]

This final example of why individuals' possession of a plurality of values is important—that it enables them to respond to others' criticisms of their values and projects—suggests that autonomy-promoting *communities* must be plural as well. Part of the way in which a community advances individuals' exercise of autonomy is by providing a wide range of (often competing) examples of how to lead a good life. It offers a range of 'collective goods'[77] in which individuals are encouraged to participate, and continually challenges members' adherence to one group or way of life via the examples of other members' living their lives in very different ways and according to sharply contrasting conceptions of the good: 'Freedom-promoting social orders are, it appears, *pluralistic*: societies of partial allegiances in which groups endlessly compete with each other and with the state for the allegiances of individuals, and in which individuals' loyalties are divided among a variety of crosscutting (or only partially overlapping) memberships and affiliations.'[78] This kind of plural public culture, however, can be maintained only with the help of liberal institutions. Thus, we see that individuals' exercise of autonomy requires the existence of liberal freedoms and institutions for the purpose of maintaining an autonomy-promoting culture as much as for the purpose of permitting individual self-assertion and self-evaluation.

We thus see that the ideal of personal autonomy is a substantive notion of higher-order preference formation within a context of cultural coherence, plural constitutive personal values and beliefs, openness to others' evaluations of oneself, and a sufficiently developed moral, spiritual or aesthetic, intellectual, and emotional personality. It is a less minimal notion than that with which I began, but I think that it is a far more sensible and desirable articulation of the notion of autonomy itself. Furthermore, its adoption within a weakly perfectionist framework provides a strong and stable justification for the establishment and preservation of liberal freedoms and institutions. If individuals are to be able to reflect upon their values and desires within a context of plurality of value as a means of establishing higher-order preferences with which they identify and upon which they are able to act, citizens must be granted freedoms of speech, association, religion, heresy, apostasy, sexual conduct, property rights, bodily integrity, etc. These freedoms are also needed to produce the kind of community necessary for fostering autonomy; thus, they are justified on a communal as well as individual level.

The task that now faces us, and with which the next four chapters will contend, is to determine what implications this picture of liberalism as a weakly perfectionist, autonomy-valuing theory has for a theory of liberal education (and vice versa). Some implications may already be obvious; others, I imagine, are far less so. The first question that must be answered is what role *children* play in this theory of pluralism, legitimation, and the exercise of autonomy. Chapter 2 addresses this problem, and discusses the role of state-regulated schooling in its solution.

2

The development of autonomy

In order for individuals to act autonomously, they must first have developed the capacity for autonomous action. This is a trivial statement; I might as well have pointed out that in order for people to tie their shoes, or to drive to Chicago, they must first have developed the capacity to tie their shoes and to drive. But it is curious that while contemporary liberal theorists often discuss the exercise of autonomy, and debate which rights and freedoms are most conducive to the achievement of autonomous action, they rarely confront in similar detail its empirical precursor—the problem of how to foster the development of autonomy. This problem, and the indispensability of formal, state-regulated schooling to its solution, is the focal point of this chapter.

2.1 DOES DEVELOPMENT FOLLOW FROM EXERCISE?

In Chapter 1, we saw that the liberal state is committed to establishing and protecting the conditions necessary for citizens to exercise autonomy. This follows from its weakly perfectionist commitment to individual autonomy as a moral good. At first glance, therefore, it may seem fairly obvious that the liberal state will (or should) also attempt to establish the conditions necessary for individuals—and especially children—to *develop* the capacity for autonomy. The argument for this is straightforward, based on an extension of Ronald Dworkin's argument quoted in section 1.3 about our reasons for exercising certain capacities. My contention there was that the simple fact of possessing the capacity for autonomy (our 'second moral power') does not in itself give us any reason to exercise it, i.e. to act autonomously. We all have many personal capacities that we choose to leave undeveloped or even to suppress—capacities for anger, for jealousy, for advancing our social standing at the expense of others, for self-absorption, and so forth. Our merely possessing these capacities does not give us a reason to exercise them. What *does* give us reason to exercise a capacity is our belief that its exercise has a certain worth and value—that is, that the capacity represents a substantive good. Thus, the argument went, the liberal cannot merely invoke the human *possibility* for autonomy and argue for liberal freedoms on that basis alone; rather, he must treat the capacity for autonomy as an actual human *good* that the liberal state must value and foster. The extension of this argument regarding development is quite simple. If the exercise of autonomy is valuable, then its development must also be a good. Mirroring the contrast above, it does not make sense to admit that there is value in exercising autonomy, but to deny that there is value in developing it (which development is, obviously enough, a precondition to its exercise).[1] As Amy Gutmann argues, 'The same principle that requires a state to grant adults personal and political freedom also commits it to assuring children an education that makes those freedoms both possible and meaningful in the future.'[2] Thus, if the liberal state so values autonomy that it works to promote individuals' exercise of it, the state should also aid people in developing their capacity for it.

The simplicity of this argument fails to engage, however, with the fundamental differences—even contradictions—between the conditions required for advancing the exercise of autonomy and the conditions demanded for its development. These arise because the conditions required for the acquisition of a skill or disposition are both logically and empirically separate from the conditions required for its exercise. Consider, for example, shoe-tying. Learning how to tie shoes requires different skills from tying them. Some characteristics, such as having control over one's hands and fingers, are required in common. Other characteristics, however, may be essential to one but utterly irrelevant to the other. Having the power to concentrate and to assimilate information is necessary if one is to *learn* how to tie one's shoes, but is then purely academic for those 'in the know'. Conversely, possessing shoes is a prerequisite to being able to tie them, but one can learn how to tie shoes (as I did under the patient tutelage of my mother) using a shoebox threaded with yarn. Finally, there are even cases in which the demands of learning to tie one's shoes conflict with the demands of tying them. The habit of thinking through every action carefully and methodically might be a tremendous aid to learning how to tie one's shoes; but someone who was never able to get past such methodicalism would inevitably lack a certain fluency in shoe-tying that more instinctive or intuitive actors achieve.

Thus we see, through the lens of this (admittedly pretty basic) example, that the development of a capacity may pose very different requirements from its exercise.[3] This is the case, I suggest, with autonomy—and it is this case that makes justifying even weak state perfectionism concerning the development of autonomy much harder than it first appears. The conditions and institutions required for the exercise of autonomy are 'built into the system' of liberalism in a way that the conditions required for the development of autonomy are not. Recall from Chapter 1 that contemporary liberalism has three distinct defining elements: (A) an acceptance of the fact of pluralism; (B) a set of formal or procedural conditions demanding free, equal, and public agreement on basic political principles as the precondition for political legitimacy; and (C) a set of substantive institutional conditions, including constitutional democracy, broad individual freedoms and civil liberties, and sometimes some measure of state welfare provision or income redistribution. We saw in section 1.3 that autonomy-based weak perfectionism best accommodates and justifies these commitments by providing a principled basis for the procedural conditions specified by (B) and generating the substantive claims regarding freedom and democracy laid out in (C). In addition, weak perfectionism responds to (A), the fact of pluralism, both by upholding the value of autonomy (and thus of certain forms of pluralism) and by showing equal respect and consideration (via the guarantee of equal citizenship) to heteronomous and autonomous adults alike. When we turn our attention to the *development* of individual autonomy, however, and especially to the notion that the state ought to promote children's development of autonomy, the liberal legitimation conditions seem to fit together much less well.

To begin with, for the state to foster children's development of autonomy requires coercion—i.e., it requires measures that prima facie violate the principles of freedom and choice affirmed by (C). For example, children are granted none of the rights and freedoms that I mentioned in section 1.1 as centrepieces or hallmarks of liberalism, such as democratic participation, the right to own and exchange private property, freedoms of speech, conscience, religion, and association, and the right to privacy. If children are permitted to vote, for example, it is feared that they may be taken in by politicians who promise them enticing freedoms and services now but who in the long run will (intentionally or simply out of incompetence) dangerously reduce their and our opportunities for choice. Unable to judge competently the claims made by competing politicians, children are thought to be made more free or autonomous in the long run by being denied the vote until their capacity for judgement is more fully developed. Likewise, full freedom of association, rights to private property, and even freedom of movement are denied to children in their own interest. The fear is that children who are permitted these freedoms—to choose their own friends without any guidance, for example, or to 'hang out' whenever and wherever they wish—run the risk of making choices that in the end reduce their capacity for autonomy and stunt its development.[4] Even the twin virtues of transparency and publicity, so vaunted by liberals at every stage of government legitimation and action, are thought to be justifiably modified at times in relation to childhood education for autonomy.[5] Furthermore, not only are children denied liberties routinely granted to adults; they are also subjected by the state to regulations—such as compulsory schooling (state or private)—from which adults are utterly exempt. While such institutions ideally aim in the long term at freeing children (by helping them to develop a capacity for autonomy), they still involve massive interference with and restrictions over children in the meantime—and as one author reminds us, 'We think that the purpose of the child is to grow up, because it does grow up. But its purpose is to play, to enjoy itself, to be a child. If we merely look to the end of the process, the purpose of all life is death.'[6]

The coercive nature of state promotion of the development of autonomy also means that children do not have the luxury of 'opting out' of public autonomy-advancing opportunities in the same way that adults do. This is true in three ways. First, insofar as adults are confronted by political *free-doms* and *opportunities* that advance the exercise of individual autonomy, they can simply decide not to take advantage of them, with no loss to or change of behavior required from either themselves or the state. The state can continue to make freedoms available to all adults, and adults can continue to make individual choices about making use of the opportunities—choices, too, which they are free to change at any future time.[7] But if children must be actively *coerced* by the state (through compulsory schooling, denial of liberties, and so forth), then there is no possibility of retreat. Given that children are viewed as not having the capacity adequately to judge their own interests, it would not make sense for the state to decide that children's interests lie in the development of a capacity for autonomy yet allow them to refuse to develop this capacity. The state may value the exercise of autonomy yet respect those adults who choose not to be autonomous; it cannot treat children the same way. Thus, in the end, children are far more profoundly affected than adults by the state's weakly perfectionist valuation of autonomy.

Second, children's co-optation is compounded by the fact that insofar as the state decides *for* children that they should develop the capacity for autonomy, it excludes them from the procedural participation that is deemed essential for political legitimacy. The liberal state values the exercise of autonomy for adults, in a certain sense, because adults agree (in theory) that it is in their interest for the state to do so. They have chosen, through the procedures specified in (B), for the state to promote their exercise of autonomy in the public sphere. And, as just discussed above, adults who prefer to live heteronomous lives can do so within (albeit in spite of) the autonomy-advancing political culture. Children, in contrast, have made and can make no such decision about the state's weakly perfectionist commitment to the development of autonomy. Unable freely to participate in the public political dialogue, they are necessarily excluded from the legitimation of autonomy (or of anything else) as a political goal. Trapped within the confines of profound political inequality, children are subject to state paternalism despite their never having participated in a procedure legitimating this relationship.

Third, the compulsory development of a *capacity* for autonomy—even if the child is never forced to *exercise* his autonomy as an adult—entails other consequences that may fall outside the state's legitimate sphere of influence. Once a child develops the capacity for autonomy, it becomes impossible for him to hold certain conceptions of the good in the same way that would previously have been available to him. As we saw in relation to Rawls' 'burdens of judgement' in Chapter 1, even passively possessing the knowledge and dispositions that underlie the capacity for autonomy—where such dispositions include toleration of others, values pluralism, openness to criticisms from others, and the recognition that reasonable people can hold incommensurable and even incompatible conceptions of the good—radically alters the way that one approaches certain professions of value and belief. Nomi Stolzenberg expresses this point powerfully in discussing fundamentalist Christian parents' concerns about 'value-neutral' state education:

fundamentalists are not concerned only with the case in which their children unequivocally reject their values; they are also concerned with the case in which their children remain attached to their parents' views, but only after coming to see those views as *such*—as subjective, contestable matters of opinion. There is a subtle but important difference between the faith that is innocent of alternatives and that which is not.[8]

She expands this point later:

The point is not simply that the objective mode of exposure exhibits options, or even that it encourages rational selection from them. It is that even if the children [continue to] adhere to their parents' beliefs, they do so knowing that those beliefs are matters of opinion. This knowledge enhances the likelihood that children will form their own opinions and deviate from at least some of their parents' beliefs. It also transforms the meaning of remaining (or in the case of children, becoming) attached to them. It is one thing for beliefs to be transmitted from one generation to another. It is another to hold beliefs, knowing that those beliefs are transmitted, that they vary, and that their truth is contested.[9]

These same children and parents might highlight a final conflict in the liberal state's commitment to helping children develop autonomy by questioning the justification for the state's interference in the essentially private matter of raising children in the first place. The family is a pre-political institution, they might suggest, whose integrity cannot legitimately be violated by the state. The family cannot be made subject to political and state control without doing violence to our understanding both of the separation between public and private—which separation is essential to liberal theory in general, and to an autonomy-based liberal weak perfectionism in particular—and of the primacy of the family over the state. In addition, it might be argued, children's interests (and human interests in general) are inseparable from the institution of the family; thus, it is nonsensical and misguided to try to assert a child's right to autonomy from outside the family sphere. These are powerful and to a large extent intuitively plausible claims in favor of family independence from political pressure and control; any political theory which calls for state interference in children's (and therefore families') lives, as liberalism does, must therefore take them very seriously indeed.

In conclusion, some of the most attractive elements of liberalism's substantive conditions—that they are compatible with heteronomous agents and heteronomous ways of life; that they permit individuals a private sphere of life into which the state does not intrude; and, most fundamentally, that they are principles of liberty and not of coercion or paternalism—are lost when liberalism declares the state's obligation to promote not just the exercise of autonomy but its development as well. State involvement in fostering children's development of autonomy violates pluralism, imposes restrictions on people (children) who were not participants in the legitimation process, denies them basic liberties, violates the terms of weak perfectionism by forcing children to develop the capacity for autonomy, and infringes the public/private divide by interfering with the family. In all of these respects, liberalism seems incompatible with a political commitment to children's development of autonomy.

2.2 PATERNALISTIC CONTROL AND THE 'FUNDAMENTAL INTERESTS' OF THE CHILD

The case for the compatibility of liberalism with state perfectionism concerning the development of autonomy looks pretty bleak, given the latter's multiple violations of both the procedural and the substantive tenets of liberalism. From all appearances so far, liberalism will at a minimum have to divorce its commitment to promoting the exercise of autonomy in adults from any efforts to help children develop autonomy—although as the Dworkinian argument that opened the chapter pointed out, it is probably conceptually incoherent to value the former as a good in itself (as the exercise of autonomy is taken to be) without thereby valuing the latter as well. Thus, if the criticisms articulated in section 1 are right, then it may be that liberalism's entire commitment to autonomy should be re-evaluated. In this section, however, I shall argue that the above criticisms are misleading, and that liberal theory *is* compatible with obligating the state to promote in children the development of the capacity for autonomy. My response will come in a slightly odd form, as I believe that the above problems are actually best confronted by responding to a further set of criticisms, this time from the children's liberationist camp. I hope that by working through the arguments set forth by children's liberationists, we will come to understand the relationships among the autonomy-oriented liberal state, adults, and children much better. This analysis will also illuminate how and why liberalism is compatible with the paternalistic violation of conditions (A), (B), and (C) mandated by the development of autonomy.

Before we step into the paternalism minefield, let me introduce one piece of symbolic notation and clarify one definitional point. First, because it is verbally cumbersome constantly to distinguish between paternalism in general and paternalism specifically toward children, I will use 'paternalism$_c$' to mean 'paternalism toward children', and 'paternalism$_a$' to mean 'paternalism toward adults'. This will make the discussion cleaner and less convoluted. Second, paternalism in general needs to be defined. At this point, I will take it loosely to mean the restriction of someone's freedom for their own good. Insofar as Chapter 1 is right that it is autonomy that the liberal ultimately views as valuable in individuals' lives, 'their own good' must therefore be understood, at least within the context of liberal theory, as relating to the capacity for autonomy. Utilitarianism, desire-satisfaction theory, and so forth are thus irrelevant to a liberal conception of paternalism, and to liberal paternalists' conceptions of others' good. There are a number of unacknowledged complexities lurking within this characterization, and I myself will suggest a modified understanding of paternalism below, but this definition should suffice for present purposes.

The problems with involving the state in fostering the development of autonomy, as discussed in the last section, can in part be summed up by the statement that, as Howard Cohen puts it, 'There is one set of rights for adults and another for children. Adults' rights mostly provide them with opportunities to exercise their powers; children's rights mostly provide them with protection and keep them under adult control.'[10] It is children's subjection to others that seems to violate the procedural and substantive conditions of liberalism. Of all children's liberationists, Cohen offers one of the most cogent articulations of this problem in his *Equal Rights for Children*. He starts from the widely recognized universalizability principle of social justice, that we must treat people equally unless there exists a morally relevant distinction among them that justifies unequal treatment. Thus, all people deserve equal rights (whatever those rights may be) unless there is a difference between them that is relevant to possessing the right in question. When we consider differential treatment toward adults and children, therefore,

> If there are differences between adults and children which are relevant to granting rights to one group but not the other, then it [differential treatment] is not unjust. But if the differences are not relevant, then the two groups are, and should be, treated alike. . . . When we call for equal rights for children—for an end to the double standard—we want the elimination of 'child' as a separate category *in all aspects of life where the distinction is not relevant.*[11]

Applying this to the problem of paternalism, we might ask what it is about children that makes paternalism$_c$ justified; or, conversely, we might raise the question of why adults are assumed to have rights *against* paternalistic$_a$ coercion. In other words, on what grounds does the state base the power of self-governance in adults? When the question is approached from this angle, the answer becomes obvious. From the standpoint of liberalism, paternalism$_a$ is wrong because adults' exercise of autonomy (which would be violated by the state's exercise of paternalism$_a$) is valuable and politically relevant. This was one of the important conclusions of Chapter 1: liberal rights and institutions—including adults' state-protected liberties and rights against undue coercion—are justified because adults cannot exercise autonomy in the absence of such liberties, and the exercise of autonomy is a valuable enterprise. Paternalism$_a$ by the state is outlawed where it would violate citizens' autonomy.[12]

The presupposition of this chapter, on the other hand, is that children are not autonomous—if they were, then our attention to *developing* autonomy in children would be both misplaced and unnecessary. If children do not possess autonomy, and the source of liberal rights against paternalistic interference is the value of the exercise of autonomy, then children seem not to merit rights against paternalism equal to those merited by adults. The distinction between children and adults *is* relevant to the rights in question; to impose paternalistic restrictions on children, therefore, seems to be compatible with social justice. As Locke adds in the *Second Treatise*, 'Thus we are born free as we are born rational; not that we have actually the exercise of either: age that brings one, brings with it the other too. And thus we see how natural freedom and subjection to parents may consist together, and are both founded on the same principle.'[13]

Once the liberal admits that adults are protected against paternalism$_a$ only because of the value attached to their exercise of autonomy, however, he opens himself up to the most probing criticism of paternalism$_c$: namely, that children are actually just as autonomous as adults are—or (on the more pessimistic and equally damning view), that many adults have just as little capacity for autonomous thought and action as children have.[14] Another prominent children's liberationist, John Harris, puts the point bluntly:

So if it is supposed that it is the comprehensive possession by adults of capacities lacked equally comprehensively by children that sustains and justifies the political disabling of children and the rule of adults, the supposition is false. False because there are numerous children whom it would be implausible to regard as incompetent and numerous adults whom it would be implausible to regard as anything else. Whatever we may finally decide about the status of children it is unlikely that the 'facts of human development', in so far as they are ascertainable, will support the rigid 'age of majority' division between adults and children.[15]

It is important to note that this argument against differential treatment of children and adults can succeed even if the previous criticisms fail. It might be right that the development of autonomy requires paternalism, this argument goes; and it might even be right that the relevant criterion for having certain rights is having the capacity for autonomy. *But*, Harris's quotation suggests, neither of these admissions gives us any reason to believe that paternalism$_c$ is justified when paternalism$_a$ is not. Autonomous people simply cannot be sorted out on the basis of age; the two characteristics are logically independent and empirically separate. Thus, if justifications for paternalism are linked to autonomy, then paternalism cannot be linked to age. If paternalism is linked to age, then it cannot be justified on grounds of helping the heteronomous. And so, unless we are willing to accept widespread paternalism$_a$, abandon democracy, and submit ourselves to a ruling elite with the power to decide about every individual whether she is autonomous and therefore free or heteronomous and therefore subject to paternalistic control, we must reject both paternalism$_a$ and paternalism$_c$ at once as being two sides of the same coin.[16]

This is an important argument. Insofar as Chapter 1 is right, that the institutional conditions of the liberal state are dependent on the state's recognizing the value of the exercise of individual autonomy, then the fact that many adults do not exhibit the capacity for autonomy does threaten its foundations. The liberal cannot permit the state to decide on a case-by-case basis who is autonomous and who is not, for tyranny would rapidly result. Massive numbers of adults would end up being denied fundamental liberal rights—or would be if we treated them like the children to whom they turn out to be similar.[17] Also, there is a real fear that if the state were given the power to decide who possesses autonomy and who does not, it could establish arbitrary and coercive requirements that would in essence give it total (tyrannical) power over all individuals' lives. At least under systems current in Western liberal democracies, people have full freedom from age 18 or so onwards, even if they may have been unjustly restricted on paternalistic$_c$ grounds before then. In the state currently under discussion, people could conceivably be restricted for their whole lives, simply because they fail to satisfy the state that they deserve freedom (because they voted for the wrong political party? because they are members of a despised religion?).

To avoid such collapse into tyranny, liberalism could abandon its links between rights and autonomy—although as Chapter 1 demonstrated, liberalism would lose much of its plausibility and normative weight if it did so. Or, more successfully, the liberal state could operate according to a *presumption of autonomy*, as opposed to a presumption of its lack; i.e., the state could assume that all citizens have the capacity for autonomous action unless there were good reason to think otherwise. As John Kleinig suggests, 'competence is presumed until disproved'.[18] The advantage of this move is that it has strong empirical as well as theoretical justification. From the perspective of liberal theory, the presumption of autonomy sets the universal provision to adults of substantive rights and freedoms back on a firm foundation, thus pulling liberalism back from the risk of dissolving into a blueprint for tyranny. And from an empirical perspective, there *is* a group about which there is every 'reason to think otherwise' about their possessing the capacity for autonomy—namely, infants and young children. It would be ludicrous to argue that four-year-olds—or even most ten-year-olds—have the capacity for autonomy in the complex sense given in section 1.3. This is not to say that ten-year-olds could not take care of themselves, or do not have articulated conceptions of the good. But it is to say that because of a combination of lack of experience, underdeveloped critical reasoning skills, insufficient emotional independence, and so forth, they do not yet have the capacity for full autonomy. Thus, while the liberal starts out by crediting all individuals with the presumption of autonomy, she does have a good reason to withdraw that presumption from young children. In other words, the presumption of autonomy is justifiably age-sensitive.[19]

Once this step is admitted, and its full significance recognized, then the rest of the argument for (some as yet-undetermined measure of) paternalism$_c$ falls into place. Given that no four-year-old possesses autonomy, we have the unproblematic right paternalistically to aid the development of autonomy in the young; at the same time, we are forbidden from imposing similar compulsory measures on adults (who are assumed to possess the capacity for autonomy). The problem then becomes one of deciding where to mark the transition between the heteronomous young and the presumptively autonomous not-young—a task which, while difficult and highly contentious, is thoroughly different from trying to justify paternalism$_c$ altogether.

Here instrumental considerations can legitimately be brought to bear. As was discussed above, it is both too impractical and too dangerous (in terms of giving the state too much power) to distinguish youth from adults by any other means but establishing a standard age (from which exemptions could possibly be sought).[20] Even if we had no fear of tyranny, it would be a tremendous burden on the state, and undoubtedly a disservice to the young themselves, to impose autonomy tests on all children every year. Thus, we must simply, and to a certain extent arbitrarily, find some standard age(s) to mark the transition from youth to non-youth, and therefore from (some measure of) justifiable paternalism$_c$ to protection from paternalism$_a$. To argue for standardization is not, however, to argue for a single age of majority. Given that the development of autonomy is itself a gradual process, there can and probably should be a gradual transition from youth to adulthood in which different rights and privileges are assumed at different times. People might gain the right to choose their doctor at age 12, to consent to major surgery at age 14, to withdraw from school at 15 or 16, to run for the US Senate at 30, and so forth. These ages are obviously contestable, malleable, and at least locally arbitrary[21]—but some set of standard ages must be chosen. So, even though it is true that 'Bold, quick, ingenious, forward and capable young people are by no means a rarity, [and] neither, unfortunately, are dull-witted, incompetent adults',[22] we have no reason to reject paternalism toward children *tout court*, nor are we obligated for the same reason to abandon liberalism in favour of strict paternalism toward adults.

While this local victory may come as something of a relief to autonomy-valuing liberals, it would be a mistake to think that in answering the criticisms posed by the above children's liberationists, liberalism's task of justification is complete. Our association of paternalism with autonomy (and its violation) left unaddressed three criticisms from section 1: first, that children are wrongly excluded from the procedural legitimation of the state (including the legitimation of the state's guiding aims, of which the development of autonomy is one); second, that because of the conceptual shifts forced by gaining the publicly promoted capacity for autonomy, children lose the ability privately to hold certain valued conceptions of the good—and that this loss can never be recovered, even in adulthood, where the public/private distinction is meant to be respected by the state; and last, following on from these public/private concerns, that paternalistic control over children should be left to the family instead of being assumed by the state, in acknowledgement of the family's integrity as a private institution.

These criticisms raise two fundamental questions that the liberal must address. First, does the child have any substantive interests (e.g. in developing the capacity for autonomy) independent of those acknowledged by the individuals who take responsibility for her—or even by herself? In other words, do liberal principles about adults tell us anything about hypothetical interests held by the child that limit what can be done in the name of her own good? Second, who has the right more generally to determine the child's best interest, especially in cases of conflict? Does the identity of the paternalistic agents matter? Should we take the claims of parents, for example, more seriously than we take the claims of other people or institutions who are interested in the child's welfare?[23]

In regard to these questions, there are two points which deserve to be made immediately. First, we must realize that the child is going to be the subject of paternalistic coercion regardless of who is determining her best interest or what that interest is judged to be. Paternalism and limitations on the child's freedom are required to foster the development of her autonomy, it is true; they are also required to inculcate in her a restricted, heteronomous conception of the good. The child is inevitably treated paternalistically, by her parents, the state, concerned adult friends and relatives, teachers, doctors, and so forth. What is at issue, therefore, is not *whether* paternalism in general is justified, but *who* has the right to determine its nature and aim. Second, it is simply false to suggest that as a private institution, the family is or should be completely independent of the state. None of us believes that parents have the right to do anything they wish to their children. The state has to have *some* notion of the child's fundamental interests, including her future interests, and has some right to interfere in the family based on this account. The task then is to spell out what that conception of the 'child's fundamental interests' is; it is not to justify the state's holding such a notion in the first place.

Given these two facts, the state's fostering the development of autonomy in children becomes easier to justify than it seemed at first blush. Consider a case in which an 'intolerant' parent raises his child to be heteronomous, believing that to be most conducive to the child's good, whereas the state believes that it is in the child's best interest to develop the capacity for autonomy. Both agents are paternalistically motivated, interested solely in the child's own benefit, and both parties assume (rightly, let us suppose) that the child does not already have an authentic developed conception of the good. Which—or whose—perception of the child's good has the right to trump? Well, as I just noted, both parties (the state and the parents) are justified in taking an interest in the child, and in positing and defending a substantive notion of the child's future interests. In addition, both parties will enact their notions through the use of paternalistic coercion. The child has no more control under the parent than she does under the state; in this sense, both of the first two criticisms raised above concerning the child's lack of choice are equally applicable to both prospective paternalistic agents. Thus from the child's (hypothetical) point of view, it is morally arbitrary who—the state or the parent—exerts coercive control over her. Both are in equal need of justification. As Gutmann comments, 'We have no a priori reason to favor one paternalistic agent over another.'[24]

Given that it is morally arbitrary from the child's perspective *who* the paternalistic agent is, the conflict must be resolved in terms of *what* paternalistic doctrine is more in the child's interest.[25] Here again the notion of choice becomes relevant. As we saw in Chapter 1, one of the primary sources of legitimacy in liberal theory is individual agreement or consent; this reliance on consent is symbolized by the legitimation conditions introduced in section 1.1 and cited throughout that chapter. Children have no opportunity for choice when young. Their lives and their values are inevitably (and rightfully) shaped by others. But the most legitimate basis for this coercion, on a liberal reading, would seem to be that which gives children the capacity for choice—the capacity to overcome the bounds of coerciveness—later on in life. The way to transfer power over their own lives back to individuals, of course, is to help them to develop a capacity for autonomy. Thus, a paternalistic doctrine that favors the development of autonomy must be judged superior (continuing with the child's hypothetical perspective) to one which inculcates heteronomy. The state is justified, therefore, in helping children to develop the capacity for autonomy, even against parents' *and children's* expressed wishes. In promoting the development of autonomy, the state is not claiming that the autonomous way of life is the only legitimate way of life, or that autonomy is a prerequisite for citizenship. It is simply trying to right the balance of power by giving individuals the ability in their adult lives to do what they could not do as children—specifically, to determine their own values and to adopt a conception of the good with which they identify (as opposed to those with which they happened as children to be identified).[26]

The autonomy-fearing parent introduced above may still protest that his child's choice is stunted because she will no longer be able to adopt her parent's conception of the good in the same way she might have before she developed her capacity for autonomy. This was the thrust of the second objection above. It is likely that there is no liberal answer that will fully satisfy this parent—for which reason I said in Chapter 1 that autonomy-based weak perfectionism provides the best, but not a perfect, means of simultaneously satisfying (A), (B), and (C). There is nonetheless a response that satisfies the demands of weakly perfectionistic liberal theory, which is what matters for my purposes. The parent's criticism, I suggest, is effectively countered from a liberal perspective by Joseph Raz's insight that 'while autonomy requires the availability of an adequate range of options it does not require the presence of any particular option among them'.[27] The liberal state must permit individuals to lead heteronomous lives because 'denying a person the possibility of carrying on with his projects, commitments and relationships is preventing him from having the life he has chosen'. But this toleration of heteronomy need not carry over to children: 'A person who may but has not yet chosen the eliminated option is much less seriously affected. Since all he is entitled to is an adequate range of options the eliminated option can, from his point of view, be replaced by another without loss of autonomy.'[28]

Again, this response will presumably not satisfy the autonomy-fearing parent, who is concerned that his child lead the *right* way of life, not that his child be able to choose among a number of what are by his definition bad lives. The point of this chapter, however—and largely of the book as a whole, as I discussed in the Introduction—is not to justify liberalism to all illiberals, which I do not think can effectively be done. In a deeply plural society no set of liberal principles and institutions will gain free, unanimous consent; not all individuals will become liberals. Insofar as autonomy-based weak perfectionism provides the strongest and most widely acceptable justification for liberal principles, it also provides a solid justification for protecting children's range of options without necessarily protecting any particular option—even if some parents do not agree. Furthermore, I suggest that just as the liberal state need not adjust its behavior when certain cultures find it hard to flourish as a result of the atmosphere created by liberal rights and freedoms, neither need the state be overly concerned about cultural attrition caused by its advancement of the development of autonomy in children. If people who have gained the capacity for autonomy choose to leave the communities in which they were raised and to develop their lives in different directions, then while this outcome might be unfortunate, it is not a violation of the state's legitimacy or of any of the principles for which it stands.[29]

It is worth making explicit at this point an argument that has thus far been implicitly developed: namely, that liberalism is not, and cannot consistently be, a neutrality-driven theory. Chapter 1 made this argument in relation to adults, suggesting that neither acceptance of the fact of pluralism nor commitment to the legitimation conditions can effectively justify traditional liberal freedoms and institutions without a non-neutral, weakly perfectionist embrace of the value of individual autonomy. Even if one were to reject that claim, however, the fact that children are inevitably subject to paternalistic coercion also deals a blow to liberalism as a neutralist theory. For insofar as a child's best interests must be determined by actors other than the child herself, the liberal state may either participate in determining the content of children's interests, or abdicate responsibility by allowing parents, family members, communities, secondary associations, etc. to make all the decisions about the child's upbringing. If it does the former, the state is obviously not acting neutrally in the sense favored by political (neutrality-based) liberals.[30] In the latter case, the state might plausibly be described as neutral, but this form of neutrality can hardly be desirable insofar as it amounts to tacit consent to the coercion of the weaker (child) by the stronger (parent/family/community).[31] The idea that abdication of this kind is a desirable form of neutrality can be traced, I believe, to the misapprehension that liberalism requires the state to be neutral among competing conceptions of the good. But if anything can be said to be entitled to neutral treatment, it is not the *conceptions of the good*, but rather the *people* who hold these conceptions. Moral doctrines or value systems have no independent political standing; they are not agents or actors or citizens. What liberals really mean to say is that the state should be neutral among individuals holding competing conceptions of the good. Children, however, do not have developed conceptions of the good. Thus, neutrality seems not to apply to the relationship between the state and children, except insofar as the state's involvement with children affects parents' abilities to pursue their own conceptions of the good. And, as I argue in the following section, parents' inclusion of children in the realization of their own conceptions of the good is again unjustified to the extent that it amounts to the coercion of the weaker by the stronger. If the principle of neutrality does not justifiably govern the relationship between the state and children, of course, then this has implications for the status of neutrality between the state and adults as well.

2.3 JUSTIFICATIONS FOR PARENTAL CONTROL

It may seem that I have now moved from one unattractive philosophical extreme to the other. Having started out by examining suggestions about the inseparability of the interests of the child from the interests of the family, I have ended up with what appears to be a radical articulation of the child's independence from the family and of the state's overriding interest in forcibly developing children's capacities for autonomy.[32] In this section, I argue that although it is true that from the child's perspective there exists 'no a priori reason to favor one paternalistic agent over another',[33] there are nonetheless compelling, child-centred reasons to grant primary control and child-rearing responsibility to the parent(s) as opposed to other agents.[34] I thus argue in favor of a presumption of the parents' *privilege* rather than *right* to govern their children's upbringing. As James Dwyer succinctly suggests, 'From a moral [and political] perspective, a parental privilege would not convey or reflect a sense of entitlement to direct a child's life, but instead would bear the aspect of a benefit contingent upon the fulfillment of attendant responsibilities, much in the nature of a trust.'[35] I suggest in this section that establishing parental privilege over the care and governance of children best respects children's needs and interests in developing their capacities for autonomy without unjustifiably infringing upon parents' autonomy.

First, there is a strong argument in favor of straightforward parental control deriving from what Judith Shklar has termed the 'liberalism of fear':[36] namely, that a state with the strength to enforce any other means of distributing control over children would inevitably be tyrannical in all aspects of governance. As Gutmann comments, 'liberals justifiably fear a state so powerful that it could, as a matter of routine practice, take all children away from their biological parents'.[37] The desire of parents to raise and care for their children is probably one of the most innate and universal of all human desires. It would take extraordinary physical strength and/or massive psychological manipulation in order to dispossess parents wholesale of their children and assign caring responsibility to someone else. All people, adults, parents, and children alike, would suffer in a state possessed of such power, since it is inconceivable that such a state would limit its actions to justified, non-tyrannical behavior. Following on from this recognition of parents' psychological link with their children, a secondary argument might also be made that the incentive to produce children is drastically reduced if biological parents run the risk of being deprived of their children at birth. While this suggestion, if true, gives extra weight in favor of biological parents' rights to keep their children, I believe that the first argument alone is enough to shift the balance of power from the state (or a similar redistributive agency) to biological parents.

That biological parents (or their surrogates) normally have the right to keep their children in the family, so to speak, does not necessarily give them rights, however, to determine the terms of paternalistic control. This in part is a restatement of the conclusion of the previous section. Drawing upon the recognition in that section that the identity of the paternalistic agent is morally arbitrary from the point of view of the child, there seems to be no reason *in principle* that a committee consisting of the state and other self-appointed interested adults might not demand to make collective judgements in tandem with the parents about the child's best interests. Locke reminds us of the ephemeral source of parental authority: 'The power, then, that parents have over their children arises from that duty which is incumbent on them, to take care of their offspring during the imperfect state of childhood. To inform the mind, and govern the actions of their yet ignorant nonage, till reason shall take its place and ease them of that trouble, is what the children want, and the parents are bound to.'[38]

There is nothing in this passage to suggest why it is only the parents who may judge how to 'inform [their child's] mind', or to 'govern the actions of their yet ignorant nonage'. If others can govern better, why should they not be granted partial control? Parents would still be allowed to keep their children and act as primary caretakers, but decisions about child-rearing would be subject to collective deliberation. A second set of arguments, therefore, is needed to justify parents' exerting primary control over the child's upbringing.

These arguments divide into three types: parent-autonomy-regarding, pragmatic or psychological, and child-autonomy-regarding. The latter two provide strong liberal justifications for parent privilege; parent-autonomy-regarding arguments, on the other hand, make uncompelling and illiberal cases for parents' rights over their children, and I address and dispense with these first.

From the perspective of parental autonomy, three arguments support the assumption of parental rights to paternalistic control over their children. The first of these is fairly simple: to rear a child may be a joy, but it is also a tremendous burden. From the day-to-day worries about day care and baby-sitters to the soul-rending crises of wondering 'Am I doing the right thing?' or 'Where did I go wrong?', child-rearing is not an easy business. Thus it is suggested that in exchange for taking on such a severe burden, parents have a right to raise their children in a way that will least disturb their own lives or cause conflicts with their own visions of the good.[39] Given that *somebody* will have to shape the child's moral outlook and mores for living, parents deserve to take primary control so that the child's mores do not cause unnecessary rifts or tears in the fabric of daily family life. This argument is parent-regarding in the weak sense that it appeals to a notion of just compensation, reimbursing parents in the form of rights to paternalistic control for what they lose in personal freedom and independence. Although this argument does give some weight to the notion of parental privilege to control their children's upbringing, it does not, however, justify the assignment to parents of a *right* to do so. Especially insofar as child-rearing is a burden (activity, joy, etc.) that adults in Western, industrialized countries can *choose* to take on or reject (via birth control before conception, and abortion or adoption after the fact), parents do not merit the *right* to control another person's future as compensation for a burden voluntarily shouldered.

A more interesting and controversial parent-regarding argument depends on a much more robust understanding of parental rights and parental autonomy. It is suggested that an essential part of one's autonomy is the right to pass one's values onto one's children. We cannot fully and autonomously enact our conception of the good life, under this reading, unless we have the right to share our conception with others, and specifically to initiate our children into this same vision. As Charles Fried argues, 'the right to form one's child's values, one's child's life plan and the right to lavish attention on the child are extensions of the basic right not to be interfered with in doing these things for oneself'.[40] A striking example of this claimed inseparability between one's own conception of the good and that of one's children is raised in an American case, *Mozert v. Hawkins County Public Schools*.[41] In 1983, a group of fundamentalist Christian parents in Tennessee tried to get permission to remove their primary-school-aged children from a reading class in which, they claimed, the mandatory reading text: taught 'that some values are relative and vary from situation to situation'; included 'various humanistic values' that were 'evil', 'polluted', and 'heathen'; and induced 'children to stray from the way of God'.[42] When permission to remove their children to the library during the reading period was denied by the school board, the parents sued the Hawkins County Public Schools for violation of the clause in the First Amendment of the US Constitution that guarantees free religious exercise. Although the case as a whole is fascinating (the parents eventually lost[43]), what is relevant in this context is the parents' argument that independent of the evil brought upon the children by reading the text, the parents themselves faced 'eternal damnation'[44] for permitting their children to participate in the reading program. This is because by doing so they were breaking the biblical commands to 'learn not the ways of the heathen' and to 'have no fellowship with the unfruitful works of darkness, but rather reprove them, for it is shameful even to mention what the disobedient do in secret'.[45] In essence, living out their own conception of the good was inseparable from inculcating that conception in their children; to fail to do the latter would be a gross violation of the former, and of everything the Bible and their lives stood for.

While the sincerity of the parents' complaint is compelling, and the conflict not an easy one to resolve, this argument seems highly suspect from the perspective of liberalism. Liberals unanimously agree that the fact that my conception of the good might include your becoming my personal slave, or your affirming my conception of the good, gives neither me nor anybody else any legitimate reason whatsoever to command your participation in or affirmation of my project. Why, then, should we consider this demand to be any more justified when it is parents making the claim in relation to their children? Fried's suggestion notwithstanding, children are widely recognized to be individuals separate from others, and not mere extensions of their parents or their parents' interests. As Kleinig drily notes, 'Although there is historical support for the view that children are the property of their parents, there is not much else to be said in its favor.'[46]

It is implausible, therefore, that the *Mozert* parents' interpretation of parental-autonomy reasons alone could make a sufficient case for parent-dominated paternalistic control over children—let alone for the stronger concept of parents' rights.

A final, related parent-regarding argument in favor of biological parents' rights to control their children's lives has been put forward by Ferdinand Schoeman. It rests on the value of *intimacy* in human beings' lives. Parents have a 'moral claim to raise their biological offspring in a context of privacy, autonomy [meaning that parents have wide latitude in determining the character and range of their children's experiences as well as their approach to discipline], and responsibility', not because that is necessarily always in the best interests of the child, but because child-rearing under these conditions enables parents to experience intimate relationships with their children, which experience of intimacy is itself a basic human good or right.[47] Intimacy, Schoeman argues, is a large part of what makes life worth living; it is the opportunity to 'share our selves' with others and have them share themselves with us that gives our lives meaning (or, less strongly, that many people see as giving their lives meaning). Thus, Schoeman concludes, 'the parent's right to raise her children in a family [including privacy, autonomy, and responsibility rights] stems naturally from the right to engage in intimate relationships, even when recognition of this right involves some comparative cost to the child'.[48] Eamonn Callan builds on this point, arguing that 'the freedom to rear our children according to the dictates of conscience is for most of us as important as any other expression of conscience, and the freedom to organize and sustain the life of the family in keeping with our own values is as significant as our liberty to associate with others outside the family for any purpose whatsoever'.[49] In other words, the liberal freedoms (C) that I said in Chapter 1 were partially constitutive of the liberal state, and without a commitment to which no theory can be considered liberal, necessarily include the freedoms to follow our conscience and associate intimately with our families in raising our children.

This is an intriguing interpretation of parent-regarding rights to control their children insofar as it binds children to their parents by blurring the distinctions between the parties' identities (because they 'share' themselves with each other) without thereby necessarily asserting that children are extensions or property of their parents. Insofar as we find this conception of intimacy and the role it plays in human lives compelling, it may provide the strongest reason yet to recognize parental privilege to control their children's upbringing. Nevertheless, it is unsuccessful in justifying a parental *right* to such control. For although liberals (and the liberal state) can coherently recognize the good of intimacy as giving meaning to many people's

lives, they also recognize that the conditions under which intimacy is established are significant both morally and politically. Intimacy may possibly be
conceived as a 'right' (which is how Schoeman must conceive of it in order
to support his claim of parental rights to an intimate relationship with their
children) when it applies to a relationship that two or more parties enter
willingly and autonomously. But we do not and should not recognize intimacy as a 'right' to force, manipulate, or prey upon the weaknesses of a
person in order to establish an intimate relationship. Rape (forced physical
intimacy), unprofessional teacher–student relationships (emotional intimacy established by manipulating an extreme difference in power, maturity,
and autonomy), and even extreme dependency between two adults
(consider Harry from Chapter 1) are all examples of intimate relationships
that are rightly legally prohibited and/or morally condemned. To the
extent that a person must rely upon some form of manipulation to establish an intimate relationship with someone, therefore, it is simply false that
a liberal state would recognize that person's 'right' to intimacy.

Insofar as children do not enter the intimate relationship freely or
autonomously, therefore, it is difficult to see how parents' production of
children in order to have the opportunity to establish an intimate relationship with them gives them a *right* to such a relationship. It might give them
a privilege—based on the parent- and child-regarding assumptions that
such relationships virtually always give deep meaning to both parties' lives
(and, as I discuss below, that they are essential to children's well-being and
healthy development)—but not a right. This conclusion is especially justified since neither the parents' nor the child's legitimate interests in establishing intimate relationships with each other seem to be harmed if one
replaces 'right' with 'privilege' regarding parents' ability to control the
upbringing of their children without undue interference. Thus, while
parent-regarding arguments may support the notion of parents' privileges
to control their children's upbringing, they do not lend support to parents'
rights to the same.

Child-regarding considerations also support the concept of parent
privilege, although not of parental rights. As I mentioned above, two
related arguments about children's psychological and autonomy-based
interests in stability and cultural coherence provide the most plausible
justifications for parental control. First, the empirical argument is often
made that parents are better able to advance their children's interests in
general than other parties are. There exists a natural, even biological, bond
of affection between children and their parents that cannot be broken
without tremendous psychological cost to both sides, as the advocates of
intimacy note. This affective bond not only offers children essential
emotional support and sustenance, it is argued, but it also inspires parents

to further their children's interests more than other agents would, by giving them greater insight into their children's needs and greater forbearance and understanding when their children fail to live up to certain ideals. As Kleinig argues,

> there is some reason to think that the developmental needs of children are likely to be met most successfully in an environment in which primary responsibility, and the authority that is derivative of that, lies with the parents. There are grounds for believing that parents, more than anyone else, will have the kind of commitment to their offspring that will safeguard and promote their welfare interests, and encourage the formation of an identity and life-plans compatible with their individual character, abilities, and talents. Parents, therefore, are permitted a wide range of discretion so far as the treatment of their children is concerned.[50]

In addition, insofar as such a bond can be established only with real people with whom one lives in close contact (as opposed to with abstract institutions such as the state, or with governing committees such as the paternalistic overseeing board suggested above), there is good reason to think that a relatively small number of adults will qualify for such mutual affection.

Finally, the most overwhelming reason to grant parents the privilege of primary paternalistic control derives from the child's particular need for cultural coherence and a well-developed and culturally embedded personality. As section 1.3 argued, membership in a community and embeddedness within a cultural and normative framework is a primary need of individuals—and an essential prerequisite for autonomy. One cannot act autonomously if one has no firm structure of beliefs on which to act. Although secondary associations such as churches, Scouts, and community groups often play an important part in teaching children values and giving them a sense of identity, families are probably most central to this process. Not only do families provide this cultural coherence and structure for their children, but they also require freedom from undue interference from outsiders in order to do it successfully. As Kleinig argues, 'If children are to develop into beings with stable and cohesive interests, it is important that they be nurtured in a secure and integrated environment, where they are loved and cared for as intimates and not aliens. To interfere too much with parents' upbringing of their children is likely to destabilize the environment whose stability is of such importance to the children.'[51] Thus, it would be counterproductive to interfere with or remove primary paternalistic control from the family on the grounds of advancing children's autonomy, because (except in cases of abuse, neglect, and the like) only the family whose integrity is respected is able (in conjunction with other secondary institutions) to provide children the cultural coherence that constitutes one of the essential preconditions for autonomy.

It is important to note that in terms of establishing cultural coherence and nourishing the various elements of the child's personality, even autonomy-fearing or -hating families can provide an adequate grounding for children's future autonomy. Families can provide a great deal of the groundwork for autonomy without intending to, which gives a further reason not to interfere in their internal dynamics. For example, parents might raise the child within their community because they believe that is the way to salvation, or because they think the community embodies the only true way of life. So long as children are able to acquire from elsewhere the further capacities and habits of thought required for autonomy, their development will actually have been advanced by being initiated into the norms and practices of a coherent community. Furthermore, the emotional stability and support offered by many families, in conjunction with basic but important lessons about trust, love, and mutual respect that children often learn in the family context, crucially help children's development of autonomy regardless of parents' intentions in this regard.

We see, therefore, that parents and the liberal state can occupy complementary roles in relation to children's development of autonomy. Liberal principles commit them both to acting in accordance with children's interests, but as very different institutions, they generally meet this obligation in different, complementary ways. The state is responsible for ensuring that children are given the means to develop their capacities for autonomy (whatever those means may be). Because of children's deep interests in having a stable home life, part of its execution of this duty lies in respecting parents' privilege to govern their children's upbringing, and thus in not violating the family's integrity unless it reasonably believes that parents are not adequately discharging their obligations (exercising their privilege) in the child's interest. Parents, on the other hand, are responsible for their children's physical and psychological well-being, development of identity, and sense of cultural coherence—in addition to many other components of their children's well-being. Because their control over their children is justified via *children's* interests in developing autonomy rather than via *parental*-autonomy-regarding considerations, parents are considered to have the *privilege* to control their children's upbringing rather than the *right* to do so. Their exercise of this privilege, however, offers them ample scope for independent paternalistic control, regardless of their stance on the moral value of individual autonomy.

2.4 THE ROLE OF EDUCATION

Thus far I have established that children have a fundamental interest in developing the capacity for autonomy, and that the liberal state has a role in

advancing this interest. I have also argued that state involvement is compatible with a strong affirmation of the integrity of the family in raising children and inculcating in them a vision of the good life. Thus far, therefore,
my analysis of liberalism, families, and the development of autonomy
seems fairly benign, demanding little if any radical social or political
change. There is much more to developing autonomy, however, than
possessing cultural coherence and an adequately developed personality (the
two elements I focused on in section 3). In this section, I argue that the
liberal ideal of autonomy not merely permits but *requires* the intrusion of
the state into the child's life, specifically in the form of compulsory liberal
schooling. I suggest that it is difficult for children to achieve autonomy
solely within the bounds of their families and home communities—or even
within the bounds of schools whose norms are constituted by those held by
the child's home community. If we take the requirements of autonomy seriously, we see the need for a place separate from the environment in which
children are raised, for a community that is defined not by the values and
commitments of the child's home, whatever they happen to be, but by the
norms of critical inquiry, reason, and sympathetic reflection. This community is the liberal school, and its achievement and provision to all children is
the duty of the liberal state.[52] In order to see where this vision of the ideal
liberal education comes from, let us first remind ourselves of the characterization of autonomy developed in section 1.3.

The liberal ideal of personal autonomy, I concluded in Chapter 1, is a
substantive (as opposed to formal or procedural) notion of higher-order
preference formation within a context of plural constitutive values and
beliefs, openness to others' evaluations of oneself, and a broadly developed
moral, spiritual or aesthetic, intellectual, and emotional personality. It is
substantive in that it denies that individuals whose volitions involve
completely subsuming their will to another can be autonomous.
Independent of the formal aspects of such individuals' actions and decision
procedures, the substance of their volition to give up their will to the
absolute control of another is itself sufficient to establish them as
heteronomous. I assume that most children who are raised in a non-abusive
or psychologically neglectful household will rise above this level of
subservience and achieve basic substantive independence.

This conception of autonomy also demanded that individuals have a
plurality of constitutive commitments. As we saw in section 1.3, plurality
serves three purposes: (1) It enables the person to question any particular
value without suffering a wholesale loss of identity, insofar as her identity
is not dependent on the affirmation of a single value, desire, or belief. (2)
Similarly, it allows the individual to criticize some subset of her beliefs
from the standpoint of the others; she can revise her assessment of love,

say, or of her career, in the context of other normative beliefs and values, as opposed to searching for a mythical objective space from which to criticize everything. (This point relates also to the need for cultural coherence: i.e., the need for a pre-established but malleable normative structure in which to evaluate options.) And (3) an individual with plural constitutive values and commitments will likely be more receptive to other viewpoints and to other people's criticisms of her own views. All of these characteristics are necessary to the process of deliberating about the values one holds, and thus eventually to basing one's life on higher-order values and desires with which one identifies.

These three elements of pluralism themselves imply other useful conditions for autonomy, the most significant of which are: the existence of a thoughtful community which offers valuable evaluations and criticisms of one's own beliefs, a lack of false consciousness on one's own part and on others', and mutual respect and toleration. As social beings, we are always comparing ourselves to, contrasting ourselves with, adjusting ourselves to, and trying to live up to the ideals of other people; this is especially true of children. To achieve autonomy, therefore, it is useful to be surrounded by other people whose opinions, values, and activities are worth taking seriously. Further, this worth is in part premised on the assumption that what they have to say, and how they lead their lives, is in some way accurate and authentic. Just as true reflection and self-definition are difficult in a social vacuum, neither are they easily achieved in a context of falsehood or ignorance; thus the achievement of autonomy by *individuals* is aided by the presence of an educated *community* free from false consciousness. Finally, values pluralism and a disposition for self-reflection are meaningful only in the context of respect and toleration for differing viewpoints. An individual must realize at the least that reasonable people can hold views about the good that are different from his own—i.e., accept the burdens of judgement—for otherwise he cannot take criticisms of his own views seriously, and thus would have difficulty engaging in critical reflection properly understood.

These are demanding conditions. What implications do they have for the development of autonomy? Truthfully, if we take the conditions seriously, their implications are almost overwhelming. The following list sets forth just some of the personal qualities that seem necessary for individuals to achieve full autonomy. (It should be noted that the length and demanding nature of the list should be taken to indicate not only how much children have to learn in this regard, but also how much we as adults have yet to learn. In this sense, the list might best be described as setting forth a set of ideals to be striven for by all individuals who value autonomy, rather than as a practical guide to be realized in twelve short years of schooling.) I suggest that in order to develop and achieve autonomy, children should: gain sufficient self-esteem and confidence to feel comfortable articulating their views in public and laying themselves and their views open to challenge—but also possess enough humility to take challenges to their positions seriously; learn to express themselves in terms others will understand, and to listen to others' responses; be imaginative, possessing the ability to step into other people's shoes and to see perspectives other than their own; be creative, observant, and sensitive to subtlety; learn to think critically and to use reason effectively and judiciously; be willing to subject their own arguments and intuitions to the demand for proof; gain the skills and knowledge to put their beliefs and values into practice, including vocational and personal skills, manual and technical competency, and social skills, among others; be exposed to and interact with people from different backgrounds, and in different contexts; learn how to read and write, and to do basic mathematics; learn about their political rights and obligations, and learn as well the history of their locality, nation, and the world; and be initiated into the social meanings of the community in order to participate as members in the cultural conversation. (The list could clearly go on.)[53]

These skills, areas of knowledge, competencies, psychological states, habits, and structures of belief cannot be acquired from only one source. They are achieved by children over time and in a multitude of contexts, of which the most important is certainly the family. But it is hard for the family to help the child achieve autonomy completely on its own. This is obviously true in the case of 'intolerant' families whose conceptions of the good preclude autonomy in the way described above. The parents in the *Mozert* case discussed above specifically objected that the reading program had 'the potential to make Christian children to be other than who they are; to create in them a desire to change from their heritage' and to cause 'the children to become more rebellious, to believe that they are their own authority'.[54] Insofar as these objections boil down to the accusation that the reading program was advancing children's autonomy, it is clear that such parents and families cannot be counted on to help their children develop a capacity for autonomy themselves. The state must take an active role, in the form of compulsory education that is regulated, if not provided, by the state.

It is not only children of 'intolerant' parents, however, who need aid from the state to develop their autonomy. Because of lack of knowledge, resources, time, interest, or some combination of these, the vast majority of parents are unable to provide a learning environment in which all of the various competencies listed above can be acquired. Most people reading this, for example, would be overwhelmed if, while trying to lead their own lives, they had also to teach a child even the essential knowledge, skills, habits, and beliefs from the list above. For these reasons alone, then, the liberal state is justified in making some sort of formal education compulsory.

Beyond the school's capacity to teach basic knowledge and skills, however, there is an additional and even more pressing reason to view the state-regulated school as intrinsic to the development of autonomy in children. This has to do with the unique *institutional* role the school is able to play in fostering the development of autonomy—a role that cannot be replicated by even the most well-intentioned and resource-laden parents. I argued above and in section 1.3 that value pluralism and critical reflectiveness can best be achieved in an environment which itself fosters pluralism and reflection. This means that children are most likely to develop the capacity for autonomy in a community whose normative structure is itself autonomy-driven—i.e. in an environment that is explicitly committed to and structured by the norms of critical inquiry and reflection, evidential justification, and mutual respect and toleration. Such a community would ideally bring together, in an atmosphere of toleration and respect, both children and adults who come from a variety of backgrounds and who hold a range of potentially conflicting beliefs and values. It would also privilege critical inquiry over indoctrination; it would value beliefs and commitments which are held evidentially and authentically, and disvalue those held as a product of false consciousness; and it would foster an atmosphere of reflection detached from the constitutive commitments of the other arenas of the child's life. Finally, such a community would provide a group of people whose evaluations and judgements of one's choices are worth taking seriously; and, more generally, establish an environment in which the various aspects and competencies of autonomy can be freely practiced and improved.

This community, I suggest, best describes the ideal liberal school. More than any other institution in the child's life, the school can—and should—establish the sort of artificial environment in which all of these norms together can be achieved. Why cannot the family, or other social institutions, achieve these norms? It is because of the very artificiality of such a community that the family is unsuitable for the role. First, even the most liberal or autonomy-loving family cannot escape the conceptual and emotional bounds of its own commitments; nor can it ensure the child's honest exposure to that which the family would find utterly foreign or repugnant. Parents who believe that religion is the opiate of the masses, for example, might be unlikely to encourage their children to find friends who are strongly religious; likewise, parents who believe in the centrality of the church in guiding their and their own children's lives might not seek out for their children friends who are avowed non-believers. Second, even though any one of the above aims could be achieved at home—many families, for example, attempt to foster critical thinking skills and thoughtfulness in their children—such aims are also sometimes sacrificed (for good reasons) in contexts other than the school. While many liberal parents may in general favor their children's thinking for themselves, interest in family harmony or the need to make an important decision might (properly) trump the child's opportunity to practice autonomous decision-making. Thus, a space *separate* from that constituted by the child's family and home community is needed in which to pursue these norms without compromise.

Further, I would suggest that no institution other than the school could achieve all of these norms, or create a community displaying all of these characteristics at once, because no other institution has the same singularity of purpose—to educate children for autonomy—as the school is able to have. Nor do other institutions reach people at the same critical age that schools do. Although intermediate associations such as the Scouts or the YMCA may also help children develop certain capacities for autonomy, their voluntary and often socially and culturally homogeneous nature makes them unfit for fulfilling all of the conditions listed above. As an institution uniquely devoted to constructing an environment in which children's interests in particular are furthered and developed, on the other hand, the school can (and should) take on the demands imposed by the liberal ideal. Detached from the inevitably partial values, beliefs, and commitments of children's families and home communities, the liberal school makes available an essential space in which children are enabled to start defining themselves on their own terms, encouraged—as well as repeatedly challenged—by an educational community in which norms of autonomy have a central place.

Children's membership in communities of this sort, however, has meaning only if they learn to use and to value the capacities and skills associated with autonomy in the first place. It might be admirable that a child's teachers try to get her to reconsider her commitments in light of evidence that is worth taking seriously, but if she does not value evidential arguments or simply has little experience in responding to such kinds of arguments, her autonomy will not thereby be advanced.[55] The conception of the ideal liberal school as an autonomy-driven community is also important, therefore, because membership and participation in such a community will help children to come *to value* and *to practice* the capacity for autonomy—both of which are essential to developing autonomy. By living and working (at least for the six to eight hours per day of school) in a community that self-consciously values and shapes itself according to the attributes of tolerance and reflectiveness, the child herself will hopefully come to adopt and to value these dispositions as well; these are crucial first steps in attaining autonomy. 'Autonomy is an excellence of character—a virtue in the Aristotelian sense. . . . If the development and exercise of autonomy are connected in this manner, then a schooling system devoted to the end of cultivating autonomy must be concerned with ensuring, among other things, ample scope for its exercise.'[56] The liberal school under this ideal, therefore, establishes a singular environment in which children's capacity for autonomy is constantly reinforced and developed through classroom discussions, written work, projects and simulations, other pedagogical exercises, curriculum design, and even the structure of the school. It provides a safe and supportive environment in which children can take the intellectual and psychological risks that are essential to becoming autonomous, and in which their interest in taking these risks is rarely outweighed by other, non-autonomy-advancing interests, as might occur in the other arenas of the child's life.

Properly understood, then, the ideal liberal school establishes a plural community whose structure and content are dictated by the overriding goal of fostering the development of children's autonomy—a community instantiated by the norms of critical inquiry, toleration, and reflectiveness. Such schools, we have seen, help foster the acquisition of essential knowledge and skills, help children develop attitudes of toleration and sympathy toward other people, and provide a reflective environment detached from children's home communities in which their capacities for critical thinking and self-reflection can develop and flourish. It may be objected, however, that they are too detached. In attempting to foster children's development of autonomy by establishing separate, artificially constructed educational communities, the liberal educational ideal may have set up a dangerous— and pedagogically backwards—opposition between state-regulated schools, on the one hand, and parents, families, and communities on the other. I examine four problems associated with this objection in the next chapter.

3

Modifying the liberal educational ideal

In Chapter 1, we saw that the most plausible reading of contemporary liberalism entails a weakly perfectionist commitment to individual autonomy. It is this commitment to the value of autonomy, I argued, that grounds liberalism's commitments to pluralism, the legitimation process, and many of the substantive rights, duties, and institutions commonly associated with contemporary liberal theory. Chapter 2 applied this analysis of liberalism as a weakly perfectionist theory to children, concluding that the liberal commitment to enabling the exercise of autonomy by adults implies a parallel commitment to developing the capacity for autonomy in children, and that this commitment should take the form in part of state-regulated schooling. After clarifying what the development of autonomy requires, section 2.4 spun out a picture of what the liberal, autonomy-promoting school would look like—and generated a surprising ideal. The ideal liberal school, I argued there, is an autonomy-driven, plural community that is explicitly detached from children's families and home communities and is not necessarily designed to reflect the values and commitments held by parents. As a state-regulated community governed by a determinate, primary aim—that of helping children to develop their capacity for autonomy—and protected from any parental influence that inhibits the development of autonomy, the liberal school is meant to ensure the freedom of all children ultimately to determine their own path in the world just as adults are free under the liberal state to chart theirs.

This ideal of the detached, autonomy-driven school contrasts radically, even violently, with many liberals' intuitive conceptions of how liberal educational institutions should be shaped. Nowhere to be found are the standard, allegedly liberal notions of democratic control over schools by all members of the community, of the establishment of a wide variety of schools reflecting a range of conceptions of the good, or of the school as responsive to parental, not state, concerns. In this chapter, I examine four objections stemming from this clash of theory and intuition, and argue that the conception of the 'detached school' should, with minor modifications, continue to provide the basis for the liberal educational ideal.

3.1 STATE VERSUS PARENT TYRANNY: OR, THE 'LIBERALISM OF FEAR' MEETS LIBERAL EDUCATION

Somewhere along the way, many liberals (and readers!) might be motivated to argue, the liberal commitment to autonomy for adults has been manipulated—even betrayed—in its application to children. The principle of freedom embodied in the ideal of autonomy, these liberals would charge, has been replaced with the practice of state tyranny. It is this manifestation of liberal principles, in the form of the 'liberalism of fear' and the criticisms of the liberal educational ideal that it inspires, that forms the core of this section. Specifically, I consider two potential forms of oppression: first, the threat of state tyranny in general, and second, the threat of the 'tyranny of sameness'. My intent is that in the process of countering these criticisms, we will come to see more clearly the internal robustness of the model of liberal education presented in section 2.4. In other words, the very reasons that the liberal educational ideal stands up to the liberalism of fear make the ideal desirable in and of itself.

I suggest that this liberal educational ideal has two major strengths that make it superior to more democratic and/or parent-centered models of liberal education. First, the detached school balances out a current maldistribution of power that unjustly favors parents. As opposed to imposing state tyranny, the detached school actually establishes a needed counterweight to the threat of parental tyranny. Second, the liberal educational ideal ensures a *substantive* as opposed to *formal* pluralism both among schools and within society as a whole. Schools can exhibit significant variation within the boundaries of educating for autonomy, thus permitting them to adjust to the specific needs or interests of their student populations. At the same time, I show that their emphasis on common education, mutual toleration, and critical engagement ensures the development and maintenance of an interactive and mutually responsive plural society, as opposed to a society composed of separate, insular, and self-protective communities which, while formally part of a diverse and multicultural whole, are internally homogeneous and disengaged from other groups in their midst. But first, let us turn to the primary objection concerning the liberalism of fear and the threat of state tyranny.

Liberalism of fear I—the threat of state tyranny

The fear of state tyranny, Judith Shklar reminds us, is most fundamentally a fear of the unchecked physical power of the state: 'while the sources of social oppression are indeed numerous, none has the deadly effect of those who, as the agents of the modern state, have unique resources of physical might and persuasion at their disposal'.[1] This statement, however, raises the question of *why* we are afraid of physical might and persuasion. What sort of 'oppression' does the power of the state threaten us with? I suggest that liberals are afraid of two different forms of state oppression that are causally linked but conceptually distinct. The primary fear is of being coerced by the state into leading a bad, unhappy, and/or painful life—the meaning of which will be clarified below. The secondary, more moderate fear (but still forceful, as Mill makes clear) is of being forced to live the *same* life as everyone else—i.e., to live a life which may be good, and with which one does identify, but whose similarity to others' lives entails an unacceptable loss of plurality. I address the more threatening form of state oppression in this subsection, and turn to the 'tyranny of sameness' afterward.

The paradigmatic threat of state tyranny is that of a state which exerts its power to force citizens to lead bad lives. Given this level of generality, all people would agree with this statement; nobody would dispute that being forced to lead a bad life is undesirable, oppressive, and ultimately tyrannical. But of course, what a 'bad life' means depends on the context of one's beliefs. From a liberal perspective, as I argued in Chapter 1, a sufficient condition of being forced by the state to live a bad life is to be forced to live a life with which one does not freely identify.[2] The principal threat of state tyranny amounts to the threat that, given undue power, the state will force individuals to live in a way which they would not autonomously choose.[3] (This statement should not be taken to belittle more fundamental concerns about avoiding torture, fear of state brutality, etc. It is assumed that one would not freely choose to live a physically or mentally brutalized life, and therefore that the free identification condition incorporates these concerns.)

It is important to understand that the state need not *intend* to force its citizens to lead bad lives in order to be counted as tyrannical. While maliciousness or indifference toward individuals' autonomy may be one cause of state tyranny (because, for example, it is to the advantage of the rulers to coerce the population to lead a certain kind of life), the state may also force individuals to lead bad lives simply through incompetence or myopia. As liberals are well aware, it is not inconceivable in an imperfect world that the state will *think* that it is establishing the conditions for free, autonomous choice—i.e., that it will operate with the best of liberal intentions—but none the less *in practice* force individuals into lives with which they do not freely identify. The goal for liberalism, therefore, is to establish a distribution of power among the state and other actors that ensures both that the state has sufficient power to establish and maintain the political conditions necessary for the exercise and development of individual freedom (as liberalism requires), and that 'the people' (and/or other actors and institutions) have sufficient power to *check* the state when it shows signs of violating or overstepping these conditions, whether the violation be intentional or unintentional. Of course one would also want to structure the state itself to be self-checking through means such as judicial review, balance of powers, etc. But one of the points of the liberalism of fear is that *no* state, no matter how carefully constructed, can be trusted not to be tyrannical. Given the massive power that is available to even the most liberal of states, even those states which are most self-regulating in form can still inflict massive pain and hardship on their members in practice. Thus, one must establish checks on the state's power from outside government as well as from within.

This goal of avoiding state tyranny through the checks and balances of power seems to be challenged—if not overtly violated—by the ideal of liberal education set forth in section 2.4. By intentionally shielding the state-regulated school from the influence of parents and local communities, it may be argued, the (so-called) liberal ideal fails to provide one important check on state power of the sort called for in order to avoid tyranny. Under this analysis, the fact that the school is explicitly conceived of as being a means of promoting children's development of autonomy is not a sufficient defense, because what matters is not what the aim of education is *said* to be, but who controls what education actually *is* on the ground. In this sense, the argument about tyranny reverses the hierarchy established in Chapter 2 between children's a priori indifference to *who* controls their development and their supreme a priori interest in *what* kind of control is exercised. Chapter 2 argued that from a liberal perspective, children's interests are best fulfilled by providing them an education that aims at developing their capacity for autonomy, and that control over education should therefore be given to whoever best fulfills (or advances) this goal. According to this approach, *who* controls education is determined by *what* the aim of education should be (which itself is determined by what children's a priori interests are thought to be). Insofar as the state-regulated, detached school is in principle best equipped to achieve education for autonomy, therefore, the state and not parents should exercise primary control over schooling. The aim of educating for autonomy dictates that the identity of the educators be the state and not the parents.

If one shifts attention from the demands of inculcating the positive liberty of autonomy, however, to the lexically prior requirements of preserving negative liberty in the form of preventing tyranny, then a very different relationship between who controls schooling and what schooling aims at emerges. For from this perspective, giving the state primary control over education is in itself potentially tyrannical, because the power of the state is intrinsically tyrannical if left unchecked. It is both naive and dangerous, this argument goes, to think that one can first dictate the aim of education and then assign the state to implement the aim, for the power of the state is so vast that no pre-established 'aim'—even that of educating for autonomy—can check its actions or educative outcomes. Rather, the fact of the state's control over education will inevitably redefine what the aim of education turns out to be.[4]

This objection carries weight whether one views the state as inevitably malicious and power-hungry, as Shklar does, or simply as occasionally prone to incompetence and mistakes. A state may begin by being liberal and therefore be accorded primary power over education, but over time reject (if power-hungry) or misconceive (if myopic) what liberal education is about and thus cease to educate liberally. In either case, Chapter 2's call to detach schools from local and parental control ends up threatening the very preservation of liberal freedoms and institutions, and thus the good of its citizens, because parents, local community members, and children themselves are unable to check the state's power over the education of future generations. Again, the fact that the aim of education—to develop in children their capacity for autonomy—has been carefully spelled out, and even that autonomy itself has been rigorously defined (see sections 1.3 and 2.4), is irrelevant in the face of the power of the state to change definitions, and to alter aims. One-off definitions are not enough, this argument concludes; one needs assurances of stability, continuity, and continuing checks on state power.[5]

This argument is right as far as it goes. Liberalism's primary political aim *is* to remove the shackles of oppression and tyranny from people's lives, and this does amount in part to ensuring that no institution has a monopoly over coercive power. People cannot live autonomously in a state that has unlimited power to direct the shape of their lives. Where this argument goes wrong, however, is in identifying the threat of tyranny with the state alone. By pinpointing the state as the sole coercive power, the liberalism of fear fails to recognize a second group of actors who possess and often exert at least as much coercive control over children as the liberal state ever can— namely, *parents*. As the power of the state stands in relation to the power of one of its citizens, so can the power of a parent stand in relation to that of his or her child. Parents have the means to coerce their children physically, mentally, and emotionally; they can control the flow of information to and from their children; they possess far greater physical and intellectual might than most children, especially young children; and they often have control over both the long-range and the day-to-day character of their children's lives. From children's perspectives, therefore, parents have the potential to be at least as tyrannical as the state—and thus to pervert the course of their education and inhibit their development of autonomy—if not checked by outside institutions (including, for example, the state).

From this perspective, the detached school does not destabilize the balance of power within the liberal state; rather, it *is* balanced by parental influence over other aspects of the child's life, and thus actually helps to right an imbalance of power that could otherwise permit the exercise of parental tyranny over children. Amy Gutmann sums up this balancing act between the family and the state as follows:

parents command a domain other than schools in which they can—and should— seek to educate their children. ... The discretionary domain for education— particularly but not only for moral education—within the family has always been and must continue to be vast within a democratic society. And the existence of this domain of parental discretion provides a partial defense against those who claim that public schooling is a form of democratic tyranny over the mind. The risks of democratic and parental tyranny over moral education are reduced (although they can never be eliminated) by providing two substantially separate domains of control over moral education.[6]

As Gutmann suggests, there is good reason for parents to have primary care of and control over their children; but from the perspective of the liberalism of fear (as well as from children's a priori perspectives) there is equally good reason for the state to place a check on parents' educative power as there is for parents to check the state. This, in brief, was the argument developed in Chapter 2. And it is hard to conceive of a better check on parental power by the state than the liberal educational ideal presented in section 2.4.

Furthermore, the existence of other liberal institutions and freedoms also helps to counterbalance the threat of state tyranny over children's education. The liberal educational ideal, after all, was constructed with the assumption that it would be implemented within a liberal state; it is not and was not intended to be a blueprint for education in all political circumstances. Thus, the ideal in section 2.4 was developed against the background of other substantive liberal institutions and freedoms, such as democracy, freedom of speech and of the press, freedom of association, and so forth. As a result, parents and other concerned community members have mechanisms available not only to find out about what children are learning in school, but also to organize, protest, and help bring about changes in schools, if necessary. Because it is presumed to be embedded within a functioning liberal democracy, therefore, even a corrupt state education system will be open to challenge via other liberal freedoms and institutions. In this context, the detached, autonomy-driven school plays a successful dual role in counteracting the liberalism of fear and the threat of both state and parental tyranny.

Liberalism of fear II—the tyranny of sameness

The notion of the detached school as a check against the potential tyranny of outside actors such as parents also answers the second objection to the liberal educational ideal presented in section 2.4—namely, the objection that autonomy-promoting schools foster a tyranny of sameness. The argument here, made most forcefully by J. S. Mill in chapter 5 of *On Liberty*, is that a standardized state education for autonomy will result in standardized people, and thus to a loss of the social and civic conditions of plurality which are essential for autonomy (as well as for other social goods). As Mill declares:

That the whole or any large part of the education of the people should be in State hands, I go as far as anyone in deprecating. All that has been said of the importance of individuality of character, and diversity in opinions and modes of conduct, involves, as of the same unspeakable importance, diversity of education. A general State education is a mere contrivance for moulding people to be exactly like one another. . . . An education established and controlled by the State should only exist, if it exist at all, as one among many competing experiments.[7]

Although he does believe that the state has the 'duty of enforcing universal education',[8] Mill argues that it should fulfill this duty primarily by forcing parents to provide schooling for their own children—even when this restriction disables the state from trying directly to advance children's autonomy through education. The state 'might leave to parents to obtain the education where and how they pleased, and content itself with helping to pay the school fees of the poorer classes of children, and defraying the entire school expenses of those who have no one else to pay for them'.[9]

How can we make sense of Mill's simultaneous support for autonomy for children and his deprecation of universal, state-controlled schools? Why does Mill view the imposition of a uniform system of state-governed schools—even well-intentioned, freedom-respecting schools—as a greater threat to individual freedom than the unmediated imposition of parents' views upon their children? I believe that there are two crucial ideas at work in Mill's argument, which depend on an appreciation, first, of the difference in scope between parental and state power, and second, of the peculiarity of education as a practice which helps to create the characters of members of the next generation. First, despite their authority within the family itself, parents have a very limited, localized power. Their power extends over their own children and within their own neighborhoods, but no further (and often, in the case of broken families, rebellious children, or decaying neighborhoods, not even that far). The state, on the other hand, has an effectively universal reach—it is able to exert at least some measure of power over all children and in all neighborhoods. (As with parents, the nature and strength of the state's power, of course, varies from family to family and child to child.) Second, education, too, has a long reach, shaping individuals in ways that impose consequences not only on the lives of the educated generation, but also on the lives of future generations to come. The adults that children become are substantially shaped by the education their child-selves undergo; to educate a generation of children, therefore, is to determine in part the character of the generation of adults they become.

Taking these two insights together, we see that the union of state and educational power generates profound social consequences of a sort which Mill believes parental control over education does not. For allowing the state to monopolize education, as the liberal educational ideal might be accused of doing, is equivalent to allowing it to colonize and homogenize the characters and beliefs of society itself. As Bonna Devora Haberman puts it, 'Without groups who educate toward different versions of the good life, our societies would veer toward some strange contentless homogeneity. We can conjure images of populations of tolerant, polite people who vote regularly, hope that democracy will continue, but have no sense of personal identification with any culture or tradition, costume or ritual, ethnicity or historical experience. What would be the colour, flavour or aroma of such a society?'[10] State control over education, on this reading, inevitably leads to social homogeneity—regardless of the content of the education itself. Parental control over education, on the other hand, results in a heterogeneous population. Although each individual child (and thus every future citizen) may be exposed to only one set of ideas, beliefs, and conceptions of the good, society as a whole will embody a plurality of opinions and ways of life. Members of this second society arguably have a much greater chance of overcoming a 'tyrannical' upbringing later in life than do members of the first, state-educated society, because they will encounter a much greater diversity of ideas and ways of living.[11] Thus, while a state-supervised, autonomy-driven education may help children develop the individual capacities necessary for autonomy, its universal imposition drastically curtails the social, civic, and cultural conditions of plurality that make the exercise of autonomy possible.[12]

This is a much more subtle criticism than the first, more general fear of state tyranny. It also resonates strongly with contemporary concerns about multicultural education, forcible assimilation, and the 'celebration of diversity'. I suggest, however, that the ideal of liberal education presented in section 2.4 can stand up to this critique fairly easily, again for reasons that further prove its desirability as a model for liberal education. Three responses are particularly pertinent.

First, it is simply untrue that plurality in and of itself enables individuals to be autonomous. Pluralism is, as Chapter 1 contended, a *necessary* characteristic of an autonomy-promoting community, insofar as an individual must have a diverse range of worthwhile options open to her in order to be able to exercise meaningful choice.[13] But social diversity is certainly not a *sufficient* condition for individual autonomy, since an individual may well be confronted by diversity but have no way to respond to it in an autonomous fashion. As well as living in a diverse society, an individual must possess the *personal* capacities for critical thought, toleration, values pluralism, and so forth if she is to be able to exercise autonomy. Insofar as parent-governed education would not necessarily help children develop these personal capacities for autonomy, therefore, it cannot be said to advance autonomy. Thus, while Mill is right to remind us that it is counterproductive to sacrifice the social conditions of autonomy to the demands of the personal, he is wrong to emphasize the social to the detriment of the personal. Attention must be paid to both, but putting schooling back in the hands of parents pays attention only to one.[14]

Second, neither is it true that state-directed education for autonomy creates uniform individuals, nor, therefore, a uniform society. This is in part because of the diverse forms that education for autonomy can take. Schools under the liberal ideal need not be mirror images of each other. They can be detached from parental control, and be shaped so as to form autonomy-promoting communities, and none the less specialize in particular academic subjects such as science or creative writing, or emphasize community service instead of sports, or establish a media studies or health science magnet program. On top of this, liberal schools will display a good measure of local variation as they accommodate themselves to the needs and interests of their particular student bodies. One strength of the liberal educational ideal, therefore, is that it permits a wide range of educational structures and practices within its remit of autonomy-promoting education. (See section 5.2 for an in-depth discussion of specialization and school choice.)

Even more important than the possible variation among liberal schools, however, is the immense amount of variation that is possible among autonomous *individuals*, and thus the falsehood of the idea that societal homogeneity along the dimension of autonomy entails homogeneity across the board, or even along any other dimension. For autonomy is not and cannot be itself a conception of the good; to say that one lives an autonomous life is to say almost nothing about the substance or content of that life. Autonomous people will choose to lead very different kinds of lives, among which the only common denominator will be that their lives are not incompatible with autonomous choice—i.e., it is not impossible to have chosen them autonomously. The fact that a society is undifferentiated along the axis of autonomy therefore says nothing about the possibility of differentiation along other axes. Society under state-regulated education for autonomy would likely be at least as plural as society under parent-directed education, and would be assured of inculcating the personal dispositions for autonomy (such as critical reflection and toleration) as well. Thus, parent-governed education has no political advantages, and at least a few disadvantages, in comparison to liberal state-regulated education for autonomy.

Finally, even if liberal schools were more like each other than I have suggested, it is still not true that children who undergo this uniform education (i.e. state-provided and autonomy-directed liberal education) would develop into the same kind of people. As I indicated earlier in responding to the initial fear of state tyranny, school is only one influence among many in the life of a child. It is only one instance of what the great historian of education Lawrence Cremin calls 'the immense diversity in the sources and sites of the education that ultimately makes a difference in people's lives'.[15] As Cremin emphasized in a 1989 lecture at Harvard:

profound changes since World War II in the rearing of children and sweeping changes in the nature, uses, and delivery of information have radically transformed the ecology of education in the United States and fundamentally altered the circumstances within which schools and colleges carry on their work. Put otherwise, changes in the education proffered by families, day care centers, peer groups, television broadcasters, and workplaces have drastically altered the overall education being offered to the American people. The result has been a cacophony of teaching, the effects of which have been at best difficult to determine and even more difficult to assess.[16]

We might add to Cremin's list the educative influences of children's increasing access to computers, summer camps and courses, after-school lessons and activities, and so forth. In particular, given the recent explosion of sources of information to which children have access (television, computers, e-mail, the World Wide Web, etc.), it is hardly tenable to claim that schools provide the only, or even the most influential, education that children receive.

In addition, these other educative institutions and activities have an important influence on how and what children learn in school itself. Cremin reminds us that 'the influence of any particular educative institution is rarely direct and unalloyed; it is almost always mediated—that is, reflected, refracted and interpreted—by other educative institutions. The family is probably the most important of these mediating agencies.'[17] In this respect, the fact that state education may everywhere be 'the same' does not mean that what children *learn* is everywhere the same; families have a tremendous influence over how their children actually learn and assimilate what is taught in school. James Coleman corroborates this conclusion in his influential report on *Equality of Educational Opportunity*: 'within each racial or ethnic group, the factor that showed the clearest relation to a child's achievement was his home background—the educational and economic resources provided within his home'.[18] Thus, even universal imposition of the state-regulated liberal school described in section 2.4 does not portend the imposition of a universal and uniform character on future generations. State-regulated, autonomy-promoting education simply does not threaten the plurality and diversity of modern, liberal societies.

In conclusion, I do not find threat of the 'tyranny of homogeneity' to be a tenable one. A uniform education does not create uniform people. A society of people who are uniformly autonomous is not uniform in any other way. And state-regulated education for autonomy enables children to make choices among diverse options in a way that parent-regulated education does not necessarily do. Liberal schools, meaning the detached, autonomy-promoting school ideal presented in Chapter 2, can display substantial variation and diversity among themselves, thus enabling them to respond and cater to a diversity of children's needs, as well as promoting an honestly plural society in which people have the critical capacities and personal abilities to engage with each other. In all of these respects, fears of tyranny are unfounded, and the strengths of the liberal educational ideal are evident.

3.2 PARENTAL INVOLVEMENT AND THE DYNAMICS OF THE FAMILY–SCHOOL RELATIONSHIP

Even if schools which are 'detached' from parental control are not tyrannical, it may be argued that they are educationally ineffective. Schools can educate successfully, it is often argued, only when they act in partnership with parents, especially by encouraging parent involvement in the school. The detached-school ideal seems to neglect this important pedagogical point. I contend in this section, however, that while parent involvement is very important in boosting students' achievement (which is the variable used in the literature to measure educational effectiveness), this does not mean that parents must be given greater control over or input into the aims and content of the school. The available research demonstrates that parent involvement programs generally work equally well when there is a gap between the values espoused by the school and by the parents as when both school and parents embrace the same educational values. Thus, I conclude that the liberal school can educate effectively and promote parent involvement without abandoning its separation from parochial norms or modifying its commitment to helping children develop the capacity for autonomy.

The following statement effectively sums up the conclusion of a vast literature on parental involvement and student achievement: 'The single most important determinant of a child's success in school, and ultimately throughout life, is not family status, education level, income, or IQ. It is whether that child's parents are involved in his or her education.'[19] As noted sociologists of education James Coleman and Thomas Hoffer concur, 'one of the most important factors in a child's success in school is the degree to which his or her parents are actively involved in the child's education'.[20] It is difficult to find anyone these days who would dispute this conclusion. Furthermore, parental involvement is shown to have a wide range of beneficial effects, of which helping students attain better grades or marks is only one: 'Involving parents in the education of their children has been found to have an associated link not only with students but also with parents, teachers, schools, and districts. These outcomes include increased student achievement, increased student attendance, lower dropout rates, increased interactions between parents and their children at home and increased positive attitudes by teachers toward parents being involved.'[21] Parents' involvement in their children's education thus has significant consequences across the board, from increasing straightforward academic achievement to improving domestic relations and decreasing school-leaving (drop-out) rates. In addition, it has been shown to be beneficial for children of all ages, all grade levels, and all socio-economic levels.[22] If anything, parent involvement seems to be especially advantageous for minority and poor students.[23] In sum, therefore, the sheer volume of studies and parent-outreach programs all reaching the same conclusion provides compelling evidence that parent involvement is essential to student achievement and learning.

This fact suggests that the discussion of liberal education in Chapter 2—and particularly the ideal of the detached school—relied on a false and debilitating dichotomy between children's upbringing and education, or between their education in general and their schooling in particular. As section 1 of this chapter reminded us, children learn a tremendous amount outside of school as well as within it, and often the former has a profound influence on how and what they learn in the latter—i.e. within the context of formal schooling. The studies of parental involvement cited above reinforce this conclusion, suggesting that schools and families (let alone schools and other institutions such as the local community) are not as separable from a pedagogical standpoint as liberals might like them to be from a political standpoint.

The detachment of the liberal school therefore causes two problems. First, parents are likely to feel alienated from an institution that does not give them a voice. Insofar as parents are explicitly excluded from the process of determining both the overall aim of liberal education (which is defined as helping children develop autonomy) and the values that will shape the day-to-day operations of the school, they may feel little loyalty to or inclusion within the liberal detached school. Second, the fact that the development of *autonomy* in particular is taken as the aim of liberal education is likely to alienate some parents. We saw in Chapter 2 that parents' opposition to teaching autonomy was not a reason in principle for liberal schools not to help children develop their capacities for autonomy. But it does threaten the success of liberal education in practice. Parents are unlikely to support or become involved in a school that has aims to which they are opposed. If parent involvement in and support of their children's schooling is essential for educational achievement, therefore, and if the detached school cannot secure that support, then the liberal educational ideal of the detached school cannot succeed at educating for autonomy.

In response, it is first important to recognize the number of different forms that 'parental involvement' can take. It does not mean only serving on the board of governors or chairing the Parent–Teacher Association (PTA), and empirical research shows that much less time-consuming or interventionist methods of involvement can be equally valuable for boosting student achievement (as well as for advancing the other goals mentioned above). As used in the literature, 'parent involvement' means anything from joining the PTA and volunteering in the library, to helping children with their homework, providing a quiet place to study, and asking questions about what happened in school, to baking cupcakes for the choir, chaperoning field trips, and organizing school fundraisers. Joyce Epstein, an influential researcher in this area, separates levels of involvement into five or six categories, all of which have been shown to be effective means of helping children learn.[24] Although she suggests that it is important for a school to have parents involved at each level, it is not necessary that all—or even more than a few—participate to the highest degree. Her studies show that indirect parent involvement, such as helping children at home and providing a quiet place to work, is at least as important as volunteering directly in the school. Likewise, parents' efforts to attend their children's school plays and parent–teacher nights can send as strong a message to their children of support for the school and for the importance of learning as would their serving on the PTA.[25]

I emphasize the number of different ways in which parents can become involved in their children's education because it is significant that few of these examples rely on agreement or harmony between parents and the school concerning the aims of education. Attending school concerts, helping with homework, and even volunteering in the library are activities that parents can and likely will support and engage in regardless of their attitude toward the school or its aims. Because these forms of involvement are often not value-laden, they can be fulfilled even by parents who are opposed, for example, to their children's developing the capacity for autonomy. Thus, the political ideal of the detached, autonomy-driven school does not necessarily conflict with the pedagogical need for parents to be involved in their children's education.

This conclusion remains true even if one takes into consideration the school's need to encourage parent involvement. For it might be objected that even if school involvement itself does not trigger value conflicts, parents must none the less be encouraged by the school to get involved and take on these responsibilities; in order for the school to speak authoritatively and convincingly, this argument runs, it must appeal to parents by articulating shared values and common concerns. But if one reads the empirical literature on how to boost parent involvement, one discovers that very little attention is paid to establishing shared values or shaping the school to mirror parents' concerns and commitments. Rather, researchers advise schools to make themselves inviting by furnishing a parent room in the school with comfortable couches and a phone,[26] or by translating school documents and forms into parents' native languages[27]—i.e., forms of outreach that are neither reliant on nor related to either the school's educational aims or the parents' values. Other suggestions include: establishing regular teacher–parent contact, with teachers being encouraged to call and even visit the child's home with good news about a child and not just when the child is failing or delinquent;[28] inviting parents to visit the school any time during the year and not just on 'Back-to-School' nights;[29] scheduling student performances, parent–teacher conferences, and other school events for nights and weekends in order to accommodate working parents; and setting up fora in which immigrant and non-English-speaking parents can learn about the structure and expectations of the school in their own language.[30] All of these measures require that schools and teachers commit themselves to reaching out to parents and encouraging parent involvement.[31] They do not require, however, that the school adjust its educational aims to meet parents' preferences or opinions, nor that parents come to adopt the school's aims as their own.

The same is true even for parents who might naturally feel disaffected by and/or alienated from the school: e.g., recent immigrants, minorities, and non- or limited-English speakers. Sociologists, educators, and researchers writing about parent involvement among these groups consistently suggest that the aims and operations of the school should be made linguistically and/or culturally *comprehensible* to such parents. But they do not demand that its aims or methods should be radically altered.[32] The focus is on giving minority parents *knowledge* and *means* (often understood as social and/or cultural capital) through which to engage with the school: 'Parents who are knowledgeable about the school's expectations and the way in which the school operates are better advocates for their children than parents who lack such skills.'[33] Likewise, schools are encouraged to learn about the socio-cultural backgrounds and needs of their students, and to shape their programs so as to meet and capitalize on these elements.[34] Responsiveness to children's needs, however, need not translate into lowering standards or changing one's educational aims. Schools are repeatedly urged to maintain their aim of educating all children to the highest level, regardless of their students' backgrounds.[35]

Furthermore, it is worth noting that virtually all parents—illiberal and liberal, minority and mainstream alike—in fact share a number of essential educational values both with each other and with the liberal detached school, values that the school can appeal to by way of encouraging parental support and involvement. Virtually all parents, for example, would like to send their children to schools that offer a strong academic curriculum emphasizing reading and writing skills, mathematics, science, history, and other traditional academic subjects. Furthermore, most parents favor schools that nurture their children emotionally and socially as well as academically, and that teach values or habits of character such as honesty, responsibility, courage, and friendship.[36] While it is true that some parents also look for other values in their children's schools—values which may (e.g. emphasis on arts education; strong sports teams) or may not (e.g. restriction to children of a certain ethnicity or social class; emphasis on a religious text as the ultimate source of truth) be compatible with the liberal educational ideal—these are generally held to be important in addition to, rather than instead of, the above values. As a result, schools can encourage most parents to involve themselves in their children's education—helping them with their homework, coming to Parent Day, attending awards ceremonies, volunteering in the library or cafeteria, etc.—by appealing to shared values of academic achievement and social and emotional development.[37]

One more potent objection must be addressed, however, before we can conclude that detached schooling is compatible with parental involvement and thus student achievement. We might call it the 'Catholic school objection'. In the early 1980s, James Coleman, Thomas Hoffer, and Sally Kilgore set off an extended and heated debate when they claimed that Catholic (private) schools in the United States are far superior to state schools in reducing premature school-leaving rates, 'adding value' to poor and minority children's education, and generally increasing student achievement.[38] Although their conclusions have been hotly contested,[39] they present potentially compelling evidence that Catholic schools benefit students more than state schools do because the former operate within the context of a close-knit community involving teachers, parents, and children—a community which no longer exists for the average American family, neighborhood, or state school. This would seem to suggest that schools are more effective when they create such communities by reflecting parents' values and commitments, and thus suggest that the ideal of the detached school is pedagogically flawed.

If one reads Coleman and Hoffer's analysis in particular more closely, however, one discovers that Catholic schools do not boast better education because they constitute a values community. Rather, it is because they form a *functional community*—'a community in which social norms and sanctions, including those that cross generations, arise out of the social structure itself, and both reinforce and perpetuate that structure'.[40] In essence, Catholic schooling is effective, Coleman and Hoffer argue, because it takes place within a community in which parents interact and talk both to each other and to each others' children. This is valuable for at least three reasons.[41] First, it enables parents to share information with each other and thus to make better choices on an individual level for their own children:

A functional community augments the resources available to parents in their interactions with school, in their supervision of their children's behavior, and in their supervision of their children's associations. . . . The feedback that a parent receives from friends and associates, either unsolicited or in response to questions, provides extensive additional resources that aid the parent in monitoring the school and the child, and the norms that parents, as part of their everyday activity, are able to establish act as important aids in socializing children.[42]

Thus, parental interaction provides the 'social capital'[43]—i.e. the network of social relationships—that enables parents to work more effectively on behalf of their children's education. Second, this same social capital enables parents to work in tandem in order to press causes of common concern, such as improving the curriculum or replacing an unpopular teacher. Organized parental pressure can be a force for the good, albeit not an unmitigated one. Parents often have privileged insight into their children's needs and desires, and by talking to other parents and comparing their experiences and those of their children, they can discover problems (or identify strengths) within the school of which teachers and school administrators may themselves be unaware.[44] Third, parental interaction within a functional community often has the effect that initially uninvolved or marginalized parents are motivated to get more involved because of peer pressure from other parents: 'In a value community, the involvement of families in the school is largely determined on an individualistic basis, while the scope of community involvement is greater in the functional community. Thus, parents who would otherwise avoid the school or be uninvolved in its activities are induced to participate through the social relationships that define the functional community.'[45]

It is important to recognize, however, that functional communities are not necessarily characterized by shared values: 'A functional community is neither a necessary nor a sufficient condition for value consistency, though the two have some affinity. Value consistency grows through the interactions found in a functional community, and when it exists it facilitates the norms that grow up in such a community. But there are value cleavages in functional communities, cleavages which may be intense.'[46] This is often true even of Catholic schools. Thus, it is neither a necessary nor a sufficient means of increasing parents' social capital to shape schools to reflect parents' values, or to try to attract parents and students whose values accord with those held by the school. For example, independent (non-religious) private schools often constitute values communities but 'ordinarily lack . . . a [functional] community, consisting as they do of a collection of parents who have individually chosen a school but who do not constitute a community outside the school'.[47] As a result, Coleman and Hoffer argue, such schools' ability to keep students in school and to boost student achievement is statistically much more similar to that of state schools. The Catholic school objection, therefore, emphasizes the importance of encouraging parents to interact with each other and with the school, but it does not suggest that schools need to structure themselves according to values that parents share.

This conclusion is further strengthened, perhaps paradoxically, by an analysis of US Catholic schools that does conceive of them as values communities. Partially in response to Coleman, Hoffer, and Kilgore's work, Anthony Bryk, Valerie Lee, and Peter Holland wrote a highly regarded evaluation of Catholic schools' achievements in which they argued in part that Catholic schools do instantiate values communities.[48] What is significant about their analysis is that even though the authors specifically dispute Coleman, Hoffer, and Kilgore's contention that Catholic schools are communities only in a functional sense, they argue that the values that link the community are traditional academic values rather than religious ones. According to Bryk *et al.*, most Catholic schools and teachers believed that all students should 'take a core of academic courses' and they emphasized regular homework, testing, and strict discipline as means to achieving these goals.[49] The core of schools' 'explicitly moral understanding of the purposes of education'[50] is also not centered in Catholic dogma or other explicitly religious wellsprings of morality. Rather, 'the emphasis was on developing a sense of personal responsibility and a commitment to hard work'.[51] A national survey of Catholic high school teachers found overwhelming support for emphasizing 'mastery of reading, writing, and mathematics skills', 'critical thinking skills', 'intellectual curiosity', 'a healthy self-concept', 'compassion', 'tolerance', and 'a commitment to justice'. In notable contrast, barely half of these teachers viewed 'building knowledge of Catholic doctrine', 'acceptance of Catholic teachings on moral values' or 'clear understanding of the Bible' as educational priorities.[52] Thus, we see that even to the extent that Catholic schools do instantiate values communities (a view that is itself still open to question, since although Bryk *et al.* show that Catholic school teachers and administrators share many educational values, they do not show that these values are equally or explicitly embraced by students and parents as well), the shared values are ones that are fully compatible with—even essential to—the aims of the detached liberal school: academic achievement, critical thinking skills, social responsibility, toleration, justice, etc. To the extent that these shared values raise parent involvement and student achievement in Catholic schools, they can and should raise parent involvement and student achievement under the liberal educational ideal as well.

In conclusion, while it is true that parents' involvement in their children's education is extremely important, liberal schools need not abandon their detachment from parents' values in order to encourage such involvement. First, research shows that parent involvement relies primarily on the school's engaging in value-neutral outreach of the sort discussed above—not on its establishing a values community reflective of parental commitments. Second, to the extent that parent involvement is responsive to schools' emphasis on values which they share, schools can appeal to the values of academic achievement and social and emotional development as a means of encouraging parent involvement without abandoning the detached status that ultimately helps children's development of autonomy. In sum, the detached school is fully compatible with parent involvement, and thus with effective schooling and high levels of student achievement in general. This is not to suggest that there is nothing more to say about the problem of creating an ethos of involvement, commitment, and mutuality among the school, parents, and other local community members. Chapter 5 will take up this issue again through the lens of school choice, examining in much greater detail whether market forces in education can and would foster the distribution of social capital among parents or increase student learning in other ways. Until then, however, we can safely conclude that liberal education can be effective education, and that students have ample opportunity and encouragement to learn and succeed within the detached school.

3.3 ABANDONING THE STRUCTURE VERSUS SUBSTANCE DISTINCTION: COMING TO TERMS WITH THE HIDDEN CURRICULUM

In this section, I examine the argument that schools are intrinsically structured so as to inculcate heteronomy instead of autonomy. Even if the distribution of political power represented by the autonomy-driven, detached school is not tyrannical (section 1), and even if it is not pedagogically counterproductive because it forbids certain forms of parental involvement (section 2), it may be that the detached school—in fact, *any* school—is none the less structurally unable to educate for autonomy. Deschoolers, functionalists, and other radical theorists argue that an ideal of education such as that put forth in section 2.4 is mired in self-contradiction, because even liberal schools are inherently structured so as to reinforce heteronomy instead of autonomy by rewarding obedience, submission to authority, and intellectual docility. These arguments, and their implications for liberal education, are addressed in the first half of the section. The second half picks up in particular on the substantive moral and cultural messages conveyed through a school's structure. Whether or not schools can foster autonomy by modifying their structures, I suggest, they inevitably transmit cultural norms that may exclude or alienate some minority children. This causes tensions within the detached school whose ramifications will not be fully dealt with until Chapter 5.

Heteronomy, capitalism, and conformity: the threat of the hidden curriculum

Schools cannot teach autonomy. This message of pedagogic self-defeat has been most forcefully articulated by members of the 'deschooling' movement headed by Ivan Illich.[53] Deschoolers such as Illich claim that the very structure of schooling as a practice suppresses instead of augments freedom, and thus is a priori unsuited for the job of educating for autonomy. As Illich charges in his famous treatise, *Deschooling Society*:

The claim that a liberal society can be founded on the modern school is paradoxical. The safeguards of individual freedom are all canceled in the dealings of a teacher with his pupil. When the schoolteacher fuses in his person the functions of judge, ideologue, and doctor, the fundamental style of society is perverted by the very process which should prepare for life. A teacher who combines these three powers contributes to the warping of the child much more than the laws which establish his legal or economic minority, or restrict his right to free assembly or abode.[54]

Although it may initially appear that Illich is merely saying that tyrannical or authoritarian teachers infringe the freedom of students, he is actually making a much deeper point. Built into schools, Illich suggests, is an unavoidable structure of power that is antithetical to both the development and the exercise of autonomy, because it establishes a cognitive and psychological relationship of dependence of the student upon the teacher that is impossible to overcome. This relationship necessarily obtains in all schools, regardless of their 'progressive' or 'liberal' nature, because the teacher's role as evaluator ('judge'), authority ('ideologue'), and therapist ('doctor') is built into the very essence of schooling. Thus, he concludes, the very conception of an autonomy-advancing liberal school is incoherent, because as compulsory institutions in which teachers have intellectual, evaluative, and emotional authority over students, schools cannot help but deform children's development of autonomy.

This notion of the self-defeating structure of liberal education is given a slightly different (and more interesting) twist by the sociologist of knowledge Nell Keddie. In her fascinating account of 'Classroom Knowledge',[55] Keddie makes the provocative suggestion that a student's success in school is structurally predicated on his being willing to accept the teacher's conception of and approach to the curriculum and the classroom. The most successful students, in other words, are those who display the least autonomy and independence of thought. Again, this is so even in the most autonomy-driven of schools, as it is not the particular ideology of a particular school but the intrinsic structure of schooling itself that generates the disjunction between individual autonomy and formal educational success. Keddie documents in detail how self-consciously 'progressive' teachers apply regressive and autonomy-stunting evaluations to those students who challenge their intellectual or disciplinary authority. Such evaluations may include ignoring or 'render[ing] invalid'[56] students' explanations of their motives and objections, and placing these students in lower-stream classes. As Keddie puts it, 'It seems probable that the pupils who come to be perceived by teachers as the most able, and who in a streamed school reach the top streams, are those who have access to or are willing to take over the teachers' definition of the situation.'[57] As a result, 'There is between teachers and A [high-stream] pupils a reciprocity of perspective which allows teachers to define, unchallenged by A pupils, as they may be challenged by C pupils, the nature and boundaries of what is to count as knowledge. It would seem to be the failure of high-ability pupils to question what they are taught in schools that contributes in large measure to their educational achievement.'[58]

Keddie's analysis, like Illich's, suggests that schools are ill equipped to teach students to be autonomous, because the structure of authority intrinsic to the practice of schooling inadvertently but unavoidably teaches a substantive message of docility and intellectual submissiveness—exactly those qualities which hinder the development of autonomous thought and action. Students learn that in order to be successful in school, they must suppress or alienate their own judgemental powers in favor of the teacher's perspective.[59] Thus, the structure of even the most ideal liberal school inadvertently conveys a substantive *hidden curriculum*[60] that teaches students to be heteronomous in even the most fundamental aspects of their lives in school. Students' suspension of judgement concerning what they learn in school might not be so troubling if the teacher's perspective echoed students' own common sense, and thus if students could rely on some measure of overlap between their own judgement and that of their teachers. But because the formal academic curriculum always requires some measure of distance and abstraction from common sense, 'It would appear that the willingness to take over the teacher's definition of what is to constitute the problem and what is to count as knowledge may require pupils to regard as irrelevant or inappropriate what they might see as problems in a context of everyday meaning. . . . This means that those pupils who are willing to take over the teachers' definitions must often be less rather than more autonomous . . . and accept the teacher's presentation on trust.'[61]

This is not to say that the overt or formal curriculum of the liberal school is itself necessarily self-defeating. Children who learn what the liberal school tries to teach through the formal curriculum (e.g. science, history, health, etc.) do presumably become more autonomous. But paradoxically, they can learn what the school is *trying* to teach only after they learn the lessons taught by the hidden curriculum (i.e., the lessons conveyed by the structure of the school)—namely, obedience and deference to authority. For only if they are obedient and surrender at least part of their judgement to the teacher's authority can children get down to the business of learning the formal curriculum. Thus, the hidden curriculum holds the overt curriculum hostage. Not until children learn from the hidden curriculum to suppress their autonomy can they begin again to develop it through the overt curriculum.

To distinguish between the overt and hidden curricula of the school on the basis of *intentionality* may itself be misconceived, because according to functionalist theorists such as Samuel Bowles, Herbert Gintis, Philip Jackson, and others, the substantive lessons embedded in the structure of the school are often at least as intentional as those imparted by the overt, formal curriculum.[62] Bowles and Gintis put the charge most directly:

To capture the economic import of education, we must relate its social structure to the forms of consciousness, interpersonal behavior, and personality it fosters and reinforces in students. ... we believe the available evidence indicates that the pattern of social relationships fostered in schools is hardly irrational or accidental. Rather, the structure of the educational experience is admirably suited to nurturing attitudes and behavior consonant with participation in the labor force.[63]

From this perspective, the hidden curriculum of the school is intentionally constructed to teach children the skills, habits, and modes of behavior best suited to perpetuating the capitalist system. Students are taught through the hidden curriculum to be docile and obedient because these are the qualities most needed in workers in the modern capitalist economy. The heteronomy and suspension of critical judgement that Keddie pointed to as accidental (albeit unavoidable) by-products of contemporary schooling is instead seen under this functionalist analysis as expressing one of the central hidden aims of modern, capitalist-driven schooling. From the lunch and recess queues one learns to stand in as a primary school student, to the time discipline instilled by the bells, deadlines, and exams imposed in middle school, to the lessons about class rigidity and separation instilled by streamed classes and graduation tracks in secondary school, children are intentionally schooled in the service of capitalism from the start of their formal education. Philip Jackson describes the situation as follows: 'As he learns to live in school our student learns to subjugate his own desires to the will of the teacher and to subdue his own actions in the interest of the common good. He learns to be passive and to acquiesce to the network of rules, regulations, and routines in which he is embedded.'[64] In this way he is turned into 'the Company Man'.[65] Thus, the functionalist argument concludes, by 'replicat[ing] the relationships of dominance and subordinacy in the economic sphere', the structure of modern schooling establishes a hidden curriculum that ensures the replication and production of the 'amenable and fragmented labor force' needed to perpetuate the capitalist system.[66]

The liberal educational ideal articulated in section 2.4 must thus confront two powerful sets of objections: first, that schools *cannot* teach autonomy, because intrinsic to the nature of formal education (schooling) are pedagogic structures that necessarily deform children's development of autonomy; and second, that schools *will not* teach autonomy, because teachers, school reformers, administrators, and even parents are fatally blinkered by capitalist assumptions and will therefore favor educational structures that diminish autonomy to advance capitalism, rather than vice versa. These objections are linked insofar as they rely on the existence of the so-called 'hidden curriculum'—i.e. on the connection between the structure and content of education. Furthermore, these objections are mere subsets of a much larger challenge to the liberal educational ideal: namely, that the structure of schools teaches a 'hidden curriculum' of substantive norms, values, sources of identification, ways of life, and so forth which themselves diminish or violate children's development of autonomy. It is this fact of the hidden curriculum that poses the greatest challenge to the liberal educational ideal, because it suggests that education is out of our control—that we cannot map aims (educating for autonomy) onto outcomes (liberal schools) in the way that Chapter 2 demands we be able to.

Let us take the latter charge first, that the modern, putatively liberal school has been intentionally structured so as to perpetuate the infelicities and injustices of capitalism. I suggest that even if this is true, it has few if any implications for the liberal educational ideal spelled out in section 2.4. For insofar as the structural threats and subversions identified by functionalists are avoidable given sufficient vigilance, liberal educators must simply learn to be vigilant. It is in fact presumably easier for the liberal school to avoid the pitfalls of capitalist-dominated education than for other schools. Since the liberal school is conceived of as being partially shielded from the direct influence of parents and the local community, it is presumably also better shielded than most from the influence and interference of the agents of autonomy-inhibiting, capitalist-driven education reform.[67] Bowles and Gintis's analysis does remind us that the liberal school must remain vigilant in order to ensure that it does not unintentionally socialize children for conformity to the unjust and autonomy-diminishing aspects of capitalist life and the capitalist system; it would seem that there is little more, however, which the ideal liberal school must do.

   Furthermore, I would question whether the character traits identified by functionalist theorists as being required by capitalists of their laborers (and thus taught by schools to their students) really are so deleterious and autonomy-diminishing as they claim. For example, Philip Jackson points out that the structure of schools requires students to be patient and willing to delay gratification, and that the capitalist workplace requires its employees to display the same qualities.[68] He concludes on the basis of this link that schools are directly structured to serve capitalist interests. But, first, as all statisticians know, correlation does not prove causation. Even if the only advantage of learning to delay gratification were that it made the capitalist machinery run more efficiently, that fact by itself would not prove that schools teach children to delay gratification for that reason. Second, and equally importantly, while these character traits are often useful to employers within a capitalist system, it is equally true that patience and the ability to delay gratification of one's desires are also important conditions of living a fully autonomous life. Most goals take time and patience to achieve; someone who was unable to delay gratification, therefore, would likely lead a frustrated and/or aimless existence. This is not to deny that one can be autonomous if one is constitutionally impatient, but patience does make full (as opposed to partial) autonomy more likely and easier to achieve. An inability to delay desire-gratification, on the other hand, does make the achievement of an autonomous life impossible. Similar associations between habits of character and autonomy are true of self-discipline, time management, deference to others' expertise, and so forth. Thus, education in those qualities of self-control and even temporary self-abnegation that functionalist writers point to with such horror as clear signs of the hegemony of capitalist interests in the classroom could be equally well interpreted as being directly intended to advance children's interests in developing their capacities for autonomy—or, for that matter, to advance non-capitalist ways of life as well. After all, successful planning and implementation of an anticapitalist revolution would also require that its proponents exercise patience and be willing to delay gratification.

Finally, I suggest that insofar as the hidden curriculum can be known and controlled, and insofar as many of its lessons actually further children's development of autonomy rather than diminish it, the hidden curriculum can be turned into a boon rather than a burden. The conception of the liberal school developed in section 2.4 provides an ideal case in point of the hidden curriculum's knowability and appropriability for liberal ends. One of the central strengths of the ideal liberal school as described in section 2.4 is that it explicitly harnesses to its own purposes many of the structural forces that are the primary of focus functionalist and radical critiques of modern schooling. It explicitly acknowledges that the kind of community created by the school is as important an educational force as the overt curriculum, and creates itself accordingly. In this manner, it consciously and openly grapples with the problem of shaping schooling so that the 'hidden curriculum' represented by its organizational structure advances the ideology of the school in tandem with the overt or formal curriculum. In the liberal educational context, therefore, the 'hidden curriculum' is neither hidden nor deleterious. Rather, it is explicitly acknowledged and appropriated as a central means of advancing children's development of autonomy. In light of this, I propose in the discussion that follows to use the term 'informal' as opposed to 'hidden' curriculum, as a means of acknowledging its separation from the 'formal' curriculum covered in textbooks and lectures, but also of emphasizing its knowable and addressable nature.[69] Regardless of functionalism's descriptive validity as applied to current educational practices, therefore, it poses no threat to the liberal educational ideal, which self-consciously shapes the informal ('hidden') curriculum to serve its own just purposes.

Although liberal education is able to appropriate some aspects of the informal curriculum for its own purposes, there are none the less still challenges to be met. I have not yet addressed the unmalleable aspects of the informal curriculum, which present a different and more difficult set of challenges to the liberal educational ideal. For example, although one can (and many schools in the 1960s and 1970s did) redistribute power in the school in response to arguments like Keddie's so as to eliminate the hierarchical divide between students and teachers, or even give students greater educational authority than teachers, it has been fairly conclusively demonstrated that this is educationally ineffective. Thus, to reveal the existence of harmful elements within the informal curriculum is not necessarily to overcome them, or to transform them to work toward liberal ends. Structures that are intrinsic to the process of formal education may at the same time be deleterious to children's development of autonomy. Likewise, in altering one feature of the structure of schooling in order better to advance children's autonomy, one may introduce a different feature that poses its own obstacles to the creation of an autonomy-promoting informal curriculum.

Keddie and Illich introduce what might be thought to be the most devastating aspects of the informal curriculum, insofar as the structural features of schooling they point to as diminishing children's autonomy include some of the most basic features of the formal educational process. But the criticisms that they raise are only part of the story, and not even necessarily the most difficult for liberalism to handle. This is because the conflict that Keddie and Illich illuminate is essentially one-dimensional: it pits the autonomy-diminishing aspects of the informal curriculum against other autonomy-promoting aspects of both the informal and formal curricula. The costs and benefits of liberal schooling raised by Keddie and Illich can thus be plotted and evaluated along a single dimension—the development of children's autonomy—and balanced out against each other accordingly. Assuming that compulsory liberal education on balance advances children's development of autonomy—i.e., that the detrimental aspects of the informal curriculum are outweighed by the autonomy-advancing elements of the informal and formal curricula—and assuming that no alternative to liberal schooling will achieve those aims as well or better (and thus rejecting Illich's proposals of such substitutes as phone books of people interested in trading knowledge[70]), then the liberal educational ideal remains on firm foundations. While the complex trade-off between children's exercise and development of autonomy goes deeper than I had initially acknowledged, insofar as it pervades the very structure of school itself, it threatens not the foundation of liberal education but merely the ease with which its aims can be achieved. So far as Keddie's and Illich's criticisms are concerned, therefore, the liberal educator simply has to make the best of a bad bargain, continuing to educate in line with the principles set forth in Chapter 2 but chastened by the knowledge that the task is harder than might initially appear.

Cultural transmission and the informal curriculum

There is a different set of intrinsic structural features of schooling, however, which teach an informal curriculum whose outcomes cannot be measured on the single scale of advancing or retarding children's autonomy, and which pose more fundamental challenges for the liberal educational ideal. These features include the moral and cultural values that inform, shape, and are transmitted by the informal curriculum of the school.[71] Unlike the evaluative structures highlighted by Keddie and Illich, a school's cultural affiliation does not intrinsically limit children's development of autonomy. But it does help to determine the shape of children's identities, and thereby both calls into question the possibility of liberal educational 'detachment', and potentially causes the school to overstep its bounds as an institution incorporated for the sole purpose of helping children develop their capacities for autonomy. In both of these respects, the moral and cultural aspects of the hidden curriculum challenge the realizability of the liberal educational ideal.

Let me make clear from the start that the problem is not moral education as such. To the contrary, moral education is an essential part of helping children to develop their capacities for autonomy. Learning to tolerate others, to value critical thinking, and to take different points of view seriously are all important moral lessons for developing and exercising autonomy, and are thus important components of the liberal school curriculum. As I briefly mentioned in section 2 of this chapter, powerful liberal cases have also been made for other aspects of 'character education', including teaching children the virtues of courage, responsibility, trust, friendship, honesty, and so forth.[72] Gutmann gives a helpful example of how schools teach liberal norms through the informal curriculum:

Schools develop moral character at the same time as they try to teach basic cognitive skills, by insisting that students sit in their seats (next to students of different races and religions), raise their hands before speaking, hand in their homework on time, not loiter in the halls, be good sports on the playing field, and abide by many other rules that help define a school's character.[73]

The problem is that it is misleading to suggest that these are the only norms of character that schools—even liberal schools—will and do teach. Instead, even the detached school will almost inevitably teach a culturally situated informal curriculum that will reflect and reinforce the norms of the dominant culture in society. Consider the testimony of Colin

Shrosbree, an English working-class child who was admitted on scholar-ship to a private school just down the road from where he grew up:

Middle-class attitudes, middle-class clothes, middle-class accents, early and irrev-ocable selection by middle-class teachers who made little concession to working-class ways or children's circumstances all made of education a barrier, not just to academic success but to a sense of owning a place in our own culture. But as chil-dren we did not question these social divisions—school was just a place apart, with different rules and alien ways, that had no place in our personal or family life.[74]

Gutmann herself offers another example by way of comparing American with Japanese school practices and organization. She points out that in Japanese schools, all school members from student to principal (head teacher) help in the day-to-day maintenance of the school, thus placing an emphasis on group responsibility for the welfare of the community and the individuals who make it up. Likewise, as Gail Benjamin points out in her excellent book on Japanese primary education, faster students are routinely expected to help slower students master the day's lesson; students work almost exclusively in groups, with praise given to the group but rarely to individual members; and on Sports Day, teams compete enthusiastically with each other for first-prize, but individual students' first place finishes in individual races are valued only in terms of their contribution to the team—the children themselves are not congratulated or fussed over, nor do they expect to be.[75] Responsibility for other members of the group, on the other hand, is not reinforced as an important norm in most American or British schools. Instead, most teachers place a premium on individual achievement, as is demonstrated in their emphasis on the following: 'doing your own work' and 'keep[ing] your eyes on your own paper'; assigning homework and other assessments (e.g. quizzes, papers) to individuals rather than groups; primarily awarding medals, trophies, athletic or academic 'letters', and other marks of distinction to individual students; and disci-plining students by emphasizing the consequences of their own behavior, regardless of the behavior of the group as a whole. To the extent that teach-ers in the United States or Britain do use cooperative learning techniques, they usually do so to help students develop group-work skills, not to teach collective responsibility.

None of these approaches—working-class versus middle-class norms, or collective versus individual responsibility—necessarily constitutes a more liberal framework for education; they are all compatible with students' development of autonomy. What is significant is their cultural particularity, and thus their effect on children's development of identity and cultural self-conception. Children who are raised in a Japanese-American or Asian-American community, for example, but are forced to attend a putatively 'detached' school that reinforces individualistic norms and behavior, may feel alienated from their culture or the school or both, and/or may feel confused about their own identities (e.g., as individual actors versus group members).[76] The same can clearly be true of working-class children thrust into a school structured by middle-class norms. Furthermore, by emphasizing their supposed cultural 'detachment', liberal schools may exacerbate these feelings as students' experiences of cultural incoherence are denied or invalidated.

This is an important challenge to the liberal educational ideal as it has been developed thus far. I do believe that this objection can be overcome, primarily by examining cultural membership within the context of civic membership. Chapter 4 takes on the task of analyzing and comparing cultural socialization with civic education. Because the relationship between civic and cultural membership is a complex one, however, and because the issue of schools as purveyors of cultural identity comes up again in the next section, I propose to leave the problem dangling for the time being. It will finally be resolved in section 5.1.

3.4 SUPPLEMENTATION OR SUPPLANTATION? BUILDING A SENSE OF IDENTITY IN THE MODERN WORLD

We could crudely summarize section 1.3 by saying that individuals' capacity for autonomy is composed of two parts. (1) Autonomy requires a sense of cultural embeddedness or coherence, of personal identity, on the basis of which one first begins to judge, weigh, and evaluate the events, opportunities, and ideas that one encounters across a lifetime. (2) Autonomy requires a bundle of personal and mental habits, skills, values, attitudes, structures of belief, etc. that taken together enable one: to recognize and take seriously a variety of ways of life and conceptions of the good; to evaluate critically one's own beliefs and commitments, and to alter them when appropriate; and to make second-order judgements with which one actively identifies as opposed to fulfilling passively one's unexamined first-order preferences and desires. As a shorthand, I shall refer to (1) as the *sense of embeddedness* or *cultural coherence*, and to (2) as the *capacity* or *conditions for choice*. An individual must possess both elements in order to be said to possess the capacity for autonomy.

Liberals typically focus on the capacity for choice as being harder both to achieve and to preserve, and thus as demanding attention from the state to a degree that individuals' sense of cultural coherence is thought not to require. This elevation of developing the capacity for choice over maintaining the conditions of identification implicitly structured my own analysis of liberal politics in previous chapters. It generated the legitimation conditions and substantive institutions discussed in Chapter 1, the conception of autonomy developed in Chapters 1–2, and the form of liberal education for autonomy derived in section 2.4. In evaluating how schools should help children develop the capacity for autonomy, for example, I focused on how to get children to become autonomous choosers, not on strengthening their personal or cultural values and commitments. The ideal liberal school, it was judged, would provide a community that was separated from, not connected to, the conceptions of the good that children were meant to be learning at home. The development of a capacity for choice was seen to be the liberal school's most important aim; the inculcation of a sense of identity in children, on the other hand, was left to parents as a task which, it was assumed in section 2.3, they could naturally (even inevitably) achieve on their own.

Many critics, however, have suggested that liberalism's obsession with establishing and protecting the conditions of choice, and its relative disdain for protecting individuals' sense of cultural coherence, is woefully inadequate in the (post-)modern or contemporary world. (When this world began is naturally a matter of dispute; estimates range anywhere from 1789 to the mid-1960s.) Protagonists as diverse as back-to-basics Tories, African-American separatists, the Christian Coalition, Blairite 'New Labour' supporters, Michael Lerner, the Archbishop of Canterbury, Allan Bloom, and the most avant-garde multiculturalists have all argued that it is the explosion of the capacity for choice, and the accompanying desiccation of cultural identification and embeddedness, that now pose the greatest threats to social stability and personal autonomy.[77] As William Galston solemnly warns, 'The greatest threat to children in modern liberal societies is not that they will believe in something too deeply, but that they will believe in nothing very deeply at all.'[78] According to this view, modern individuals lack a clear identity and purpose in life because they lack cultural coherence. This lack of purpose in turn occasions more general feelings of fear and anomie, which on their part pose the most serious modern threat to the maintenance of both political and personal freedom. Deprived of a standard by which to evaluate their and others' choices and afflicted by low self-esteem, modern anomic individuals either move aggressively to impose their values on others (as a means of stoking up their failing confidence), and thus violate the demands of political stability, or they follow others' leads instead of relying on their own judgements, in violation of the demands of personal autonomy. In either case, freedom is sacrificed as a result of the ascendance of choice over cultural coherence.[79]

Three arguments are typically put forward to justify the claim that the relative strengths, and therefore the relative political and educational relevance, of the capacities for choice and personal identity have shifted position. First, it is argued that there has been an explosion in the number and range of choices available to children in modern times. The very forces that I argued in section 1 counteracted the threat of state tyranny, such as children's exposure to television, the World Wide Web, and other forms of mass media, also counteract parents' attempts to provide their children an integrated cultural upbringing. As Galston remarks, 'the basic features of liberal society make it virtually impossible for parents to seal their children off from knowledge of other ways of life'.[80] Children have become increasingly sophisticated about the range of different lives people lead, and thus about the range of options potentially available to them in their own lives. Schools are therefore not needed to help children achieve a greater sense of choice than they already have, since children's capacities for choice are well developed in contemporary times.

Second, this increase in children's range and knowledge of choices is said to lead to a decrease in their identification with any one conception of the good. The capacity for choice and a sense of embeddedness are opposed attributes, according to this view, in that an increase in one must always be matched by a decrease in the other. This counterbalance is especially true for children, for whom a sense of options from a very early age can translate into a sense of interchangeability or indifference among choices. The prevalence of children's and teenagers' attitudes that 'all values are relative' is the most obvious instance of this phenomenon. Children and adolescents perceive standards to be arbitrary or even dangerous in the face of the multiplicity and supposed equality of available options, and they consequently either lose or abandon their ability to evaluate choices on the basis of a coherent set of values and cultural commitments. As a result, this argument concludes, the prevalence of choice in the modern world has led to a drastic and ultimately devastating loss of cultural coherence among children.

Third, critics argue that this movement toward the abandonment of standards of evaluation and the ascendance of the fetishism of choice is further exacerbated by a breakdown in families, neighborhoods, institutions, and community structures that would otherwise work in concert to reinforce children's initiation into an integrated way of life. Families move more often and over longer distances; parents divorce and remarry, or never marry at all; life is no longer centered around the church or other stabilizing community institutions; neighborhoods change character as gentrification occurs or public council housing is built; single and working parents have neither the time nor the personal resources to inculcate in their children a stable sense of community and identity; small, home-grown businesses and traditions are replaced by faceless conglomerates and mass-produced products; one can generate multiple examples. For all of these reasons, and many more besides, this argument concludes that children's senses of identity, like the character of human lives in general in Western liberal democracies, have become fractured and disjointed. The capacity for choice exercises its own kind of tyranny over children's lives, depriving them of the sense of embeddedness which is so central not just to personal autonomy but also to the capacities for identity and agency themselves.

If these arguments are right, their implications for liberal education are manifold. At the very least, they would suggest that the ideal of the detached school needs to be substantially rethought. The concept of the detached school was developed as a vision of an educational community in which students are able to learn the habits, dispositions, and skills that ground the capacity for choice. It was designed to promote toleration of other points of view and ways of life, to promote critical thinking skills, and to provide a space in which children could step back and question the (supposedly) ingrained values in which they had (supposedly) been inculcated by their parents. But according to the arguments presented above, students do not need to become members of yet another community that presses them to develop the capacity for choice; instead, they need a community that develops their sense of cultural coherence and reinforces the values and commitments that are being taught, however ineffectually, at home. Schools are needed to build up parents' attempts to inculcate a sense of cultural coherence in their children, not to tear them down. From the ages of 5 or 6 to 16 or 18, children live nearly as much of their waking life in school as at home. Parents must be able to rely on the school to help reinforce their values, to be 'connected' instead of detached, because otherwise they have no hope of battling the other social factors that contend for the minds and allegiances of their children.

I suggest that the liberal educational ideal can generally stand up to the first two objections. First, the fact that there has been an explosion in children's exposure to choices and to different ways of life does not mean that their capacities for choice, in the senses relevant to autonomy, have also increased. It is important that children become aware of and receptive to a variety of ways of life, values, ideals, etc. But as I discussed in section 1, such awareness is not sufficient in and of itself to ground the capacity to make autonomous choices. In order to develop autonomy, children must also be able to evaluate critically the choices that are available, to imagine options that do not immediately present themselves, to assess the short-, medium-, and long-term outcomes of the choices they make, to integrate the choices they make in one sphere of life with their goals and interests in other spheres of life, and so on. Thus, the liberal, autonomy-promoting school must still teach the skills, habits, beliefs, and knowledge that ground the capacity for choice, despite children's growing awareness of the availability of different ways of life and conceptions of the good.

Second, I reject the idea that there is a necessary trade-off between the capacity for choice and a sense of embeddedness, so long as the liberal school educates in an age-sensitive and age-appropriate manner. Very young children, it is true, may well experience confusion and distress if confronted with a plethora of choices too early, or with teachers who tell them that their way of life embodies only one possibility among many. In this context, age matters. The early grades are an appropriate place to teach patience, listening skills, how to express oneself to others, and how to find one's way around the neighborhood, all of which are important for the development of autonomy; they are not the appropriate context in which to teach radical doubt or critical thinking skills. Studies in child development and psychology support this conclusion: children are simply not cognitively equipped before a certain age to engage in the sort of critical thought and analysis that ultimately provides the foundation for the capacity for choice.[81] As Benjamin Barber puts it, 'Teach the child what she needs to know, but also teach her what she is ready to learn.'[82]

The fact, however, that very young children are not equipped to think critically does not mean that children can never do so successfully, or that there will always be a trade-off between choice and cultural coherence. As children develop they certainly become able, like adults, to learn about other cultures and conceptions of the good while remaining confident in their own way of life. It can be argued, in fact, that being in a school that teaches respect for other traditions may actually *strengthen* children's commitments to their own traditions.[83] When a student sees other students learning respect for his way of life, he feels proud and learns to see his culture as something worthy of respect. Also, in contrasting his own traditions with others', he learns what is distinctive and noteworthy about his own. Finally, in a school that teaches about a diversity of traditions, children see their own traditions taught to other people from an external perspective, and thus see how and why others are led to understand and respect their own ways of life. In all of these ways, the detached liberal school may actually advance children's senses of embeddedness at the same time as helping them to develop the capacity for choice.

The third contention—that the breakdown of family, neighborhood, social, and cultural institutions has deprived children of important sources of identification and cultural membership—poses the most difficult challenge to liberalism and the liberal educational ideal. This is in large part because the loss of 'social capital' in modern societies is closely connected to the development of 'modern culture'. Many Western democracies, such as Great Britain and the United States, have both spawned and been partially taken over by a culture of modernity—by a way of life that derives from, plays off of, and perpetuates the distinctively 'modern' elements of contemporary society. It is this fact, that liberal democracy tends to breed a culture of modernity and discourages traditionalism, and not the fear that liberal democracy breeds no cultural identification, that I believe really lies at the heart of some of the criticisms articulated above. The claim that the conditions of modern life have produced cultural incoherence and identity confusion, in other words, should properly be understood as a different claim in disguise: namely, that the conditions of modern life *have* fostered cultural identification, but it is identification with an intrinsically distasteful (because valueless, unworthy, secular, reason-obsessed, modern, Enlightenment-driven, anti-traditional, capitalist, etc.) culture of modernity that should be rejected. Under this interpretation, the detached school is seen as yet another agent of liberal cultural imperialism, one which not merely withdraws from the task of reinforcing parents' attempts at cultural reproduction, but actively substitutes its own cosmopolitan, culturally opportunistic, and choice-ridden set of values in place of parents' conceptions of the good.

It is hard to know how seriously to take this assessment. On the one hand, I have made clear my belief that liberal principles do not privilege parents' chances of passing on their cultural traditions over other groups' opportunities to do the same. Section 2.3 acknowledged that children do in general have a better chance of developing a stable identity if it is done within the context of the home, and if this attempt by their parents is respected by outsiders. Thus, liberalism encourages parents to provide their children with such an upbringing, and respects the integrity of the family in part for this reason. In addition, liberalism may even perceive it to be a loss for aesthetic or other reasons if too many children abandon a particular way of life and that culture goes defunct. Many liberals do view the fact of pluralism as an active good, rather than merely as a value-neutral condition of the world. But it is not an *injustice* toward parents or their children if children do not end up identifying with their parents' way of life, so long as they end up turning toward some other set of substantive cultural forms and practices instead. As I have argued before, liberalism does not have the responsibility to rescue or artificially preserve cultures that would otherwise die out or change character, so long as a sufficient range remains available to promote future autonomy. Autonomy is achievable despite not identifying with one's parents' way of life, and ultimately it is the development of children's autonomy that matters to liberal theory in this context.

In addition, as Jeremy Waldron cogently points out, it may be both historically and normatively misrepresentative to suggest that *anyone* growing up in a multicultural society is truly grounded in one culture—including adults who grew up decades ago: 'in the modern world—in the wake of imperialism, global communication, world war, mass migration, and frequent flying—people are not able to absorb their cultures whole and pure. . . . In what seems like chaos or anarchy . . . each of us makes a discovery about herself. We are not so lost or timid that we cannot build an identity for ourselves without the guiding hand of a pre-established framework.'[84] From this perspective, it does not make sense to speak of preserving 'a culture', or to speak of children growing up in and adopting 'the same culture' as their parents. Every person's identity is a mélange, Waldron argues, of disparate cultural influences. Although modernity and especially self-conscious cosmopolitanism may represent two particularly distinctive forms of mélange, it is wrong to contrast it with other, more unified constructions of individual identity.

That said, on the other hand, modern culture itself really may not be valuable. Such a judgement is not necessarily illiberal: insofar as liberals (and the liberal state) would fight against a child's coming to identify constitutively with a culture of criminality even if it fostered her cultural coherence, liberalism must evaluate the worth of cultures, at least in a very basic way. Thus, if modern 'culture' really is as shallow and superficial as many of its detractors claim, then liberal schools should not self-consciously create the conditions that promote it.

Furthermore, even if modernity can provide a valuable source of cultural identification, there will none the less be cases in which children will not develop the sense of embeddedness and identity that they need to be intentional, directed, and ultimately autonomous agents. First, it is possible that because of the fragmentation of families in certain areas, especially when combined with a lack of cultural, social, and economic resources in the community as a whole, some children will be deprived of the attention and cultural participation that are necessary to develop a sense of cultural coherence and embeddedness. Whether or not identity is a mélange, after all, children need something (or many things) from which to build an identity. If few stories, visions of history, rituals, rites of passage, etc. are shared and practiced as a child grows up—whether these stories and practices derive from one culture or many cultures—then it will be hard for a child to feel embedded in any discernible way (or ways) of life. Such children therefore require an alternative source of participation and identification if they are to develop the embeddedness that is a prerequisite for autonomy. Insofar as the ideal of the detached school is not designed to acculturate children in this way, it fails to meet these children's needs. Such children may not benefit from the ideal of liberal education as it now stands.

The second group of children who may have difficulty forming a stable, healthy sense of identity are those who come from cultures and traditions that are in a minority or are in some way discriminated or selected against in the larger society. Children who suffer discrimination, of course, often experience lowered self-esteem, lack of confidence, and shame about their culture or background. Although many children rightly fight back and overcome this disadvantage, these feelings are nonetheless at the time deleterious to the construction of a healthy and stable self.[85] Even when discrimination is not a factor, children from minority backgrounds can still feel excluded from or on the outskirts of mainstream society. This feeling would not be problematic from the perspective of identity formation if minority children felt fully comfortable in their 'home' culture, i.e. in the culture of their parents. But such membership is often equally elusive, as children evaluate their parents' practices and customs according to the standards of the self-styled 'normal' world beyond. Able to judge each culture with the eyes of an outsider, such children fail to become full 'insiders' in either, torn between the conflicting demands and practices of their overlapping yet competing worlds. As I suggested in the conclusion to section 3, this problem is exacerbated by the informal curriculum of so-called 'detached' schools which, via their structure and language, in reality (and inevitably) promote the norms of the dominant culture. Although many people successfully adopt composite identities, taking and rejecting elements from both cultures at will, many others may fail ever to develop a sense of personal strength, identity, and belonging in which they feel confident and from which they can act.[86] The detached, liberal school would seem to fail these children as well.

Thus, although I am not sympathetic to some of the objections raised above about cultural identification—I believe that children need to develop a capacity for authentic or autonomous choice, that age-appropriate education need not trade off choice for membership (or vice versa), that many children even in this day and age do have a stable sense of identity, and that modernism can sometimes provide an adequate replacement for traditionalism—it must be acknowledged that some children do and will lack a sense of embeddedness or cultural connectedness. How must the liberal educational ideal be altered to take this problem into account? I would reiterate that it should not retreat from developing children's capacities for choice. The liberal school must still teach children toleration, critical thinking skills, respect for other points of view, etc. The qualities of the detached school are still important in this respect, as are the skills, habits, and beliefs that were listed and discussed in section 2.4. But it is possible that, in deference to people's need for cultural embeddedness and membership, and in recognition of the pre-eminence of identity over autonomy (insofar as the former is a precondition of the latter), the liberal school should be more accommodating to particular cultural traditions. It might be argued that if education for choice (via the detached school) and education for cultural coherence (via a culturally 'connected' school) conflict, then the latter should take precedence over the former. If it is possible, especially, to teach children the knowledge, skills, and dispositions necessary for civic membership in a liberal polity, it could be suggested that schools should not attempt to educate for autonomy as well. Chapter 4 addresses this possibility by examining whether a state can educate for citizenship alone while respecting students' cultural convictions and safeguarding their cultural membership. The arguments examined there will point to a final conclusion about the connections among autonomy, choice, culture, and citizenship in section 5.1.

4

Culture, choice, and citizenship:
schooling private citizens in the public square

Chapter 3 closed on a questioning note. It ended by asking: can education for choice and education for cultural coherence be made fully compatible—or in other words, is education for autonomy truly possible in a deeply plural society? If not, it was suggested, then despite the liberal commitment to the value of individuals' development and exercise of autonomy, it may be that liberal education is better focused on helping children develop a coherent identity—one that will sustain them as adults and enable them to function as healthy, stable individuals and citizens—rather than on their capacity for choice. In this respect, adults' and children's development and exercise of autonomy would still be valued and supported by liberal state institutions, but they would not be directly pursued as aims of liberal schools. Rather, schools would educate for cultural coherence and civic virtue, as these are the fundamental mainstays of individual agency and the liberal state, respectively. Children's development of choice would be incorporated to the extent that it did not conflict with their development of cultural coherence; ultimately, however, liberal schools would emphasize different capacities and have a different character from that sketched in the last two chapters.

In order to determine whether this would be a practical form for liberal education to take, we first need to clarify what the components of this education would be. One important component, of course, is a substantial commitment on the part of the school to protecting—and potentially even promoting—children's sources of personal identification and cultural coherence. A second, equally important component is a commitment to education for civic virtue. As most theorists and practitioners agree, civic education is essential to any coherent program of liberal education, whether it strives to educate for autonomy in full realization of the liberal educational ideal or adopts a more modified and limited set of aims.[1] This is because civic education is critical to ensuring the stability and sustainability of the liberal state, which in turn is an essential prerequisite for maintaining liberal democratic institutions and freedoms, and therefore for protecting individuals' ability to exercise their autonomy. Even a truncated form of liberal education, there-fore, cannot be limited to the inculcation of cultural coherence alone. An accommodation must be found with the goals of educating for civic virtue. The nature of this accommodation—and three models demonstrating how it might be achieved—take up the bulk of this chapter.

Before I examine the accommodation between civic education and the preservation of cultural coherence, however, it makes sense to clarify the nature of civic education itself, and to explain why it has not been included in my investigation of liberal education until now. I do this in section 1. In that section, I analyze the character of civic education in a liberal polity, and demonstrate why and how such education is essential to the maintenance of the liberal state. I also examine the relationship between autonomy and ci-tizenship. I argue that children's development of autonomy and acquisition of civic virtue are compatible, and even in some ways mutually reinforcing, aims. Because the skills, habits, dispositions, and knowledge central to autonomy are to a large degree coextensive with those central to civic virtue, I suggest, the detached school is ideally equipped to teach children the civic virtues neces-sary for the stability and preservation of the liberal state. As a result, the aims of civic education did not need to be addressed until now; their achievement was already virtually built into the liberal educational ideal.

To demonstrate the compatibility of civic and autonomy-based education, however, has little significance if autonomy-based education—especially its component of education for choice—is itself under suspicion as being worse on empirical grounds than a purely civic education that explicitly respects rather than challenges children's cultural and personal identities. In sections 2-4, therefore, I analyze three different models of political liberal civic educa-tion that also purport to respect personal identity, expressed in terms of three countries' systems of education: England, the United States, and France. Because of the transformative nature of civic education and its correlative effect on individuals' construction of their own identities, I shall argue, none of these three models manages to balance education for cultural coherence and education for citizenship any more effectively than an autonomy-based approach to liberal education does. As a result, I conclude that the liberal educational ideal presented in this book remains both the strongest theoreti-cal conception and the strongest empirical realization of liberal education.

4.1 THE STATUS OF CIVIC EDUCATION

Autonomy and citizenship: compatible ideals

Civic education is crucial in a liberal state, I suggest, because no matter what institutions and freedoms are built into the basic structure and constitution of the state, their realization will always depend on the character and commitments of its citizens—and we cannot trust that children will 'naturally' develop appropriate characters and commitments without being specifically educated in the liberal civic virtues. To understand why character matters, simply consider the following examples. A state that has passed the most stringent anti-discrimination laws in the service of equality of opportunity, even if these laws are applied conscientiously and consistently by politicians and other employees of the state, cannot overcome the insidious but lethal effects of private prejudice and discrimination. Similarly, an apathetic, ill-educated, and non-participatory citizenry can allow shocking violations of democracy or infringements of liberal rights to take place, even if liberal democratic structures are formally in place. In both cases, this is because the liberal state is a collective good, sustained via the collective practices of active citizens. It depends for its stability and preservation on the existence of a sufficiently high percentage of citizens who behave in public *and private* in ways that advance freedom, democracy, toleration, and non-discrimination. By contrast, if too many people take a passive or anti-democratic stance toward politics or even toward their fellow citizens, then the social order may quickly become illiberal and the political order become dominated by an unrepresentative, often fanatical few who compete to shape the state to their own, illiberal ends. In such a case, the stability and sustainability of the liberal state will be threatened.

In other words, the character of liberal citizens matters. Consequently, civic education also matters. Future citizens must be taught to exemplify the virtues characteristic of a liberal democracy. Insofar as liberal states are democratic, for example, future citizens of a liberal state must learn to participate in and uphold democracy. This means not only that children must learn about their rights, but also develop the skills and habits of character to exercise their civic responsibilities. They should be taught to respect and value the democratic process, the constitution or similar codifying documents, and the constitutionally or legislatively protected liberties that help establish the basic structure of the liberal state. They should also develop such habits as paying attention to public issues, voting, and exercising their rights as citizens. Liberal democracy weakens with disuse, and one of the best antidotes to disuse is producing more citizens who take it seriously and who have developed the habit of public involvement.

Children must also learn to evaluate the arguments made in a democratic and political world, as well as to put forth such arguments themselves. In practice, this means that children need to develop many of the same skills as those listed in section 2.4 in relation to their development of autonomy, to wit: to learn to read and write; to understand at least basic history, economics, civics, political science, mathematics, and natural science; to separate style from substance; and overall to think critically and carefully. If they cannot do these things, then they will not be able to construct, analyze, or take thoughtful positions on the multitude of issues facing adults in the political world, and therefore will not be ideal liberal citizens. Empirical evidence buttresses these claims; as study after study has shown, 'Formal education is almost without exception the strongest factor in explaining what citizens do in politics and how they think about politics.'[2] Increased education reliably increases individuals' attention to, ascription of value to, and involvement in democratic politics.[3]

Civic education is also needed to teach (and has been shown to be effective in teaching) students to tolerate and respect other citizens and their differences. As Chapter 1 emphasized, toleration is one of the hallmarks of both a liberal state and the liberal citizen. The legitimacy of the liberal state rests in part on citizens' accepting that it is right to tolerate others' differences given the fact of deep pluralism (i.e. it rests on citizens' accepting the burdens of judgement). Furthermore, Amy Gutmann makes a compelling argument that political education cannot stop at teaching toleration, but must also extend to teaching 'mutual respect—a reciprocal positive regard among citizens who pursue ways of life that are consistent with honoring the basic liberties and opportunities of others'.[4] Toleration may help guarantee that individuals or groups do not try to use state power (including legislative power) to impose their conception of the good on other citizens. But as Gutmann points out, it does not guarantee that individuals or groups will not discriminate against each other in the private sphere, or that people will experience equal opportunity. If white and black people (or Protestants and Catholics, long-time residents and recent immigrants, etc.) tolerated but did not respect each other, for example, then they would 'live and let live', but presumably not hire each other, attend similar private schools,[5] or socialize together. Any pre-existing social, economic, or other inequalities would at best remain, and more likely be exacerbated, by such a situation. Public life would become stratified as well, and while equal opportunity might remain theoretically institutionalized, it would be stripped of any meaning in practice. Thus, for purely civic reasons of maintaining the liberal state, children must be taught to respect each others' differences as well as tolerate each other.

As has become obvious, the skills, habits, values, and beliefs that underlie the capacity for autonomy—for example, critical judgement, toleration, mutual respect, reflectiveness, the ability to read a newspaper—also underlie the capacity for citizenship. It happens to be the case that 'most (if not all) of the same skills and virtues that are necessary and sufficient for citizenship in a liberal democracy are those that are also necessary and sufficient for educating children to deliberate about their way of life, more generally (and less politically) speaking'.[6] In this respect, education for autonomy actually *incorporates* education for citizenship; in other words, as children develop and learn to exercise their capacities for autonomy, they simultaneously develop the skills and habits necessary for effective and productive citizenship. As I said above, this is one reason that discussion of the aims of civic education could be delayed until now; they were already realized within the liberal educational ideal.

Furthermore, I argue that those capacities and habits of character which are necessary for liberal democratic citizenship but are not directly inculcated through education for autonomy nonetheless can and should be incorporated within the liberal educational ideal. This is because the existence of active citizens is a precondition for the maintenance of a healthy liberal democracy, which in turn is a precondition for individuals' exercise of autonomy. Thus, to the extent that the purposes of citizenship education—namely, to ensure the stability and preservation of the liberal state, and to give citizens the ability to participate effectively in the political sphere—are essential conditions of an individual's being able to exercise his or her autonomy, education for autonomy must by definition involve education for citizenship. This is also true insofar as it is important for citizens to know about their rights and opportunities if they are to take advantage of them as potentially autonomous individuals. Children must learn that heresy is not a political crime, that freedom of speech is a basic right, that they have the rights as adults to accept any legal job and/or marriage offer they wish, and that certain forms of sexual and racial discrimination are illegal (among many other rights and freedoms). By definition, therefore, an autonomy-driven education must help children develop the capacities for and habits of effective citizenship, and to learn about their rights and obligations as citizens. If there are particular skills, habits, or areas of knowledge that are essential to effective citizenship but not to autonomous action outside the political sphere, they must none the less be taught by the liberal school. In this way, we see that education for citizenship is fully compatible with—even essential for—education for autonomy.

It may be objected that one important aspect of autonomy conflicts with children's development of the habits of active citizenship. Autonomy requires that one be able to opt out of certain enterprises as well as being able to participate in them. Part of the point of living in an autonomy-valuing liberal society is having the opportunity *not* to do things that one does not wish to do. Active citizenship may rightly be seen as one of these options. An individual can perfectly autonomously—and rationally—decide that it is not worth his or her while to participate in politics. In modern industrialized countries such as Britain or the United States, individual actors can rarely if ever exert significant influence over the impersonal, cumbersome lumberings of the bureaucratized state. Thus it may be rational for any particular individual to reject the obligations of active citizenship and to devote his or her energies to other projects. This is especially true insofar as liberal democracies can sustain themselves, and even flourish, with many passive citizens, so long as a critical percentage (whatever that may be) of individuals take their duties as citizens seriously. Thus, while some or even many people need to learn to accept the burden of active citizenship, it may be a violation of individual autonomy to teach *all* children that they must do so, since many of them could rationally and autonomously reject the world of politics without the liberal state's falling into disrepair.

There are two responses to this argument that serve to affirm the legitimacy of educating for citizenship within the context of an autonomy-promoting education. The first depends on clarifying what active citizenship means. It is true and even unproblematic that many people will reasonably decide not to engage actively in the civic sphere—because, say, they have adopted a disengaged or even anti-civic conception of the good (e.g. they are deeply committed to the hermetic life, or they look to Nietzsche as the guiding force in their lives), or because they reasonably believe that the conditions of liberal justice are being met and would therefore prefer to direct their energies elsewhere (e.g. to their family or to marshalling support for a new sports arena). These are predictable and undisturbing outcomes of a civil society that encourages people to make autonomous choices about how to lead their lives. What cannot happen, however, is for the number of civically uninvolved citizens to get so high that the stability and maintenance of the liberal state is threatened. Part of teaching children to become active and effective citizens, therefore, should be to teach them that it is their duty to engage in political and civil action when they see liberal justice, freedoms, and/or institutions being endangered.[7] To be an active citizen under this conception is not necessarily to engage in politics or other civic action on a regular basis—although it is certainly important that some critical mass of people do exercise citizenship in this way, and thus that all children are enabled to do so through civic education. Rather, active citizenship entails monitoring the civic sphere to a sufficient extent that individuals do take action when justice and the liberal state seem threatened.[8] Under this conception of active citizenship, it cannot be a violation of children's development of autonomy to teach them the habits and dispositions of good citizenship, because the duties of citizenship impose themselves on the lives they have autonomously chosen only when liberalism itself (which provides the security for their chosen lives) is under threat.[9]

Picking up on this notion of citizenship as a protective function, we can understand the second reason that teaching all children to be good citizens is not a violation of their development of autonomy: namely, it does not violate children's developing autonomy to teach them not to free-ride. The stability and perpetuation of the liberal state is a public good which, like all public goods, is freely and equally available to all. To enjoy the benefits of a public good without contributing to its maintenance and preservation, however, is to free-ride. Passive citizens in a liberal democracy, therefore, end up free-riding on the responsibility and dedication exercised by their more active compatriots. It does not violate children's future autonomy to teach them not to free-ride any more than it violates their autonomy to teach them other moral virtues such as honesty, generosity, and sympathy. We must have a common foundation of basic moral beliefs, including a belief in reciprocity and 'pulling one's weight', in order to live together in peace and stability over time. Teaching all children to fulfill their duties as active citizens who fight for liberal freedoms and institutions when they come under threat rightly works toward this aim.[10] In sum, education for autonomy can provide a sound and mutually compatible basis for education for citizenship.

Citizenship and cultural coherence: more compatible ideals?

To demonstrate that education for autonomy and education for citizenship are mutually compatible or even mutually reinforcing, however, is not to demonstrate that education for *choice* and children's development of *cultural coherence* are similarly compatible. This was the challenge that remained at the end of section 3.4. At this point, therefore, I propose to shift the focus a bit, and to examine whether *political liberalism* might provide a more tenable framework for liberal education than autonomy-based liberalism provides. One might wonder why I turn to political liberalism at this stage of the argument, since I carefully analyzed and forcefully rejected it in Chapter 1, and have focused on autonomy-based weak perfectionism for the past two chapters. I do so for three reasons. First, political liberalism provides the best framework within which to analyze the possibility of structuring liberal education around children's development of citizenship and cultural coherence alone. Political liberals explicitly favor individuals' development of civic virtue and cultural coherence while remaining ostensibly indifferent to children's development of autonomous choice. In this respect, they offer an obvious 'escape hatch' for liberals who are concerned about reconciling choice with cultural coherence. If political liberal education could be successfully achieved, therefore, it might be thought a preferable (and more widely acceptable) alternative to autonomy-driven liberal education. Thus, political liberalism poses an important challenge to autonomy-based liberalism in the realm of education, and provides an important framework within which to determine whether there is a viable alternative to the autonomy-based liberal educational ideal I developed in earlier chapters.

Second, I focus on political liberal education because it provides the *strongest* challenge to autonomy-based liberal education. I tried in Chapter 1 (and, I hope, succeeded in my effort) to discredit political liberalism's claim that it provides a consistent, non–autonomy-based liberal theory. Some readers, however, may still view political liberalism as a viable alternative to autonomy-based weak perfectionism on empirical grounds, possibly for some of the reasons discussed in section 3.4. This chapter will demonstrate that the practice of political liberal education suffers from failings similar to those of political liberal theory, in that both end up resting on individuals' development of the capacity for autonomy. I hope that this will serve to remove any lingering doubts about the status of the liberal educational ideal as it has been developed in previous chapters, and to confirm that political liberalism cannot offer a competing educational ideal.

Third, I analyze the relationship between citizenship and cultural identity in the context of political liberalism because I believe that this approach will best reveal both the complex nature of civic identity and the role of the civic culture in constructing individuals' personal identities. This is important because I will argue in Chapter 5 that civic identity can provide a bridge between cultural coherence and choice—i.e., that the presence of a certain kind of citizenship education within an autonomy-driven school can help children achieve both cultural coherence and the capacity for choice, and thus help them achieve full autonomy. Although the full meaning and significance of this argument cannot be clarified until section 5.1, this chapter's analysis of the nature of political liberal education is central to its justification.

Political liberal education: setting the stage

What do I mean, then, when I say that I am interested in exploring the shape of political liberal education? First, I should reiterate my statement in Chapter 1 that there are many 'political liberalisms', all of which place different emphases, to greater or lesser extents, on pluralism, civic virtue, reasonableness, and the separability of private conceptions of the good from the process of public consensus-building within the political sphere. That being said, however, I suggest that political liberalism is generally characterized by two different commitments. On the one hand, political liberalism privileges the private component of individuals' lives, attempting to shield individuals from interference by the state, government, and other secondary associations to the greatest extent possible consistent with protecting all citizens' basic liberties and opportunities. As a result, political liberalism favors a strong public–private distinction that protects individuals' identities, and attempts to place as much of people's lives as possible (i.e. as is consistent with the maintenance of liberalism) in the private domain so as to protect them from public interference. The civic dimension of political liberalism, on the other hand, is concerned with the public character of individuals' lives, as well as with individuals' obligations to preserve the institutions of public life. Recognizing the maintenance of liberal democratic institutions to be an essential prerequisite for the maintenance of political liberalism itself, the civic element of political liberalism finds expression in its insistence that citizens come to identify with the political community and learn and demonstrate the civic virtues of toleration, mutual respect, and critical reflection concerning the demands of public life.

It is the means by which schools—and by extension, society at large—can accommodate this tension between private non-interference and public citizenship that will be the focus of the next three sections. In particular, I will explore how school provision might actually be structured so as to minimize the tension between the principles of private non-interference and respect for individual identity coherence on the one hand and public 'character building' on the other. To this end, I will examine both the potential *curricular* demands imposed by political liberalism, and the *institutional* demands of structuring school provision so as to meet the civic and privacy-regarding requirements of a plural society.

In exploring the possibilities of public school[11] provision for the private individual, I will present three competing visions of the school as a politically liberal institution, expressed in terms of a schematic representation of three countries' approaches to education: England, the United States, and France.[12] These competing structures of education, I will argue, reflect important differences of commitment to, and can profitably be distinguished on the basis of, the relative weight given to privacy/identity-coherence and citizenship. If we think of these two elements as defining the endpoints of a political-liberal spectrum, England's approach to school provision will be represented as lying very near the privacy-protecting end of the spectrum (and therefore relatively far from concerns about inculcating civic virtue), with France at the other extreme, and the United States positioned somewhere in the middle.

The division between the demands of the political and the private will be seen to be linked to a second divide among political liberals—namely, the place of *pluralism* in public life (and therefore also in the life of the public school). In tandem with its privileging of the private over the public, England will be seen to pursue a policy of 'divided pluralism', in which pluralism is treated as a condition of private life to which public life and schooling must conform, but not as itself a public good. The US, on the other hand, will be seen to embrace individual pluralism as an intrinsic—and intrinsically desirable—feature of public life; France, under this analysis, will be seen to link its republican emphasis on the inculcation of a single national character to an explicit disavowal of pluralism as a public good. Thus, the chapter will follow through both sources of tension—the balance between private non-interference and public civic education, and the place of pluralism in a liberal society—in its attempt to set forth the institutional possibilities and practical conflicts latent within political liberal education.

By focusing on the specific systems of educational provision represented by these three countries (as opposed to confining the analysis to a purely abstract level), I hope that we will better come to understand the possibilities and limitations of political liberalism in the civic and educational spheres. Theorizing about education conducted without reference to specific experiences of educational practice can be problematic for two reasons, as Chapter 3 made clear. First, the nuances characteristic of relationships among principles, ideas, and praxis are often lost when they are considered in purely theoretical contexts. Empirical study can reveal tensions and subtleties of influence among ideas and practices that seem straightforward and unproblematic at the level of abstract theory. (Ensuring parent involvement in a school governed by liberal principles is a case in point.) Second, reference to experience is useful because of the special link between the construction of national identity and the construction of education and the school. As I will try to demonstrate throughout this chapter, education cannot be abstracted from its national and local context. Working through politically and legislatively located, empirical examples of educational institutions and approaches is thus the best means of coming to understand even in theory what a politically liberal education can achieve. Although there is no room to give further justification here, I hope that the chapter will itself provide a demonstration of this methodological assertion.

I should note, however, that theoretical rather than empirical questions ultimately drive this chapter, and thus direct the use to which the empirical material is put. In particular, I do not mean to claim that English, French, or American education policies are or ever have been motivated primarily by political liberal concerns, nor that my characterizations of the possible outcomes of these policies always occur in practice. Rather, the descriptions that follow are intentionally simplified and schematized 'ideal-type' models of what are in practice extraordinarily complex sets of pragmatic institutional aims, motivations, and practices. This is especially true insofar as these models are limited to each country's *public education* policies. Private schools occupy a surprisingly privileged place in all three countries—France's funding of private Roman Catholic schools in spite of its fierce attachment to secular education being the most noteworthy example. Private schools thus end up playing a role in society that can be sharply divergent from the state's primary educational stance.[13] Although the exclusion of private schooling from this discussion obviously reduces the chapter's descriptive validity and effectiveness as an empirical analysis of comparative educational practices, its omission is warranted, I believe, by considerations both of space and theoretical clarity. In the end, while I do hope that the theoretical discussion will prove at least somewhat empirically illuminating, any insight gained into current education practice is welcome but secondary.

4.2 PRIVATIZING THE PUBLIC: THE ENGLISH MODEL

As we saw in Chapter 1, political liberalism's 'claim to fame' is that it avowedly makes minimal demands on individual citizens, especially in the private arena of personal commitments. Citizens must exhibit such traits of character as will uphold and maintain the institutions of liberal democracy, and they must respect the rights and liberties of others. But, they need not affirm any state-wide conception of what defines the good life or the good person. Insofar as liberals measure legitimacy by the range of people who could reasonably support a particular set of political principles (under a variety of more and less artificial conditions), political liberalism's undemandingness is what sets it apart as a desirable and viable political theory in the eyes of many thinkers. Extending this approach to the question of education, then, any public schooling should, according to this conception of political liberal theory, respect the private lives of children and families by leaving their private lives and commitments essentially untouched—or at least unchallenged—if possible. This approach thereby also protects children's development of cultural/identity coherence. Education in the civic virtues would, under this analysis, ideally take place within a context that respected or even affirmed children's private commitments (assuming that the affirmation of one set of commitments did not interfere with those held by other children).

This weighting of private identity coherence versus public citizenship suggests that the philosophy of school provision exemplified by England might best satisfy the demands of political liberalism.[14] Under the English model, families are (in theory) permitted to separate themselves into more or less homogeneous groups based on common interests and commitments. The state then partially funds ('maintains') schools that cater to these private interests.[15] According to the 1985 Swann Report delivered by the state-sponsored Committee of Inquiry into the Education of Children from Ethnic Minority Groups, 'The right of ethnic minority communities to seek to establish their own voluntary aided schools is firmly enshrined in law. Under the provisions of the 1944 Education Act ethnic minority communities, along with any other group of individuals, are entitled to make proposals for the establishment of a voluntary aided school to cater for their children's educational needs.'[16] If we consider religion, for example, we see that in England today, the state supports voluntary Anglican, Catholic, Methodist, Seventh-Day Adventists, and a few muslim Jewish schools, and may eventually approve assisted or grant-maintained Muslim schools as well.[17] Although these schools may not discriminate among prospective students on the basis of ability, they can discriminate on the basis of religion;[18] thus, a publicly maintained Catholic school, for instance, can refuse entrance to all non-Catholic children. In practice only 32 per cent of English state schools are church-affiliated,[19] and even many of those display minimal or limited religious adherence. In theory, however, this model (and English law) permit the public school essentially to accommodate itself to private commitments, functioning almost as an extension of the child's private upbringing as opposed to establishing a rigidly differentiated public space or institution. The state satisfies the public as a whole by providing 'something for everyone' in the form of a compilation of state-funded private spaces. But, at least in theory, no single school need encapsulate the entire 'body public'.[20]

Nor is religion the only axis along which families may separate themselves within the state school system in order to form the equivalent of 'independent state schools',[21] as former Prime Minister Margaret Thatcher approvingly terms them. Since the establishment of numerous parental choice schemes in the 1980 and 1988 Education Acts, parents and children can 'privatize' public education to meet their particular needs and commitments in a number of ways. The most obvious of these until recently was the Assisted Places Scheme, established by the 1980 Education Act[22] and only abolished by 'New Labour' in 1999, which explicitly provided money for deserving students to attend private schools. State financing of private as opposed to public schools might have been the logical response to political liberalism's call for state non-interference with individuals—but it remains to be seen whether such action could be compatible with a similar maintenance of civic virtue. Even within the context of public schools, 'open enrolment' and parental choice rights detailed under the 1994 'Parents' Charter' provide extensive opportunities for parents and children to segregate themselves into schools that reflect their particular commitments or associations. For instance, every school must publish an annual prospectus that details not only exam and attendance statistics, but also 'the aims and values of the school and its approach to teaching' and 'how they provide moral and spiritual guidance for their pupils'.[23] Parents are encouraged to use these statements of purpose in order to choose a school for their child—and thus to ensure that their children are educated in a school whose ethos explicitly favors the particular commitments and values held by the family.[24]

In addition, class differentiation and segregation has re-emerged in some public schools as a result of parents' increased powers to choose. Popular schools with more requests than places can decide which students to take in a process that *The Economist* acknowledges often leads to 'pupils being "selected" by schools (offspring of the middle-classes preferred), rather than vice versa'.[25] Furthermore, some schools have reintroduced selective entrance exams—exams which, again, have been criticized as a shorthand method of reintroducing class-based segregation within supposedly public schools.[26] In sum, the English model of school provision permits parents and children considerable latitude in separating themselves from other students who are 'different' (be it on religious, moral, intellectual, or class-based grounds), and thereby allows them, too, to shape the public school to reflect and reinforce their private aims and values. In this respect, at least, the 'privatization' of the public school in the English model seems well on its way.

Unlike truly private schools, of course, even voluntary (denominational), grant-maintained, and specialized public schools in England are required to teach the National Curriculum—a comprehensive syllabus for 5–16-year-olds that is ostensibly intended to take up 70–80 per cent of school time.[27] The National Curriculum thus might be seen as a unifying public force in an otherwise divided school system. It is notable, however, that the presumptively most public element of the curriculum—Education for Citizenship—is not included in the list of the ten 'core and foundation' subjects in which students are formally assessed for competency and achievement. Rather, as one of a group of subjects designated to be 'cross-curricular themes' (the others being health education, economic and industrial understanding, careers education and guidance, and environmental education), citizenship is designed to be taught only within the context of the other disciplines.[28] It is not thought to warrant a class on its own. Nor are teachers or students given much guidance as to what citizenship (or citizenship education) is meant to entail. In contrast to the massive government publications that detail with exquisite precision every dimension of the core and foundation subjects, the National Curriculum Council has published a single workbook about citizenship education, and provides no standards for assessing students' progress.[29] While the theory behind this division between 'core and foundation subjects' and 'cross-curricular

themes' may (or may not) be sound, in practice it leads to the marginaliza-
tion and effective exclusion of citizenship education from the public school
classroom. Thus, I suggest that not even the National Curriculum succeeds
in reinstating the body public within the potentially divided and privatized
space of the publicly maintained school.[30]

This analysis of the English model of school provision also reveals the
source of my claim that such a system may foster and/or arise from
'divided pluralism'—i.e. a pluralistic national community composed of a
number of mutually uninterested monoreligious, monocultural, monolin-
guistic, and/or monoeconomic subcommunities. By providing schools that
reinforce families' private values and experiences, the state helps to perpetuate a polity that is composed of a number of separate, thriving cultures. In
a sense, therefore, such a system fosters a multicultural national society.
Multiculturalism itself, however, is not treated as a public good; in an
important sense, pluralism is merely an accidental public by-product of a
private-regarding school system. Nor does pluralism necessarily *become*
part of public culture or the public identity of citizens and the state, since
future citizens (i.e. children) are not necessarily encouraged in school to
embrace or even experience communities and values other than their own.
This is not to deny that the National Curriculum Council pays lip-service
to the demands of multiculturalism. As one of the two 'dimensions' of
cross-curricular education, multiculturalism is credited with being at the
core of a successful curriculum: 'A commitment to providing equal opportunities for all pupils, and a recognition that preparation for life in a multicultural society is relevant to all pupils, should permeate every aspect of the
curriculum.'[31] This written acknowledgement of the importance of multiculturalism, however, is as far as the National Curriculum Council and the
state go in actually establishing education for a multicultural society.

While the English model of schooling admirably fulfills political liberalism's promise to leave citizens alone to develop and pursue their own
private conceptions of the good, therefore, it seems less successful in inculcating the public virtues needed for the maintenance of a liberal democracy.
The nearly total weight placed on individuals' protection of privacy and
maintenance of personal identity, as opposed to their development of civic
virtue and identification, leaves this model of school provision open to
challenges from within political liberalism itself. Four objections to the
English model present themselves.

First, the English model neglects the nature of toleration within a liberal
democracy. As we saw in Chapter 1, in order to be tolerant, political and
other liberals generally agree, it is necessary that we possess some measure
of detachment from our own personal commitments. We can accept other

people's conceptions of the good as reasonable—and therefore as worthy of respect and toleration—only if we are able to see our own commitments as in some way contingent. This sense of contingency demands in turn a level of intellectual, if not emotional, detachment from our own conceptions of the good; i.e., we must accept some version of the burdens of judgement. The appropriate sense of detachment, however, cannot be adequately fostered in a school that is purpose-built to reflect the personal aims and conceptions of the good of children and their families (as the English model is). A more separate, *public* space must be established instead, one which provides an environment distanced from the commitments promoted by children's home communities and families. Only in this way can toleration reliably be achieved, because only in such a setting can children best come to recognize the contingency of their own attachments.

Following on from this, a more public conception of school, in which children from many backgrounds learn together, is needed because it is so hard for students to learn to be mutually tolerant and respectful of other people, traditions, and ways of life unless they are actually *exposed* to them. It is not enough to talk about tolerating others within the safety of mutually reinforcing, homogeneous groups as the English approach allows, even if such a setting did permit individuals' formation of intellectual detachment from their own commitments. Instead, toleration and mutual respect for others can best be acquired only by interacting with others in a setting that is itself challenging, heterogeneous, and mutually respectful. This is essentially the argument developed in favor of the detached school in Chapter 2, that students should encounter and interact with each other if they are to learn to tolerate and respect each other.[32]

Third, I suggest that further implications follow from this vision of the school as an explicitly public space that is differentiated from the private spaces of children's everyday lives. Because of the radical pluralism that characterizes modern society, a necessary condition of individuals' becoming a 'people' or 'public' is that they be able to identify—and to identify with—a shared, communal space or institution. It is out of the common commitment to the visible, even physical, institutions of public life that citizens come to tolerate each others' private differences. Children, as future citizens, develop these attachments best within the context of a public school that models in miniature this national public square. Just as it is not enough for adults to overcome the mutual mistrust and intolerance implied by radical pluralism in the absence of a set of common spaces and institutions to which they all feel connected and for which they feel mutually responsible, neither is it sufficient for children to discuss the principles of liberal democracy abstractly and from positions of mutually exclusive difference. Instead, I would conclude, a public space or body must be

created in which children participate in common and with which they identify. This aim is clearly not fulfilled by the English model of schooling
presented above.

Finally, in contrast to the minimal 'book-learning' in civic virtue that
children experience in the 'privatized' public schooling represented by the
English model, I would suggest that children can practice the civic virtues
and establish them over time as habits of character only within a truly *public*
school. This gets back to the argument developed in section 2.4 that children need opportunities to exercise virtues of character (such as citizenship
or autonomy) in order fully to develop them. As the American educational
reformer Theodore Sizer terms it (presumably following Aristotle), the
capacities for critical reflection, detachment, and toleration are dependent
upon children's developing proper *habits* within a suitably designed and
structured community: 'Habit grows from a mixture of conviction . . ., of
practice . . ., and of reinforcement from the community. . . . It is the habit
of thoughtfulness, of bringing an informed, balanced, and responsibly
skeptical approach to life, that schooling addresses.'[33] The public school,
under this reading, should thus be intentionally constructed so as to
provide a true model in miniature of the body public, in which children
interact and participate so as to build the habits of civic virtue necessary for
the long-term preservation of liberal democracy.

Two responses are possible to this set of objections against the English
model of political liberal education outlined above. One might attempt to
refute each of the four objections, to prove that the divided, 'privatized'
public education represented by English school policy *is* adequate to teach
the civic virtues and habits of character necessary for democratic citizenship, and thus is adequate to preserve the structures of liberal democracy.
Such a refutation might rely on broad theoretical and empirical arguments
that apply to most states and most children; it might also be made in reference to a smaller field such as a single state which is distinguished by
certain unique characteristics. 'In most communities,' this latter argument
would run, 'the objections to separate culturally, linguistically, religiously,
or economically homogeneous public schools are sound, but not in *our*
community, for the following special reasons' (whatever they might be).

Many liberals, however, will not find the wholesale rejection of the
objections outlined above to be adequate. A second response to the problem of political liberal education, therefore, is needed—one that engages
more directly with the issues that are involved, especially with the need to
foster reasonable detachment from one's own commitments and to establish
the school as a public space in which all children share and with which they
all identify. I would suggest that a partial solution to this problem can be
found in the policy of *neutrality* represented by the French and American

school systems. As we shall see below, both countries consciously establish the school as a public place by adopting a policy of public non-identification with private conceptions of the good. Religion, for example, is strictly excluded from the curriculum and public life of the school in both countries. Public schools are non-denominational; prayer within the classroom and school assemblies is strictly forbidden; and school officials remain officially neutral among and/or silent about both specific religions and religion in general.[34]

In this way, each state's policy of neutrality serves to maintain a strict division between the private and the public by refusing to allow any public school to take a stand on or intentionally to bias individuals' private commitments. At the same time, their neutrality permits children from all backgrounds to enter the school as equals, and presumably to identify equally with the school as a shared (because non-discriminatory) public space.[35] The French and American systems thus seem to respect the integrity of individuals' private commitments, as the English model does, but in a way that also responds to political liberalism's concern that the school maintain a public character in which to foster the development of civic virtue.

On the other hand, this surface similarity between the French and the American approaches conceals an essential difference underlying their two 'solutions' to the dilemma of political liberalism, as we shall see in the following pages. Although each country does pursue public neutrality, the two models are intriguingly and importantly distinguished by their contrasting means of achieving this neutral public character—and by implication, their means of achieving (and conceiving) their national civic identity. As I will show in sections 3–4, these differences will have important implications for how each balances the tension between citizenship and privacy, as well as for how each incorporates pluralism into the public school and the public culture. Neither model, however, will be seen fully to resolve these tensions; in certain ways, in fact, weaknesses in both positions will bring us back full circle to aspects of the English model. The conclusion of this chapter, therefore, will address the absence of a single educational 'solution' to the tensions inherent within political liberalism, and briefly discuss the collapse of all three models into a more coherent, weakly perfectionist, autonomy-driven model of liberal education.

4.3 BUILDING A 'MOSAIC': AMERICAN EDUCATION AND POLITICAL PLURALISM

One can achieve neutrality among a given set of competing claims (values, commitments, conceptions of the good, etc.) in two ways. One way is to exclude all claims from consideration; by ignoring them all, one shows preference towards none. This 'exclusionary' approach is characteristic of the French model of public education and will be discussed in section 4. A second method of achieving neutrality is to adopt a policy of equal inclusion instead of exclusion. By somehow accommodating all conceptions of the good within the purview of the school, one can at least in theory create an overall neutral environment in which all people have an equal stake. This, I suggest, is the aim of American education—to create a public school, a public space, and even more ambitiously, a public national identity, in which all private individuals and identities find inclusion.

Two problems immediately present themselves in trying to accommodate private difference within what is meant to be a shared public space. First, one must explain how this approach distinguishes itself from the English model, which also apparently attemps to accommodate private conceptions of the good within the public sphere. The answer is that under the American model, the inclusion of difference takes place on a local as opposed to (or as well as) a national level. Every school, and not just society taken as a whole, is meant to incorporate difference within its walls. As emphasized in section 2, the English model neither creates a local public space with which children can identify, nor fosters the exposure to diversity and personal detachment from one's commitments that is necessary for the development of toleration and civic virtue. Because of the localization of difference within every school, the American system is able in theory to do both.[36]

Second, the attempt to accommodate the public school to a diversity of private commitments without losing the public character of the school poses both a logical and a practical challenge. If the 'accommodation' or 'inclusion' of the private within the public means that the public space must be shaped to *promote* the competing demands of individuals' private commitments and values, then the enterprise seems doomed. It is impossible coherently to express *A* and not-*A* simultaneously; yet, given the radical plurality of modern industrialized societies like America, this is what shaping the public space to reflect individuals' competing conceptions of the good would require. In addition, even if the claims of reason were somehow met, there is a practical difficulty. One of the primary aims behind modeling the public school after the public square is to establish a shared space in which children from a plurality of backgrounds feel equally welcomed, involved, and committed. Only thus, it was suggested at the end of section 2, can children learn toleration, mutual respect, and identification with the civic community. If the public school starts promoting all of the diverse and competing commitments held by its students (and their families), however, then many students will presumably feel alienated, since the school will appear to embrace values which they and their families reject. Thus, the inclusionary approach to public (educational) neutrality can succeed only if the *accommodation* of competing viewpoints and values can be distinguished from the *promotion* of them.

One might well ask, then, what is meant by the claim that the American model of school provision respects the public–private distinction and children's construction of identity coherence even as it creates through the school a public space that accommodates the private commitments held by children and their families. I would suggest that under the (in many ways uniquely) American principle of accommodation, the public space of the American public school is created out of the overlap of individuals' private spaces and interests. On both a structural and a curricular level, United States schools have arguably adopted and are perpetuating a conception of shared civic identity and education that is built out of the interaction and accommodation of individuals' separate, private identities.[37]

In structural terms, children and parents often 'bargain' with the school to get special treatment in light of religious, ethnic, linguistic, or other cultural differences. Although each school nominally offers the same curricular choices, activities, and structure for all non-special-needs students,[38] students are frequently excused from lessons or other obligations as a result of their conflicting private commitments or beliefs. Thus, strongly religious students are excused from health class on the grounds that it contravenes their (or often their parents') religious or moral beliefs by teaching about contraception; they may also be released from biology class if it presents evolution as fact without giving equal time to 'scientific creationism.' For similarly religious reasons, children of Jehovah's Witnesses are excused from the quintessentially public activity of pledging allegiance to the flag (an exercise that takes place every morning in most of America's primary school classrooms) because they see it as idolatrous.[39] And non-English speakers are accorded the right by some states to study the full curriculum in their native language if a critical mass of similar students is present in the school or school district.

In all of these cases, the public space of the school shapes and reshapes itself to accommodate the private needs, desires, and commitments of its students. In order to keep up its public character (and thus to satisfy the political liberal demands of teaching civic virtue within a context that respects the public–private distinction), it must attract and retain in one place an often overwhelmingly diverse set of students with an equally diverse set of expectations, needs, and demands. As a result, the American school arguably tries to be (or become) all things to all people, all of the time. The challenge, of course, is to keep up the show. As I suggested above, if the school *obviously* accommodates itself to such a diversity of private interests, it runs the risk of alienating its students and thus losing its status as a truly public space. The public school under the American model, therefore, must take on a multiplicity of simultaneous identities, hoping both that each facet of its 'personality' will attract some set of students and families (who might otherwise retreat to private or parochial schools), and that out of the overlap of these identities a shared public space will be achieved in which students will confront sufficient diversity and heterogeneity to come to embrace the virtues of toleration, mutual respect, and critical reflection.[40]

We see the same pattern of (re)constructing the public identity of the school—and more generally, the civic identity of the American public square—in the newly developed 'multicultural' curricula in use in many US primary and secondary schools. The self-conscious recognition of the private within the public is especially notable in two elements of the modern curriculum: the (re)presentation of American history not as a single linear process but as a discontinuous history of a number of different types of 'hyphenated Americans' (African-Americans, European-Americans, Latina-Americans, etc.); and related to this, the alteration of the classroom metaphor of America as a 'melting pot' to America as 'mosaic'.[41] Both of these elements are notable, I suggest, because they represent the abandonment of an older, assimilative ideal of the public school and of public life, under which newcomers (children as well as immigrants) were considered to become 'true Americans' only when they had learned to share in a unitary civic identity adopted and lived by all. This older vision played itself out in the classroom in the form of civics classes that emphasized the 'melting pot' conception of American identity, citizenship contests and 'school pride' activities (still represented by frequent 'pep rallies' in most secondary schools), and the daily 'Pledge of Allegiance' mentioned above. While such activities and curricular requirements seemed to fulfill the *civic* element of political liberalism, they did so in a way that violated individuals' private identities and personal or cultural integrity.

In contrast, the new multicultural ideal expresses a potentially truer form of political liberalism by replacing the goal of assimilation with that of toleration, and the unitary with a plural conception of American identity. Students are now taught that only out of the preservation of difference, and of mutual respect among different individuals with different histories and commitments, can the 'mosaic' that constitutes 'hyphenated America' be maintained. Schools' growing recognition of difference also expresses itself in the increasing number of classes on the secondary school level that concentrate on the racial, ethnic, and/or gendered aspects of the American experience (to say nothing of the proliferation of such classes, as well as full degree programs, in many US universities).

Thus, at the level both of curriculum and of school structure, the American model of school provision can be seen as providing an explicit, self-conscious response to the dilemma of simultaneously educating for civic virtue and cultural coherence. By constructing the identity and curriculum of the public school out of the union of students' private identities and commitments, the American model appears to achieve a balance between the demands of private non-interference/identity-coherence and the demands of civic virtue. This springs in part from a much more positive conception of pluralism than we have yet seen. In contrast to the English model of 'divided pluralism' presented in section 2, the American construction of the public school and public identity embraces pluralism as a truly desirable, public good that should be fostered and appreciated at both the national and personal level. By 'celebrating' and modeling itself after the pluralist, national public square, the American public school establishes a neutral space into which all individuals are equally welcomed, and thus ultimately achieves the public character that the English school lacks. These characteristics arguably equip it to meet the four objections to the English model discussed at the end of section 2, and (at least in theory) to inculcate toleration, mutual respect, and civic identification among its students. Likewise, the very neutrality that establishes the public, civic character of the school also fulfills the political liberal demand that the private be kept free from public interference or manipulation. Students' identification with certain private commitments is respected and even welcomed into some aspects of the public life of the school, but no set of commitments is actually endorsed by the public school. The public character of the school is built out of, but is distinct from, the private spheres of student life.

Within this 'celebration' of the American conception of pluralism and the American model's apparent solution to the dilemma of political liberalism, however, lurk two potentially fatal weaknesses. Both stem from the incorporation of the private into the public. First, there is the risk that the show of realizing the private within the public will work too well. I suggested above that in order to draw all students and families into the school, the American model of the public school has to take on a number of simultaneous identities, accommodating itself in a continual process of reconstruction to meet the expectations of a diverse population. At the same time, however, the school cannot diversify completely. It must retain and even emphasize elements which are common to all students, for as I argued at the end of section 2, it is only in recognizing the *common* demands of civic identity and public life as represented by the school that students will come to participate and to acknowledge each other as equal partners in the political process. If under the American model, therefore, the public school fails to establish clearly enough its shared, public character, then private identifications and commitments may continue to hold sway. Students and families would identify with *their* vision of the school—but not with the public institution taken as a whole. Such a scenario would in effect return us, whether wittingly or unwittingly, to the English model of school provision. The only difference would be that a number of effectively separate, homogeneous schools would co-exist under one school roof in the American model, as opposed to being divided up among separate school buildings as in the English model. Although the proof of this claim falls outside the scope of this book, it could well be argued that such a divided co-existence has already implicitly taken place within American public life, finding its political expression in the proliferation of interest- and identity-group politics and the increasing division of the polis. If such a retreat from civic identification and democratic virtue to local identification and interest politics is a *necessary* outcome of the celebration of the private within public life—i.e. if the Balkanization that many would argue describes American society and political life is a necessary outcome of the accommodationism of American culture and education—then political liberal education on the American model seems doomed from the start.

This problem becomes even more pointed as we move to consider the other risk posed by the American model of school provision—that the public face of the school could itself actually overpower, rather than be overpowered by, the integrity of individuals' private commitments. Toleration and civic identification require for their development conscious (and conscientious) reflection about one's civic or public identity, and about one's relationship to others in the public sphere. By conceptualizing their private identity as part of—even as constitutive of—their public persona, as the American model leads people to do, individuals implicate their private identities in the activities of their public selves. Thus, when the public school encourages a student to reflect critically upon her civic responsibilities—her duty to discount a person's sex in evaluating his abilities to fill a job, for example—it requires that she also reconsider the commitments of her private self—say, her religious commitment to a God-given distinction between the sexes—in this same context, because of the overlap between her civic and personal identities. This seems patently to violate the public–private distinction central to political liberalism. This is not to suggest that civic education can ever be kept fully in the public sphere; as I noted in section 1.2 and in my second objection to the English model above, the public habit of toleration itself requires that one has come to recognize the contingency of one's private commitments and to adopt a stance of public detachment from one's private values.[42] But there is a difference between coming to recognize the contingency of one's private beliefs in order to learn to tolerate others—a virtue essential to the preservation of liberal democracy—and subjecting one's private beliefs to wholesale analysis within the public sphere of the school.

I suggested above that the American approach may fail to surmount the private divisions between people and thus fail to establish a truly democratic education in civic virtue. If in this case we see that the same approach may also fail adequately to preserve the public–private distinction and violate individuals' identity coherence, the American project seems doomed as an adequate response to the dilemma of political liberalism. In sum, the American model's delicate balancing act between the claims of individual privacy and the common experience of civic education may fail adequately to satisfy *either* element of political liberalism. By forcing the incorporation of each individual's private identity into the public sphere, the American approach may violate the integrity of children's and families' private lives; it also runs the risk of fostering a public square characterized by civic instability and identity politics as opposed to democratic virtue and civic identification.

We must therefore seek out a third solution to the dilemma of political liberal education—one that seeks to construct the public character of the school aimed at by the American model of school provision, yet manages to separate individuals' private commitments from the public body of the school in a manner different from both the American and the English models. This third way, I suggest, can be found in the French approach to school provision, an approach to which I now turn.

4.4 SECULARISM AND CITIZENSHIP: THE FRENCH MODEL

The English and American models left us with two important challenges. First, in order to avoid the failings of the English approach, the politically liberal school system must establish schools as public spaces that are properly representative of the public square. They must, as far as reasonably possible: bring together a range of students representative of the national society; inspire widespread communal identification and attachment; and consciously and conscientiously inculcate the habits of civic virtue, including toleration, civic identity, and critical reflectiveness. These requirements have implications both for the overall structure of school provision (e.g. public schools should probably not select students on the basis of class or religion or be otherwise exclusionary) and for the curriculum that gets taught—implications that for the most part the American model picks up on. The very failure of the American model even so to achieve a politically liberal system of school provision, however, implicitly conveys the second challenge: namely, that the public character of the school must be achieved without sacrificing a robust distinction between individuals' public and private lives.

It is to these two challenges that the third, French model of political liberal education should be seen to respond. Like the American approach, this model takes a commitment to neutrality as its starting point for constructing the public space of the school and the public identity of its students/future citizens. In contrast to the American model, however, the French neutral public school is created not through a principle of equal *accommodation* of the private within the public life of the school and the individual, but through a principle of equal *exclusion* of the private from the public. Students (as well as all teachers and school staff) are expected to shed their commitments at the school door in order to enter as equals the 'public square' represented by the school. For example, they are forbidden to wear 'ostentatious'[43] symbols of religious affiliation, to claim excused school absences stemming from religious festivals or obligations, and to omit any portion of the national curriculum on cultural, religious, or other private grounds. Students are treated as solely public beings from the moment they enter the school gates.

Likewise, the school itself is purged of particularistic commitments in favor of constructing a unified, national character. On a structural level, public schools are resolutely secular and similar, making few if any accommodations for local or regional variations in language, culture, or ethnicity, and no accommodations for religious commitment.[44] All are bound to teach the national curriculum (as are many private schools), and none may violate the ostensibly secular code by which its schedule is governed. In this sense the school is explicitly intended to mirror the secular neutrality of the public square, as Jules Ferry, the architect of the modern French public school system, declared in a speech to the Chamber of Deputies in 1880: 'Religious neutrality in the school . . . is, in my eyes and the eyes of the government, the consequence of the secularization of civil power and of all social institutions.'[45]

On the curricular level, too, anything which smacks of religious affiliation or identity politics is excluded: religion classes are banned; French history is taught in terms of supposedly universally apprehensible ideas and movements, as opposed to being taught in terms of the hyphenated histories of difference and individualism favored in American classrooms; regional languages such as Breton were until recently not taught or spoken in public schools; and, most tellingly of all, French educators and politicians explicitly acknowledge that the aim of the curriculum is to teach students to be 'French'. Although this nationalizing vision was first instituted by Jules

Ferry's 1870s school reforms, François Bayrou, the current Education Minister, gives one of the most striking recent articulations of this aim, and is worth quoting at length:

In France the national and republican projects have been identified with a certain idea of citizenship. This French idea of the nation and republic by nature respects all convictions, particularly religious and political beliefs and cultural traditions. But it rules out the breaking down of the nation into separate communities which are indifferent to one another, and which respect only their own rules and laws and only engage in a simple coexistence. The nation is not only a group of citizens who hold individual rights. It is a community with a destiny.

This ideal is constructed firstly at school. School is the space which more than any other involves education and integration where all children and all youth are to be found, learning to live together and respect one another. If in this school there are signs of behavior which show that they cannot conform to the same obligations, or attend the same courses and follow the same programs, it negates this mission. All discrimination should stop at the school gates, whether it is sexual, cultural, or religious discrimination.

This secular and national ideal is the very substance of the Republican school and the foundation of its duty of civic education.[46]

As this quotation potently suggests, the French model explicitly commits itself to the inculcation of democratic virtue and civic identification within its students, consciously shaping the 'Republican' public school to mirror and to establish the unified and 'destin[ed]' character of the national square.

How does such an approach square with the demands of political liberalism? I would suggest that at least on the face of things, the French model of achieving public neutrality through private exclusion is able to balance respect for private commitments with civic concerns quite well. It preserves the public–private distinction by encouraging—indeed forcing—the private to remain fully separate from public life. By giving no public space or attention, be it affirmative or negative, to the private dimension of individuals' lives, it arguably preserves in a liberal fashion the integrity and distinctiveness of the private sphere. At the same time, the exclusion of private differences from the public sphere frees up the public space of the school—and the public identity of the individual—to be shaped in the service of citizenship more fully than either the American or the English models allow. No longer is the public character of the school constrained by private needs or demands; as a result, the school can devote full attention (or whatever level of attention is appropriate) to achieving the civic educational goals initially set out at the end of section 2 and reiterated at the beginning of this section.

It is worth noting that the aims of civic education are easier to achieve in this setting, too, because by redefining people wholly in terms of their public selves, the French model shifts the brunt of liberal education from teaching toleration of *private others* to inculcating mutual respect for *public similars*. Civic virtue under this model does not require toleration of difference, because people's differences do not enter the public square. Instead, students are taught to see and respect each other as equal, even undifferentiated, inhabitants of the same public space and public character. The French model thereby completely avoids the American trap of blurring the public and the private through conveying substantive messages about the value of others' private commitments (i.e. that they deserve respect). Individuals' private identities and commitments simply do not enter the picture.

Despite its apparent success at integrating the privacy-regarding with the citizenship-regarding demands of political liberalism, however, the secular, exclusionary neutrality that motivates the French model may be a double-edged sword. Three objections to the French model present themselves in particular: that individuals' private differences are in practice swallowed up rather than protected by a homogenizing national public character; that the republican character of the French model is anti-liberal; and that an exclusionary neutrality of the sort represented by the French model must itself be non-neutral and incompatible with political liberalism. While it is possible to pursue these objections on theoretical grounds alone, I will examine them through the lens of *l'affaire du foulard*—a now decade-long series of cases in which Muslim girls in France who started wearing headscarves to public school touched off a nationwide debate about nationality, immigration, minorities, education, the republican tradition, and the future of France itself.

The initial incident is deceptively simple. In September 1989, three Muslim schoolgirls wore the traditional Muslim headscarf, the *hijab* (misleadingly translated as *foulard* in French), to class in the Parisian suburb of Creil. The headmaster barred the girls from entering, citing a 1937 law prohibiting religious symbols in school; he later offered to permit them to wear the scarf, which covered their hair, ears, and necks but not their faces, in the schoolyard but not in class. A three-month standoff occurred, until finally two of the girls declared they would remove the *hijab* in class and the fracas temporarily subsided.[47] In the meantime, however, the incident sparked a raucous and hotly contested national debate about the nature of religious neutrality in the 'republican' school. In November 1989, Prime Minister Michel Rocard took a stand, declaring that 'France could not be "a juxtaposition of communities"', it could not follow the Anglo-Saxon models that allowed ethnic groups to live in geographic and cultural "ghettoes", and resulted in "soft forms of apartheid".'[48] The following spring, the Conseil d'État ruled on the case, taking the more lenient view that each school had the right to set its own policy, with future incidents being decided by local authorities and school officials on a case-by-case basis.

Three years later in November 1993, *l'affaire du foulard* erupted again, this time with four girls being suspended from school in Nantua. In conjunction with this action, the government deported a local Turkish imam who had declared 'Allah's law takes precedence over French law', and placed an Islamic 'advisor' to the girls' family under house arrest.[49] In response, an estimated 700 Muslim girls started wearing headscarves themselves, until at its peak, approximately 2,000 children (out of an estimated 150,000 to 250,000 Muslim girls attending French public schools) were wearing the *hijab* to class.[50] Although this amounted to only 1 per cent of Muslim girls who attended public school, and less than 0.02 per cent of the French school-age population as a whole (estimated to number twelve million),[51] it caused massive public and governmental outcry. On 10 September 1994, Bayrou announced that he was reversing the Conseil d'État's decision, and would ban headscarves from all public schools:

it is not possible to accept the presence and multiplication of ostentatious signs in school whose meaning involves the separation of certain students from the rules of the common life of the school. These signs are in themselves part of proselytization. . . .

I would therefore ask you [heads of schools and teachers] to propose to your administrative councils to include in your internal rules the banning of these ostentatious signs while recalling that more discreet signs which indicate attachment to personal conviction should not be treated in the same way, as the Conseil d'État and administrative jurisprudence have already stated. . . .

I would also ask you to ask all teachers of all disciplines, all educational personnel, and the rest of your team to explain to the pupils in their charge the double meaning of respect for personal convictions and firmness in the defense of the republican project in our country.[52]

As a result, between September and December 1994, 68 girls were suspended from school and the number of girls wearing the scarf dropped from 2,000 to approximately 600.[53] This standoff persisted until April 1995, when first a court in Lille, and then the Conseil d'État, decided that wearing a headscarf was not 'in itself' necessarily ostentatious and proselytizing.[54] Since then, school heads and other local school officials have been able to exercise considerable judgement in determining whether to admit, suspend, or expel girls wearing the *hijab*. Predictably, some schools have chosen to admit students wearing headscarves with little incident, while others continue to expel those girls who insist on covering themselves.[55]

Although it has periodically flared up since, the conflict has generally subsided. Fewer than 10 per cent of the original girls are estimated still to be wearing the *hijab* to school, and no further legal or practical changes have taken effect since 1995.[56] It is notable, however, that regardless of how teachers and schools respond 'on the ground', the principle banning ostentatious and proselytizing symbols still stands unchallenged. To this extent, the notion of exclusionary neutrality in the service of civic education remains central to French schooling.

The outcome of *l'affaire du foulard*, I suggest, signals the failure of the third and final model for a politically liberal education that effectively balances the principle of respecting individuals' private commitments with the principle of inculcating civic virtue in future citizens. Let us return to the three objections to the French model enumerated above. First, I suggested that the wholesale exclusion of students' private commitments and beliefs from the public sphere of the classroom can result in those students' private identities being swallowed up and replaced by the homogenizing norms and identity of public life.[57] This seems to be the aim of French schooling, insofar as educational and political officials across the political spectrum in France speak with horror of a pluralistic, multicultural society along American lines. To support an 'American' right to difference, former Socialist Minister of Education Jean-Pierre Chevenement warned, would be to prepare France for 'a Lebanon'.[58] Bayrou speaks of the need to 'build a united, secular society, specifically where schools [are] concerned',[59] while conservative deputy Pierre Lellouche starkly declares, 'Multiculturalism would be the end of France. You can be what you want to be here—Christian, Jewish, or Muslim—but we're all Gauls. The alternative is to create cultural ghettos.'[60] For the French, at least, the exclusion of the private from the public space of the classroom not only has the *possible* and *unintentional* outcome of the withering up of individual identity, but has such a loss as an *explicit* aim.

Is such an anti-pluralistic and ultimately illiberal stance the only possible outcome of the French model? Might it not be possible in theory to separate the constructive, exclusionary neutrality of the French model from its more sinister (i.e. less liberal) outcomes in the empirical sphere of French politics? In one sense these are impossible questions to answer, or at least to answer quickly; they share the historical and empirical complexities inherent in the question about American identity politics and fragmentation posed at the end of section 3. But in another sense, a negative answer seems fairly clear: liberal respect for and protection of private difference cannot coexist with the wholesale exclusion of private difference from the public sphere, especially the sphere of the public school. This is true for two reasons. On the one hand, it is difficult to separate the two strands of one's identity in the way one would have to do in order to preserve the pretense of 'keeping the government out of one's private life'—it seems well-nigh impossible for children to effect such a separation. The relationships children develop at school are often the sole relationships they have outside of the family, and are consequently central to their personal, intellectual, and emotional development. It is simply bizarre to think that a Muslim girl could form friendships at school based on a fully secularized public identity and yet maintain a fully intact and encumbered Muslim identity at home and in her private life. On the other hand, private differences are often based on identification with and obedience to the laws of a particular collectivity, such as the Muslim community. The restriction of difference to the private sphere thus requires that individuals violate the religious or other laws to which they have committed themselves whenever they enter the public sphere of the school. In this respect, children's private commitments as expressed through identification with non–public associations are effectively negated within the walls of the public school.

The second objection to the French approach, that its republican character is ultimately anti-liberal because it desiccates the private sphere, is also implied by the model's rejection of pluralism, of individuals' collective identification with non-public communities. Whether or not it is psychologically possible for individuals, including children, to maintain mutually separate or disengaged public and private identities, I suggest that the *state* under this model cannot remain indifferent to individuals' private commitments, as is favored by political liberalism. As the state's conception of the demands of civic virtue increases, the space left over for individuals' private lives necessarily decreases—and decreases substantially. The public–private distinction may nominally be preserved, but the range of private commitments that are seen not to interfere with the public sphere is shrunk almost to invisibility. Thus, the girls' 'ostentatious' identification with Islam through wearing the headscarf was interpreted in France not only as illegitimate 'proselytization' to other students which violated those students' rights as public citizens, but also as: the encroachment of fundamentalist Muslim terrorism on the French state;[61] an anti-democratic and anti-egalitarian subjugation of women that had the potential to reduce the girls' own empowerment as citizens;[62] and the anti-republican 'ghettoization' of French society. People from the political left as well as the right argued for banning the *hijab* in school on all of these grounds—all of which, notice, are overtly spun in terms of the *public* rights and duties of citizens. While such reasons ostensibly make no claims upon the private sphere of individuals' lives, I would argue that they depend on such a thick notion of the state and of civic virtue as to be incompatible with liberal aims.

Finally, I would also suggest that 'neutrality by exclusion', which constitutes the foundation of the French model, is itself non-neutral in a way that conflicts with political liberalism. In order to exclude a private conception of the good such as religion from the schools, someone must decide what is to count as religious display or practice—and, correlatively, what is to count as non-religious display or practice, i.e. as religiously insignificant or irrelevant. This requires the adoption of a public norm from which religious practice is seen to diverge. The problem is that it is impossible to conceive of such a norm which is not itself religiously charged. Consider Bayrou's distinction between 'ostentatious' and 'discreet' symbols of religious affiliation. A symbol of religious affiliation is ostentatious by definition only if it departs substantially from the norm. By banning ostentatious symbols from the school yet permitting subdued displays of religious affiliation or belief, Bayrou is in effect identifying the public space of the school with the prevailing religious norm. In practice, this means that Muslim headscarves are excluded as ostentatious, while crucifixes are officially deemed to be discreet. Such a distinction hardly seems compatible with the ideal and maintenance of the secular school! The religious norm of the community, in this case Christianity, is thus implicitly embraced by the supposedly secular school, and Christianity comes ultimately to define the boundaries of the public square.

It is worth noting that this conclusion would hold even if 'discreet' symbols were banned from school, as becomes clear if we turn even cursory attention to the rules, structure, and schedule of French public schools. For example, French schools forbid the wearing of hats or other head coverings inside the school building, but this ban is interpretable as 'secular' only within the context of a Christian society. For Jews and Muslims, going bareheaded is as much a mark of Christian religious affiliation as covering one's head is seen by Christians to be a mark of Jewish or Muslim religious affiliation. The same is true for the attendance schedule in French schools. As Norma Moruzzi reminds us, 'the French school week runs through part of Saturday, and the only full day of rest on the weekend is Sunday. That practice is a happy compromise of the religious and the secular, unless your religion is other than Christian, in which case the secular school week may seem very much religiously defined.'[63] Regardless of the exclusion of 'discreet' versus 'ostentatious' religious symbols, therefore, religion can never be fully excluded from the construction of the public school (or the public square). In this case, at least, exclusionary neutrality is a contradiction in terms.[64]

In sum, I suggest that while the French model ostensibly attempts to achieve the same aim as the American model does—namely, to balance equally the demands of citizenship and the necessity of preserving the public–private distinction—it does so in a way that ends up ransoming the private dimension of individuals' lives to the public demands of civic identification and virtue. Insofar as the 'cosmetic' exclusion of private difference from the public school (i.e. excluding overt symbols of religious commitment) is buttressed by an explicitly assimilationist (and thus antipluralistic) curriculum that attempts to turn all children into 'French(wo)men',[65] the French approach effectively sacrifices liberalism to democracy and political liberalism to the republican ideal.

4.5 CONCLUSION

In searching for a response to the defects of the French model, we might return, full circle, to England—to an ideal of political liberal education that neither pretends to achieve neutrality within the space of a single school, nor attempts to shape individuals' private selves and commitments to fit the public mold of civic obligation. But of course, recovering the English model is not a solution, for the original problems that drove us to develop the American and French models in the first place still remain—i.e. the English model's lack of attention to civic education, and its indifference to establishing a truly public space in which pluralism and toleration can flourish. Personal integrity and public citizenship are no better balanced by the English system of privatized public schools than they are by a French system that 'publicizes' private selves, or for that matter, by an accommodationist American system in which individuals' public and private identities nestle uneasily inside each other like Russian *matrioshka* dolls. Each of the three models has strengths that the other two lack. But each also has weaknesses that make it unfit as a universal template for political liberal education.

Instead of continuing to cycle through our three models of political liberal education, therefore, I suggest that we return to an autonomy-driven conception of liberal education. To the extent that political liberal education is successful at teaching the civic virtues (i.e. in the American and French models), it arguably loses its characteristic virtue of accommodating a greater range of social diversity than autonomy-based liberalism allows. This is certainly true in the French model, and as we saw it is also a potent possibility within the American model, which threatens to collapse individuals' private identities into the public sphere in order to avoid creating a Balkanized, unstable, and ultimately anti-democratic politics of identity. Neither cultural pluralism nor cultural coherence is better protected in political liberal schools than in autonomy-driven schools—except in the case of the English model, which in turn fails adequately to inculcate children with the civic virtues. Ultimately, we are led to agree with Gutmann: 'The social diversity accommodated by liberalism depends as importantly on the strictly political requirements of liberal democratic citizenship. We therefore find a remarkable degree of convergence between those political and comprehensive liberals who embrace a demanding view of the political requirements of civic education.'[66]

Political liberal education (and political liberalism itself) thus has no practical or empirical advantage over weakly perfectionist liberal education (and weakly perfectionist liberalism itself). Because of the identity-shaping character of education for civic virtue—characteristics which, as I noted in section 1, bring it close in effect even if not in intent to education for autonomy—children's maintenance of cultural coherence is no more guaranteed under a political liberal conception of civic education than it is under a weakly perfectionist ideal of education for autonomy (and citizenship, insofar as the former incorporates the latter). Ultimately, from a practical standpoint, political liberal education may be scarely distinguishable from weakly perfectionist liberal education:[67] both end up teaching most of the attitudes, skills, dispositions, habits, and knowledge needed for children to develop and exercise autonomy, and do so within an institutional structure similar to the detached school. Furthermore, insofar as I showed in section 1.2 that political liberalism rests on the same theoretical foundations of valuing autonomy as weakly perfectionist liberalism does, the former may simply turn into the latter. To the extent that it is theoretically and practically coherent, political liberalism must adopt the aims and outcomes of autonomy-based liberalism. And to the extent that political liberals try to hold on to the purely 'political' character of their theory, or to the solely 'civic' character of their education, weakly perfectionist liberalism and its accompanying autonomy-promoting education must be judged superior on both theoretical and empirical grounds. Finally, I suggest that the remaining weaknesses within autonomy-based liberal education—i.e. the potential conflict between children's development of choice and their achievement of cultural coherence—can be partially resolved by incorporating into it the conceptions of civic identity developed in this chapter. How this resolution can be achieved will be discussed in the next chapter.

5

Making sense of it all: transforming political theory into educational policy

Having concluded at the end of the last chapter that autonomy-promoting liberal education is superior on both normative and empirical grounds to political liberal education—at least to the extent that they are distinguishable—I discuss in this chapter what steps need to be taken to implement the liberal educational ideal in practice. I first tie up loose ends in section 1, clarifying the ways in which choice, cultural coherence, and citizenship fit together within an autonomy-driven education, and then addressing three other possible liberal or educational aims that should potentially help guide the implementation of the liberal ideal. Section 2 reviews the characteristics of the liberal educational ideal, and constructs a public policy of liberal education, arguing for strict state regulation of schools (whether public or private), as well as for a very limited 'market' in education in the form of 'controlled choice'. Finally, in section 3 I discuss the changes that would need to take place in the areas of legislation, pre-service and in-service teacher training, public dialogue, school accountability, and cultural attitudes about education in order to make the liberal educational ideal a reality in modern liberal democracies, especially the United States and Great Britain. Given the obvious distance that exists between current practice and the proposed changes, I conclude by assessing the implications of my theory for both liberal theorists and educational practitioners in the 'here and now', and I discuss the directions in which I hope future work in liberal and educational theory and practice will go.

5.1 FORGOTTEN AIMS?

We have seen that civic education has significant implications for individual identity. Crucially, 'personal' and 'political' constructions of identity are not separable in the way political liberals would like, either in theory (as I showed in section 1.2) or in practice (Chapter 4). This fact, while posing a fundamental challenge for most forms of political liberalism (i.e. any versions that are not actually weakly perfectionist autonomy-based liberalism in disguise), actually serves to resolve the remaining problem for autonomy-based liberalism left hanging from sections 3.4 and 4.1: how can education for autonomy balance education for identity coherence and education for choice? I now suggest that students who lack the resources to form a coherent identity within the context of their families and communities (because of familial and social breakdown, and/or because of tensions between their minority status and the majority culture) can and will often construct a coherent identity based upon the civic components of identity—components which are inevitably cultural as well.

As we implicitly saw in the last chapter, civic identity is 'thick': it encompasses and/or gives life to a complex combination of commitments, practices, beliefs, rituals, etc., which help to shape the lives of individuals and communities within the state.[1] These components of civic identity inevitably include cultural, social, historical, and linguistic aspects; without such elements, the nation or polity could hardly function as a source of identification at all. This helps in part to explain the formal and informal curricula taught by state schools—embodied by such features as the language of instruction, mandatory literature and history classes, and so forth. Aside from the practical necessity of teaching in a common language, for example, and even of promoting some common rituals, beliefs, and values, these features can be justified in part on the basis of the need to initiate children into and perpetuate the national culture. Without such a common curriculum, including a common language or languages, history, and literature, a common civic identity would be difficult if not impossible to achieve.

This curriculum has the further justification of providing a stable source of personal identitification and cultural coherence for those students who might otherwise grow up without one. Because states are cultural as well as political constructs, and because civic identification therefore inevitably includes a cultural component, schools which educate children for civic membership can also help children achieve a sense of cultural membership. Thus, children who grow up in the fragmented or culturally impoverished environments mentioned above can achieve cultural embeddedness within a detached liberal school. Their membership will be in the public culture taught by the school, rather than in a private, ethnic, or religiously based cultural community. But as I emphasized previously, the source of this cultural identification does not matter; so long as public cultural membership provides the necessary prerequisites for agency, it satisfies the important aim of education as socialization.

Furthermore, depending upon the way in which civic identity is constructed at the local level, children raised in minority cultures but educated in a detached school may be able to achieve simultaneous cultural coherence in both their home culture and the civic culture. No single policy can be imposed to ensure that all children from all minority cultures will always feel at home in a detached school that educates for autonomy and citizenship. But a liberal state whose civic identity in some way incorporates or responds to individuals' private identities (as in the American model), including minority identities, may be able to reinforce children's development of cultural coherence while encouraging their identification with the liberal polity. In this case, an autonomy-driven school could serve minority children's interests in developing cultural coherence even while educating for choice, and thus overcome the dilemmas posed at the end of sections 3.3 and sections 3.4. If children's home cultures were partially represented by, or even just compatible with, local civic identity, children could feel that their personal cultural identities and senses of cultural coherence were being reinforced even while they develop their capacities for effective citizenship and autonomous decision-making. This synergy may be possible only in particular states whose construction of liberal civic identity incorporates or is compatible with minority cultures' constructions of their own identities. As Chapter 4 illustrated, the relationship among citizenship, cultural socialization, and choice is a highly contingent one. But at least in those liberal states that exhibit these characteristics, children who learned in a school that was structured by (and therefore taught an informal curriculum of) dominant civic and autonomy-based norms might simultaneously be able to develop their capacities for choice, cultural coherence, and liberal democratic citizenship.

Finally, I suggest that education for citizenship is at least as important a liberal aim as education for socialization into a non-public culture, because members of minority groups who cannot reconcile cultural with civic membership (including participation in a common school) will inevitably be both marginalized and disenfranchised within the liberal state. This is a great loss for the majority as well as the minority community; it turns children within such communities into 'internal exiles within the state'[2] whose opportunities for any kinds of choices are extremely limited, and increases prejudice and misunderstanding between the majority and minority groups. In addition, if there are more than a few such minority groups, then their presence fundamentally weakens the state; as Chapter 4 emphasized, liberal democracy can be preserved only if future generations learn to identify themselves with the virtues of citizenship as well as with their more local communities. Ultimately, groups which cannot reconcile cultural socialization with liberal education cannot and should not maintain themselves unchanged in a liberal state: 'What must happen . . . is that existing national identities must be stripped of elements that are repugnant to the self-understanding of one or more component groups, while members of these groups must themselves be willing to embrace an inclusive nationality, and in the process to shed elements of *their* values which are at odds with its principles.'[3] This process will inevitably challenge some children and their parents, especially in the first generations of its implementation, but it is necessary and justified, and the numbers will reduce rapidly with each succeeding generation.

To conclude, we have seen here that one revered aim of education that may appear to have been neglected within the liberal educational ideal—namely, cultural socialization—is already satisfied by the ideal because of the cultural and identity-forming components of civic education, which is part of liberal education. Three other aims of liberalism and/or education, however, may still seem to remain unacknowledged: economic competitiveness, democratic self-reflection, and equality. In the following subsections, I address each in turn, arguing that while all three goals are important, they are either already included within or are trumped by the goals of educating for autonomy and citizenship. Thus, I conclude that the liberal educational ideal as developed in the previous three chapters remains an important and reliable guide to the implementation of liberal education, and need not be altered to incorporate these other aims.

Economic competitiveness

Education has long been seen as a means for increasing both society's and individuals' economic competitiveness. When countries or individuals are faced with economic threats, they typically turn to education to provide the solution: 'Teach our children more mathematics, more foreign languages, better vocational skills,' they cry, 'if we are not to lose the battle for success in the marketplace!' In current times, this subordination of education to economic concerns (often deemed economic 'imperatives') has translated into increased involvement of businesses in education, revived interest in vocational education, and especially an increased comparison—to an almost obsessional level—of one's own educational system with those of other countries deemed economically successful or competitive. Ron Dearing's 1996 report on post-16 education in Britain exemplifies this trend perfectly: despite a high-flown initial summary paragraph about education's aim to develop 'all the talents, abilities, and faculties of young people',[4] the report then focuses almost exclusively on vocational education, workplace needs, and the economic threat posed by Germany's and Japan's superior education systems.[5] Again in Britain, the Conservative government's early 1990s establishment of revamped General National Vocational Qualifications (GNVQs) and 'Applied A-levels', along with its creation of City Technology Colleges through the 1988 Education Act, stemmed directly from a belief in the importance of education's following economics. Since its election in May 1997, Tony Blair's 'New Labour' has shown little inclination to reverse this trend. Vocationalizing education has thus become a commonplace in Britain, even though, as I shall argue below, these policies in many cases themselves badly misinterpret economic needs. Similar trends are evident in the United States as well. Many states have been aggressively courting business involvement in the schools for over two decades, restructuring their vocational education programs, and eagerly studying foreign schools in order to increase national and local economic competitiveness. East Asia and especially Japan were the model school systems of choice until recently, when interest dropped precipitously with the Asian economic crisis and Japan's deepening recession. Although the US's commitment to reshaping state education to serve current economic interests is at least as strong as Britain's, American love affairs with foreign education systems are fickle things, swept hither and thither by the latest international test results and economic indicators. (The same is true, it might be noted, of many school districts' commitments to education reform and innovation in general—but that is a different matter, to be addressed in section 3.) In any case, regardless of the short-termism that infects many business- and economics-oriented education reforms in both the United States and Britain, it remains true that economic 'imperatives' are taken seriously during debates about and engineering of educational policy reform. To the extent, on the other hand, that the liberal educational ideal developed in previous chapters focuses exclusively on helping children to develop their capacities for autonomy, it may fail to realize the legitimate goal of using schools to promote economic competitiveness. If this is the case, then for both political and principled reasons the ideal may need to be modified.

In response, I assert two things. First, education for autonomy will create an economically competitive workforce; as is the case with citizenship and autonomy, the goals of economic competitiveness can also be incorporated within autonomy-driven education. Second, to the extent that children's development of autonomy conflicts with economic growth or competitiveness, the former should trump the latter both because individuals' development and exercise of autonomy is a more fundamental interest and because such an economic order will likely be illiberal.

These two assertions are justified for three reasons. First, by definition, developing children's autonomy involves teaching them to be self-sufficient, which in turn must include teaching children the skills, knowledge, and habits necessary to find (preferably fulfilling) employment. Unless they are born into an independently wealthy family, most children will be able to achieve their future aims, whatever those might be, only by joining the workforce and earning a living once they have grown up. In many cases, having a particular job or career will constitute an intrinsic realization of part of their conception of the good; for many others, having a job will be an extrinsically necessary means of earning the resources required for realizing their chosen way of life.[6] Either way, children will need to learn the skills and knowledge required to become productive members of the workforce in order to become autonomous, self-sufficient adults.

Second, I suggest that for contingent reasons related to the structure of the modern, information-based economy, individuals who develop the capacities for autonomy simultaneously develop many of the exact capacities needed in the workforce today. This is because the modern economy demands of both individuals and societies that they be adaptable and self-reliant: the prizes go to those who adapt themselves to new technologies, who can anticipate and set trends rather than following them, and who can take responsibility within a horizontally structured work environment, rather than to those who have a fixed set of skills which they only deploy in response to orders imposed from above.[7] This has not always been true, of course. Until quite recently, in fact, both individuals and nations could succeed quite well by offering unskilled, industrial labor. Thinking for oneself and making independent choices were not valued characteristics on the factory floor or the assembly line. But modern individuals and nations can no longer afford to develop a fixed set of skills and fill others' orders. Economic success now relies on flexibility, creativity, adaptability, an ability to learn new skills quickly, and self-reliance—exactly those characteristics which one learns in the process of developing one's capacity for autonomy. Thus, while it is true that education for autonomy does probably preclude the narrow vocationalism and work-based training that found favor among the British Conservative Party in the 1980s, I suggest that individuals' development of autonomy actually helps to increase economic competitiveness and success on the part of both individuals and the nation as a whole.

Third and last, I suggest that to the extent that a state's (or individual's) economic competitiveness depends on the existence of a supply of workers who cannot direct their lives authentically and autonomously, then the state is itself probably illiberal. In this case, it is the illiberality of the economic culture or societal structure as a whole that should be of concern, and not the putative incompatibility between educating for autonomy and educating for economic competitiveness.[8] As I have argued throughout this book, the aim of liberalism is to create a society that guarantees individual freedom—i.e., to create a society within which adults can lead fulfilling and autonomous lives. In contrast, an economic order which relies for its success on the existence of a non-autonomous workforce essentially relies on coercion, be it economic, psychological, or intellectual. Such an economic or social order cannot be liberal; we should therefore be unconcerned if education for autonomy does not support such an economy. For all three of these reasons, therefore, I conclude that the liberal educational ideal of helping children develop their capacities for autonomy is compatible with the aims of educating for economic competitiveness in a liberal society.

Democratic self-reflection

Another potential liberal and educative good that may appear to have been neglected by previous chapters is that of democratic self-reflection—in other words, adults' democratic engagement with formulating educational goals. Let me explain. In Chapter 2, I rejected the claim that children can or should be used as a means to realizing their parents' ends, and in particular that they should necessarily be educated so as to realize their parents' conceptions of the good. In this respect, parental control over children's schooling has been seen in this book as permitting an illegitimate exercise of power by the strong (parents) over the weak (children). In contrast, schooling under the liberal ideal is meant to benefit children, not to further parents' or groups' interests. As such, it was designed in Chapters 2 and 3 to be shielded from some forms of parent involvement and control, and in particular to aim at helping children develop their capacities for autonomy, regardless of parents' preferred educational aims. To permit the aim of educating for autonomy to be tampered with would be illiberal, and would treat children as means rather than as ends.

A potential problem with this approach is that not all of the benefits that accrue to adults when they participate in determining the shape and content of children's schooling come about as a result of treating children as means rather than ends. Rather, the very process of debating and disputing what the aims and content of education for children should be is itself educative for adults. As Francis Schrag argues, 'the idea of public schooling should be defended in part because of the opportunity it affords citizens to continue their own education by participation in policy making in an arena that is close to them geographically and emotionally'.[9] On a civic level, debate about the aims of education is one of the best means for prompting democratic self-reflection about the aims of society itself. What are we striving for as a society? What would we like to change? How do we conceive of ourselves as a national (provincial, state, local) community? What makes us distinctive that we wish to pass on to our children? Public consideration of these questions is essential to maintaining a healthy and self-reflective democratic community, and is arguably best prompted by public debate about the aims and content of education. Insofar as 'we value democracy because it is the best way by which we can discover what a community values for itself and its children',[10] even more should we value democratic debate about education. This debate also has individual importance: the process of reconsidering educational aims causes us each individually to step back and consider what the aims and content of our own lives are and should be. We lose something valuable if we are denied the opportunity to reflect upon, and especially to discuss with others, the education of the next generation, and thus the character and direction of our own lives.[11] If the aims of education are predetermined in a liberal state, however, then this public educative act of debate is denied to its citizens. How can this loss be justified?

Three arguments are relevant, I believe, in response to this problem. None of the arguments is fully satisfactory on its own; but taken together, they justify the liberal insistence on positing the aim of education to be the development of autonomy, independent of the outcome of public debate.

First, enshrining educational aims can be justified in the same way that enshrining other rights or claims of justice can be justified: some things are too important to try to balance against other claims, social claims included. They are 'trumps', to borrow Ronald Dworkin's language; or in Rawls' terms, the right of children to develop the capacity for autonomy through state-regulated schools takes priority over the good of democratic reflection.[12] Although losing the opportunity for public discussion about the direction and aims of society is unfortunate, children's rights to an autonomy-directed education trump this social loss.[13]

Second, it is important to recognize that debate over an issue does not cease just because it is enshrined in a constitution or otherwise made difficult to change.[14] The ongoing debate over free speech in the US, for example, makes this vividly clear. Public disputes about the legality of flag burning, the regulation of the Internet, federal funding for offensive art, and the status of 'hate speech' all attest to the vibrant—if sometimes vitriolic and almost always politicized—character of public discourse about the nature and limits of speech. Thus, the fact that something is enshrined in the constitution does not shield it from public examination, debate, and even disagreement. For better and for worse, this would be true for education as well.

Third, to say that the aim of education is to help children develop their capacities for autonomy is to leave many of the most difficult questions unanswered. What capacities are required for autonomy in 1999, in 2015, in 2050? While such characteristics as toleration, critical thinking, and literacy will always be important components of an autonomous person, many other elements will both develop and be replaced as society changes. What these elements will be, and how they should fit into an autonomy-driven curriculum, is necessarily left to the public (in conjunction with teachers, school administrators, educational experts, etc.) to decide. Furthermore, even stable elements of autonomy such as literacy take on radically different meanings over time: for example, notions such as 'cultural literacy' and 'computer literacy' have recently come to the fore, and even the kinds of reading and information processing that autonomous individuals are required to do now is very different from that required of people 100, 50, or even 25 years ago. Thus, the existence of democratic conversations about education—and by extension, about the construction of our lives both on an individual level and as a society—is fully compatible with (and fully necessary within) a liberal state that defines the aim of education as advancing children's development of autonomy. The problem of realizing the aim of autonomy-driven education in practice is one that will provide the grist for an ongoing and irresolvable public debate, for there is no way to answer these questions once and for all even if we wanted to. To assert that education should be autonomy-driven is not to withdraw education entirely from the realm of politics, especially not from the realm of justified political debate.

Equality

Just as this book may have seemed until now to ignore other legitimate educational aims (socialization, economic competitiveness, democratic self-reflection) in its single-minded pursuit of educating for autonomy, it may also be thought to have unjustly neglected liberalism's own diversity of aims and governing principles. For liberal theory is and historically has been motivated by a number of different aims. Sometimes these aims are pursued in isolation; at other times, liberals call upon a complex set of principles to justify their positions. But in any case, there is more to liberal thought than the value of autonomy; by focusing my discussion of education on autonomy alone, therefore, it might be argued that I have failed fully to explore the shape of *liberal* education.

I agree that many liberals adhere to (and are inspired by) principles other than autonomy. I would argue, however, that only one liberal principle demands further attention here—that of equality. Of the many forms of liberalism, I can distinguish five that seem to be current in contemporary theory, other than autonomy-based liberalism. These five (and their variations or composites) are based on the following concerns or commitments: non-sectarianism (which has replaced an older and less sophisticated commitment to neutrality), fear, diversity, negative liberty, and equality. The first four, I suggest, have been sufficiently addressed in other chapters.

Non-sectarian liberalism is best symbolized by John Rawls' *Political Liberalism*, and has been thoroughly addressed in Chapters 1, 2, and 4. Nothing more needs to be said here about the chimerical attractions of non-sectarianism, especially neutrality. The liberalism of fear, as articulated by Judith Shklar, was discussed briefly in section 2.3 and in detail in section 3.1, while the demands of diversity, which find their most passionate liberal articulation in William Galston's writings, were addressed in various parts of Chapters 2, 3, and 4. Again, I do not have anything to add to my judgements in those chapters. Negative liberty is embraced by libertarians as liberalism's most important commitment; I do not consider libertarianism to be a coherent liberal ideology, however, and I briefly discussed my reasons for rejecting it in my treatment of autarchy and autonomy in Chapter 1. Furthermore, I believe that negative and positive liberty cannot be coherently separated, and thus reject libertarianism for this reason as well.[15]

Equality, therefore, is the only potential liberal commitment or principle that I believe does deserve attention here. Obviously, I cannot say much about equality in the space I have left: given that one could write encyclopedias about equality and education, a few pages may seem an irrelevantly short space in which to try to say something interesting. I suggest, however, that a good case can be made for a liberal commitment to equality of opportunity, and for its compatibility with the value of autonomy.

To begin with, the political value of equality has to be circumscribed. A state cannot be committed to the achievement of equality *as such*—at least, not if it is to avoid being tyrannical. Rather, it must choose a particular good or goods to equalize, such as opportunity, resources, outcome, or welfare. In assessing the role that equality should play in a theory of liberal education, therefore, we must ask what liberal equality should be *of*: i.e., what is or are the good(s) that liberalism should equalize? In the context of this book, we might think that liberal citizens should be provided or achieve 'equal autonomy'. But equality of autonomy is an opaque concept, to say the least, especially when applied to adults rather than children. It is a contradiction in terms to coerce somebody to act autonomously, and anyway weak perfectionism mandates against forcing adult citizens to live more autonomous lives. Furthermore, insofar as the exercise of autonomy represents a complex balance of realizing, revising, and adopting one's commitments, adults' varying displays of autonomy are often incomparable. Is an adult who reflectively values and lives up to the constitutive nature of his previous commitments more or less autonomous than someone who reflectively values a continually examined and ever-changing life? It is impossible to know. It also does not matter. The value of autonomy lies in its exercise, not necessarily in its maximization. For these reasons, then, it does not make sense for a liberal state to be committed to providing adult citizens equal autonomy.

Rather, it makes more sense to talk of equality of *opportunity*—where opportunity refers in this case both to the opportunity to develop autonomy and the opportunity to exercise it. What matters, after all, is that all individuals have the same opportunity to structure their lives authentically and autonomously; according to weakly perfectionist principles, it is not up to the liberal state to ensure that all individuals equally do so. Thus, my justification of substantive liberal freedoms and institutions in Chapter 1 implicitly relied on a commitment to adults' equal opportunity to exercise autonomy, and children's equal opportunity to develop autonomy also drove the construction of the detached, common school ideal in Chapter 2. Equality of opportunity is thus a likely ideal within autonomy-driven liberalism and compatible with it.

In addition, equality of opportunity is a comprehensible and desirable liberal ideal even when it is tied less closely to the ideal of autonomy as such. First, equality of opportunity and equality of resources are the two forms of equality that are most favored by contemporary liberal theorists in general. Equality of outcome is rejected as being insufficiently sensitive to choice,[16] while equality of welfare unjustly skews resources toward individuals with 'expensive tastes'.[17] To the extent that liberals embrace equality, therefore, they concentrate on equality of opportunity or resources. These two concepts are not easily distinguishable, especially since resource egalitarians such as Ronald Dworkin argue that distribution of resources should be sensitive to individual handicaps resulting from 'brute bad luck' (such as being born blind or having a compulsion with which one does not identify).[18] It is hard to tell in such a case what separates equality of resources from equality of opportunity. In the context of developing a liberal theory of education, however, I choose to concentrate on the latter, because it is more directly applicable to children. Resource egalitarianism is often justified as a means of enabling individuals to fulfill their conceptions of the good, but children do not yet have fully formed conceptions of the good. Equality of opportunity, therefore, is more appropriate to a theory that takes children into account as well as adults.

Second, whether or not equality of opportunity is understood in autonomy-regarding terms, I suggest that a commitment to equality of opportunity generates many of the same outcomes as a commitment to the value of autonomy. This is because equality of opportunity has the same aim as education for autonomy has: namely, to ensure that individuals' outcomes should not be dependent on their origins—i.e., that we should not be able to predict children's ultimate achievements as adults (educational, socioeconomic, and otherwise) on the basis of their parents' backgrounds.

Children should have an 'equality of life chances'.[19] Insofar as children's education tends to have a tremendous influence on their life chances, this suggests that children's educational opportunities should not be sensitive to their origins. A child's religion, race, ethnicity, and gender should have no relation to the quality of school he or she attends. Furthermore, educational provision should not be sensitive to families' abilities to pay.[20] Schools should be permitted to charge fees only if the state provides a tuition subsidy for poorer families, and such schools' fees should be capped so as not to exceed the level of the grant provided. Although these judgements are generated by opportunity egalitarianism, the liberal commitment to autonomy generates equivalent conclusions. Autonomy is valued, after all, in part because of the opportunity it gives individuals to divorce their life choices from their background origins. As Chapters 1 and 2 argued, it is good for people to determine authentically the shape of their own lives, rather than being unduly directed either by other actors (such as parents or an illiberal state) or by forces beyond their control (such as gender, race, or childhood poverty). The value of autonomy, therefore, requires that education—which, as noted above, enormously influences children's life choices and chances—be provided to all children without regard to class, gender, race, religion, etc. Thus, the same conclusions flow from the liberal commitment to autonomy as are generated by egalitarian principles.

I conclude, therefore, that autonomy-based liberalism is compatible with opportunity-based egalitarianism, and in fact anticipates many of its outcomes. Neither the liberal educational ideal nor, more generally, the theory of contemporary liberalism that has been developed over the last four chapters, needs to be modified in response to egalitarian concerns. Furthermore, insofar as the same question about aims must be answered for equality of opportunity ('opportunity *to do what?*') as has to be answered for equality itself ('equality *of what?*'), autonomy provides a promising object for liberal egalitarianism. Equality of opportunity is best understood in a liberal context, I suggest, as the equal opportunity to develop and exercise one's capacity for autonomy. Thus, the liberal commitments to autonomy and equality are in overlapping partnership, with autonomy as the driving aim; together, they generate (and often overdetermine) the conclusions reached in the previous four chapters and the policies to be developed in the next section.

5.2 SCHOOL CHOICE AND THE PUBLIC POLICY OF LIBERAL EDUCATION PROVISION

In this section, I look at how the theory that I have developed over the last four-and-a-half chapters should be applied within a liberal state. I focus particularly in this section on an ideal implementation of liberal education provision, insofar as I ignore such practical impediments as the existence of political opposition to liberal education, or the existence of contrary laws and systems of educational provision in current Western liberal democracies. (Section 3, in contrast, addresses the problem of 'getting from here to there'—of what changes would need to be made in order to achieve the liberal educational ideal, and of how to convince current citizens, states, and governments to adopt and implement the system of liberal education developed in this section and throughout the book.) At the same time, I try to balance political idealism with educational pragmatism. As I have tried to emphasize throughout this book, any theory (let alone practice) of liberal education must take into account the practicalities of pedagogy, educational efficiency, and human behavior. Thus, this section tries to build an ideal political public policy on the basis of a pragmatic assessment of educational practice and outcomes.

Let us start by summarizing the conclusions reached thus far. Many policy recommendations have been both implicitly and explicitly developed in previous chapters, and it makes sense to review them before moving on. I suggest that a public policy of liberal education, if developed in accordance with recommendations made in Chapters 2–4 and section 5.1, would exhibit a number of identifying characteristics. To begin with, schools should be 'common', in that children from all segments of the population should be welcomed into and enroll in them without prejudice or restriction.[21] This commonality is important both for building a sense of citizenship and civic identification among students, and for advancing children's development of autonomy. This latter goal, to educate for autonomy, is taken to be the primary educational aim of all schools in the liberal state. As a result, schools should not attempt to advance or to shape themselves in accordance with fundamental or divisive conceptions of the good; rather, all schools must be structured as autonomy-promoting communities which are 'detached' from local and parental control. Although significant forms of parent involvement in their children's education should be encouraged, parents and other groups should not be able to control schools' curricula, ethos, or aims.

Schools should nonetheless be sensitive to children's developing sense of cultural coherence, especially in younger grades; more generally, since children develop over time, schools should make sure always to teach age-appropriate material. Thus, while children's development of autonomy may be the school's ultimate educational aim, it should help foster different skills and capacities at different times. For example, the school might help children develop community awareness, creativity, and basic writing and listening skills in lower grades, and critical thinking, advanced writing skills, political awareness, and independence in upper grades. Likewise, 'detachment' from parents and local organizations need not and should not mean indifference to them. Schools should encourage parent and community involvement through outreach programs, regular and consistent communication with parents about their children, sensitivity to parents' work schedules when planning school events, emphasis on common academic and social goals, and so forth.

Detachment in the service of autonomy also need not mean uniformity. There should be a diverse range of schools within the liberal state, all of which take children's development of autonomy as their educational aim but which vary in other respects. Schools which specialize along academic, artistic, or vocational lines should be encouraged, as should schools which diversify along administrative or pedagogic lines. Depending on their needs, interests, and learning styles, children should have the opportunity to choose between large or small schools, traditional and open classrooms, progressive and traditional teaching styles, and so forth, in addition to selecting schools with academic or vocational specializations. A good school for one child is not a good school for every child. As a result, children and parents should be able to choose among a diverse range of schools—so long as the requirements that schools be common and take children's development of autonomy as their aim are not compromised.

Finally, it should be noted that private as well as state schools may fulfill these conditions; nothing has been said which would require that schools be state-owned and state-operated.[22] Private schools would be subject to the same requirements and regulations as state schools: they would have to be common (i.e. open to all children) and adopt the aim of educating for autonomy as well as display the other characteristics listed above.[23] In the service of the former goal, private school fees should be restricted by state law to no more than the maximum amount provided by the state, in the form of a voucher, tax credit, or assisted places scheme, to low-income families in order to meet the cost of schooling. The liberal educational ideal forbids educational discrimination on the basis of wealth or class just as it forbids racial or religious discrimination; all three violate the principles of citizenship, equality, and autonomy. All told, therefore, there would in practice be little if anything to distinguish private schools from state schools—which is exactly the way it should be. Given the extent of these regulations, individuals and organizations may have little incentive to open private schools, and a state which implements the above requirements or principles may in practice include few private schools. But there is no reason in principle to forbid private ownership of schools or school services.[24]

These requirements raise a number of questions about implementation. Four problems are especially pertinent:

The myth of the common school. First, it is widely recognized that the ideal of the common school is unenforceable. Even if no private schools existed which selected students or charged fees, common schools could still not be legislated by the state unilaterally. This is because wealthy families can always exercise school choice, even absent the private school alternative, by means of exercising residential choice: families who can afford to, especially in the United States, often choose what area to live in based on the comparative quality of local schools.[25] Children of such families thus can never be legislatively forced into a particular school, as James Coleman forcefully points out:

the enrollment of a child in a given public school is not determined by the government. It is a joint result of the government's decision that makes school assignments and of the parents' decision on whether to remain in the same residential location, whether to send their child to a private school, or whether to move into one school district or another if the family is moving into a metropolitan area. The fact that the child's enrollment is the result of a joint operation of these two decisions means that government policies, to be effective, must anticipate parental decisions and that the government must obtain the active cooperation of parents in implementing school policy.[26]

Furthermore, the educational choices exercised by wealthier families have implications for the character and quality of schooling available to all other children. As families who can afford to do so segregate themselves residentially in order to ensure that their children attend particular schools, the neighborhoods and neighborhood schools which are left behind become correspondingly segregated as well. In the United States, this has resulted in the creation of schools (and neighborhoods) segregated by race as well as by class, as well as in gross inequities in school funding between rich and poor districts. Two decades of busing minority and white students into each other's neighborhoods has done little to mitigate the situation.

A liberal education policy built upon the lines laid out above must therefore address two objections. First, the common school is not an enforceable ideal in the absence of such an extraordinarily coercive (and illiberal) measure as dictating where families live. Second, given that some families (the wealthy) have de facto school choice, liberal egalitarianism mandates that choice be extended to all families if possible. It is not just for poor families to be denied school choice in the name of detachment or the common school while rich families exercise school choice with impunity. Both of these issues throw into question the liberal policy ideal of common schools detached from parental control.

School choice. This pragmatic/egalitarian push toward school choice is further buttressed by a recent barrage of studies and pilot programs purporting to show that school choice is a positive educational benefit for children. As I shall discuss below, researchers and politicians in virtually all Western, industrialized countries have been arguing that parental choice of their children's schools promotes educational efficiency, effectiveness, and achievement. There is hardly a school reform program in the United States or Europe that does not at least gesture toward school choice or the creation of a parent-driven educational marketplace. Many of the policy recommendations set forth above, however, potentially conflict with the extension of parental power to encompass school choice. This conflict must be resolved. Since even an ideal liberal public education policy must be pragmatic about the effectiveness of various educational approaches and institutions, it would be foolish to ignore the vast number of claims that have been made over the past ten to fifteen years about the manifold benefits of school choice.

Diversity versus commonality. I stated above that schools can and should exhibit substantial variety in the areas of curricular specialization, size, teaching style, and administrative structure, but that a liberal school could neither endorse a fundamental or divisive conception of the good nor fail to endorse the educational aim of helping children develop their capacities for autonomy. At least two important questions are raised—and left unanswered—in this formulation of the scope of school diversity. The first, glaring question is how we identify 'fundamental' and 'divisive' conceptions of the good, and how they are distinguished from the apparently more innocuous pedagogic, administrative, and curricular commitments that liberal schools are permitted to take on. The second, related question is whether education for autonomy requires any particular administrative, pedagogic, and/or curricular approaches. By endorsing school diversity in these areas, I implicitly suggest that children's development of autonomy is unrelated to a school's chosen pedagogy or curriculum. But this is clearly false. To what extent do schools need to exhibit commonality of administration, pedagogic approach, size, and/or curricular content in service to their commonality of purpose to educate for autonomy?

Enforcing education for autonomy. The previous question articulates in a limited way the most general—and fundamental—policy question raised by this book, namely: how can we encourage and enforce the principle that schools in a liberal state should educate for autonomy? What kind of institutions should be established to ensure that teachers and schools adopt and maintain the aim of helping children develop their capacities for autonomy? In the absence of an answer to this question, the implementation of the liberal educational ideal cannot even get off the ground.

These four problems or objections guide the rest of this chapter. I address the first three in this section, and consider the realization of autonomy-driven schools in section 3, the concluding section.

School choice and the myth of the common school

School choice can without exaggeration be described as the most radical movement for educational change to sweep Western(ized) industrial democracies in the last fifteen years. It has taken root, in various forms, in countries from England to New Zealand, Denmark to the United States, Italy to Norway and Spain. In Great Britain and the United States, for example, politicians on both the right and the left have proposed subjecting all schools, from nurseries and pre-schools on up, to the harsh judgement of market forces. Parents are being promised sweeping new powers to choose their children's schools; schools which do not manage to attract a sufficient share of students will have their funding gradually withdrawn while successful (i.e. popular) schools will establish market dominance. Similar proposals to enhance parent choice are being discussed in Denmark and New Zealand at the primary and secondary school level,[27] while across Europe market principles are being applied to higher education in the areas of institutional autonomy, curriculum, funding, and student selection.[28] In all cases, parent choice and the application of market forces to state schooling are seen as the keys to improving education.

As is to be expected with such a politically potent term, 'school choice' has taken on very different meanings in different political and social contexts. In all cases, however, 'school choice' is taken to include the ability of parents to choose (or participate in choosing) the school their children attend. Depending on the program, parents may choose among schools within a particular district or education authority,[29] schools in the parent's plus neighboring districts, or schools throughout the region or state. In many school choice programs, parents are aided only if they choose state schools, but an increasing number of programs include private schools as well.[30] School choice may amount simply to a loosening of administrative restrictions over which schools children are allowed to attend (in order to encourage voluntary desegregation, for instance, by allowing minority children to attend predominantly white schools in the suburbs, or white students to attend inner-city schools), but it is more often accompanied by substantial financial rewards and penalties—incentives that may be offered to parents and schools alike.

These financial carrots and sticks generally take one of two forms: either vouchers,[31] which channel state funding directly to the school chosen by the parents, or tax credits, which refund money directly to parents who choose not to use the state system. Tax credits are designed to prevent the 'double jeopardy' that parents who pay both private school fees and state school taxes currently face. They are sometimes justified in fairness terms—parents who prefer private schools, for whatever reason, should not have to pay for their children's education twice—but more often the justification is an egalitarian one. By overcoming the financial 'double jeopardy' posed by private school attendance, it is argued, tax credits permit lower-income families who could not previously afford it to send their children to private schools, and thus move some distance toward equalizing educational opportunity between rich and poor. Tax credits are also a popular idea in the United States because by channeling money directly to families rather than to schools, they potentially avoid the unconstitutional entanglement of the state with religion caused by direct state funding (e.g. through vouchers) of religious schools.[32]

Vouchers, in contrast, channel money directly from the state to schools, with funding levels generally determined by the number of children each school has managed to attract. Under voucher schemes, funding follows children, and is thus directly sensitive to choice. If a parent chooses to move his daughter from the neighborhood school to a school across town, the money associated with educating her also moves to her new school.[33] Likewise, in voucher plans that permit private school choice, parents can apply their vouchers to offset the cost of tuition, although usually funding levels for private school vouchers are lower than the per capita cost of education in the state sector. For example, parents may be given a voucher that assures their children a free education at any state school in the region, or pays $2,000 toward the cost of a private school. In all cases, however, voucher schemes offer schools potent financial incentives to attract new students, and punish unpopular schools with the equally potent prospect of losing funding as they lose students. Schools are led to compete with each other for students and the resources they bring with them.

This injection of competition into the previously 'monopolistic' arena of state education provision is a crucial component of most justifications of school choice. Competition within an 'educational marketplace' has been credited with achieving the following goods:[34] greater educational efficiency, higher student achievement, greater responsiveness to children's and parents' needs and/or desires, increased educational innovation, easy identification of successful and failing schools (according to which schools attract and lose students, respectively), reduced bureaucracy, greater flexibility and responsiveness to new ideas and technologies, and replacement of the 'pathologies' of the 'public monopoly'[35] in education with market-based virtues. This last reason provides a good example, as well, of the rhetorical shift that has accompanied the above justifications for school choice and competition. The 'educational marketplace' is no longer viewed as a metaphor. Rather, in the language of today, schools *are* producers and parents (or children or both—it is never exactly clear) *are* consumers, and thus market forces *should* govern school–parent interactions just as they should (e.g. for efficiency reasons) govern all producer–consumer interactions.

The justifications for school choice do not end, however, at the free market line. Independent of the benefits of competition per se, school choice is also credited with: creating value communities, increasing parent involvement, encouraging voluntary racial desegregation (mostly through the creation of 'magnet' schools offering particular specializations designed to draw white students into black schools), and successfully matching children who exhibit a diverse range of needs, interests, and learning styles with the specific school that serves each child best. Furthermore, it is argued that school choice programs lead to greater equity. As our identification of the 'myth of the common school' made clear, wealthy parents have always been able to choose their children's schools—either by choice of residence in the case of a state school, or by paying for private education. School choice plans are thought to extend these opportunities to all families, by making residence irrelevant to school assignment and by offsetting the costs of private school tuition with public vouchers or tax credits. Finally, there is evidence from an American study that given the opportunity, a higher percentage of minority families than white families will take advantage of choice programs.[36] Thus, school choice may help to promote racial as well as economic equality of opportunity within education.

These are hefty claims for the benefits of school choice: in essence, school choice is credited with achieving every educational and political virtue imaginable and then some. When one examines the evidence gathered from studies of school choice programs, however, a different picture comes to light. At best, evidence in favor of school choice is highly inconclusive and sometimes contradictory; in no cases other than 'controlled choice' programs (described below) can it be shown that school choice achieves more than a few of the aims listed above.[37] This absence of definitive evidence in favor of school choice is due in part to the fact that districts which adopt school choice measures also usually undergo other financial or administrative changes at the same time, which makes isolating the effect of school choice in particular almost impossible to assess. New York City's East Harlem district (also known as District 4), for example, has a nationally acclaimed middle school choice program for 11- to 13-year-olds which has been credited with, among other things, raising reading scores from the worst in New York City's 32 community districts in 1981 to 16th out of 32 in 1989.[38] The association between East Harlem's remarkable turnaround and its adoption of school choice has inspired the creation of numerous school choice programs across the country. Simultaneously with implementing its school choice program, however, East Harlem was awarded millions of dollars of federal funding that raised its per-student expenditure to the highest in the nation;[39] it opened up its schools to high-achieving students from other districts, thus raising its pool of above-average readers; it permitted schools to select their own students, resulting in 'advantaged out-of-district students sometimes gain[ing] admittance to the more selective schools at the expense of less advantaged in-district students';[40] and it also made schools smaller, reformed the curriculum, gave teachers more autonomy, and increased teacher and principal accountability.[41] These latter changes are clearly essential to understanding District 4's success, but they have strangely been ignored by most advocates of school choice. Furthermore, reading scores have actually fallen in District 4 since 1989; while this decline in part reflects a city-wide trend, it is far more precipitous in East Harlem than across the city as a whole.[42] It would be foolhardy, therefore, to give school choice all of the credit for causing the possibly temporary improvements in East Harlem's educational achievement and efficiency, much less to tout school choice as the solution to the world's educational ills.[43]

Even apart from the problem of isolating the effect of school choice from the effects of other changes made in the course of school reform, studies of school choice programs reveal few consistencies in the benefits they purportedly deliver. Claims of increased reading scores in one school choice district are counterbalanced by evidence from other 'schools of choice' of flat reading scores and non-existent achievement gains. Early analyses of Milwaukee's program, for example, show that 'in the first year of the program choice students [who come from low-income families] gained more than low-income MPS [Milwaukee Public Schools] students in reading but were behind in mathematics. In the second year, choice student scores dropped considerably in reading and remained approximately the same in mathematics.'[44] Likewise, in Alum Rock, California, site of the first American school choice program, students showed no improvement in reading scores during the five-year experiment.[45] Similarly, as mentioned above, scores in New York's District 4 did rise impressively (mirroring, it should be noted, a simultaneous increase city-wide), but then dropped drastically to well below New York City averages in the early 1990s. School choice may have nothing to do with this drop, 'But if choice is not responsible for the decline in reading scores in the late 1980s, it may not have been responsible for the earlier gain in reading scores either, especially when we consider the broad range of reforms, beside choice, implemented in District 4 in the 1970s.'[46]

Just as district-wide student achievement is not necessarily raised through the introduction of school choice, neither do parents necessarily choose individual schools for their achievement records. Although schools' academic reputations (and, far less often, test scores) play a vital role in some parents' choice of schools,[47] parents cite proximity to workplace, ease of transportation, what school their child's friends attend, availability of day care, greater likelihood of their child's making the varsity sports team, disciplinary attitude, and even racial homogeneity as other important reasons for choosing one school over another.[48] Furthermore, many parents and students say their choices were based on little to no information at all: in particular, parents with poor educational backgrounds themselves relied on 'reputation', hearsay, or blind luck to make their choices.[49] As a result, those schools which are successful in attracting students may not be those which actually boost student achievement or educate most efficiently. To make the point clear: marketplace success is not necessarily a good indicator of educational success; likewise, competition does not necessarily breed better education. This conclusion is further buttressed by numerous studies showing that parents generally feel more satisfied with schools that they have chosen even when there is no evidence that teaching quality, student achievement, or other measures of educational quality are better at the chosen school.[50] Although parent satisfaction may increase in districts featuring school choice, this seems to be an artifact of choice rather than a reflection of actual improvements in the schools. It is possible that increased parent satisfaction will have 'knock-on' effects that eventually do lead to increased student achievement or other educational improvements. But for the moment, school choice and the competition it inspires seem to breed parents who are more satisfied with unimproved educational results.

Choice programs have not been in place long enough to determine conclusively whether they lead to an increase in educational innovation or a decrease in bureaucracy.[51] A number of well-conducted studies show that in England and Wales, however, schools of choice (both grant-maintained state schools and private schools participating in the Assisted Places Scheme) have generally decreased innovation and become more traditional rather than less.[52] This is in part because parents associate educational quality with 'old fashioned teaching standards'[53] and practices that mimic those they remember from their own days at school. Furthermore, at least in the first few years of choice, those parents who bother to choose schools select those schools that are traditionally known to offer a strong educational program. These schools are thus encouraged to maintain their current practices, rather than being encouraged to innovate. The Assisted Places Scheme typifies this conservative tendency, as 'some schools which might otherwise have felt constrained to diversify in order to attract more fee-paying customers were sponsored by the government to remain the same'.[54] Similarly, government funding priorities for grant-maintained schools (favoring technology and physical improvements, indifferent to many other curricular needs) have cramped schools' plans for expanding in other directions.[55]

Furthermore, it is interesting to note that increased school choice often leads to the state's creating and imposing increased standardization measures on schools—the most obvious example being the National Curriculum introduced in England and Wales in 1988. Many analysts have rightly suggested that this apparent paradox derives from the association between school choice and market values.[56] Because a market is justified only if people can make rational choices, and rational choice depends in turn on similar products being comparable with one another, choosers within the educational marketplace must be provided with the tools to compare schools if the market is to work efficiently. Since the most significant outcomes of schooling cannot be judged until many years after the fact, school choice advocates must create a proxy for judging educational outcomes—in this case, by comparing standardized exam scores which are in turn based on standardized curricula. It may or may not be that standardized curricula and examinations help children and promote the aims of liberal education. But one thing that the 1988 reforms in Britain made clear is that national curricula and standardized testing do not reduce bureaucracy or increase educational flexibility and innovation.

I would suggest further that the 'delivery' (better understood as the practice) of education should not be understood in market terms. Normatively, the notion of the educational marketplace is misleading and deleterious. As I have emphasized throughout this book, liberal education is about creating future citizens and individuals; it is not about delivering a product to a consumer, still less to a parent as consumer. On a conceptual level, as well, most descriptions of education in market terms are simply confused. Consider the following typical statement: 'Clients (parents and students) provide the raw material for schools and, by their choices, they deliver important signals about their preferences for what is learned in school. Providers (teachers and administrators) bring the expert knowledge of content and pedagogy necessary to capitalize on the talents and preferences of consumers.'[57] Numerous questions spring to mind on the basis of this quotation. Are parents and students clients, raw materials, or consumers? What do parents as consumers consume? Can a piece of raw material (presumably a child) simultaneously be a client (or consumer)? Upon what kind of 'consumer preferences' should the 'producer' 'capitalize'? Again, does this mean that the raw material, simultaneously a consumer, should also be able to express preferences? Or is it only the raw material's talents that should be taken into account? If parent and child have conflicting preferences, to which ones should the school respond? Who is the *real* client/consumer? I hope that these questions go some way toward revealing the descriptive and normative poverty of much of the school choice/competition/marketplace rhetoric.[58]

Finally, most school choice programs do not live up to their promise of equalizing educational opportunities between rich and poor children. Programs in which there is a limited number of schools of choice, or in which families do not *have* to choose (i.e. there is a default neighborhood school option), show worrisome inequalities between students who participate in the choice programs and those who do not.[59] Students in such programs who attend schools of choice tend to have more highly educated parents who are more involved in their children's education both at school and at home, have better jobs, and are more assertive than the parents of children who do not take advantage of school choice. They are 'active' as opposed to 'passive' choosers[60]—and thus seek out better educational opportunities than passive choosers do. Likewise, school choice programs which permit schools to select some or all of their students similarly discriminate against children from less privileged backgrounds. A well-regarded study of magnet schools in Boston, Chicago, New York City, and Philadelphia, for example, 'found that these schools favored students with good academic, attendance, and behavior records at the expense of those with learning problems. ... Transfer practices returned undesirable students to their neighborhood schools and contributed to the disparity between neighborhood and magnet schools. Competition for students who were already performing well reduced district interest in improving education for all students.'[61] Likewise, evidence shows that racial and ethnic self-segregation have resulted from school choice, and discrimination is evident along class lines.[62] Selection based on academic achievement adds to this class discrimination, since middle class and poor students are disproportionately represented in accelerated and remedial classes, respectively.[63] Whether or not schools streamed by academic ability are educationally sound, therefore (and there is much evidence suggesting that comprehensive schools are educationally most effective),[64] schools that select according to achievement in fact discriminate by class rather than by ability. Thus, school choice programs that do not require all families to choose a school (i.e. by eliminating the possibility of a 'default' option) and/or which allow schools to impose selection conditions on students (e.g. by requiring a clean discipline record or a minimum grade-point average) do not seem to advance equality of educational opportunity.

In sum, school choice programs do not usually live up to the expectations listed above. The specific benefits of school choice are not easily separable from the outcomes of other school reforms which tend to accompany school choice programs. Most school choice programs have not raised children's achievement or increased educational efficiency. Parents do not necessarily choose their children's schools based on academic quality, but instead are swayed by other, non-academic concerns (such as proximity to workplace or presence of child's friends). Thus, the market feedback mechanism that school choice was meant to put in place is misleading, as popular schools may not be educationally superior. Parents do feel more satisfied with schools of choice than with local schools, but students' educational achievements do not show a corresponding increase; paradoxically, therefore, schools of choice actually face less demanding or assertive parents rather than more, and school accountability is diminished. School choice has caused in many places a decrease of educational innovation and an increase of bureaucracy through the rewarding of traditional schools and the imposition of standardized curricula and state-wide examinations. School choice expressed as the application of the market metaphor does not make normative or conceptual sense. Finally, school choice often increases inequality as opposed to promoting equality. For all of these reasons, therefore, school choice is not the panacea that many people have suggested it is.

This is not to say that school choice has no benefits. Parent involvement seems to increase in schools of choice,[65] and parents do seem to feel as if they form more of a community when they have all chosen a particular school for their children.[66] But as the above analysis demonstrates, school choice programs must be extremely carefully designed in order to be beneficial to students, families, and society as a whole. I suggest that school choice best lives up to (some of) its promises when it is in the form of 'controlled choice',[67] meaning the following: all schools are 'schools of choice', with no default options available; consequently, all families must actively choose a school (or submit an ordered list of preferred schools), with the help of an energetic and effective system of school choice counseling at centers located in families' neighborhoods and open at times convenient for working parents; families choose by a deadline, with school assignment determined after the deadline rather than on a 'first come, first served' basis;[68] schools do not select their students, or establish any admission criteria—rather, school assignment is determined solely by family preference weighted in order to achieve common schools[69] (and also weighted in favor of families with siblings in the same school); and free transportation is provided for students within the area. Furthermore, controlled choice should be available within a broad geographic area, rather than within already demarcated districts or local education authorities.

This is to prevent a withdrawal by wealthy families from controlled choice districts to geographically proximate but institutionally separate districts (e.g. from a city to a suburban district), as occurred in the United States during implementation of desegregation orders in the 1970s and 1980s. Students and parents should have the right to apply to all schools within a fifteen- or twenty-mile radius, say, regardless of district.

These conditions incorporate the beneficial elements of school choice without succumbing to the various injustices perpetrated by some school choice plans discussed above. This system of 'controlled choice' also has the virtue of addressing both objections concerning the 'myth of the common school', insofar as it attempts to turn the 'myth' into an egalitarian reality. By divorcing school assignment from students' residence and compelling *all* parents to make 'active' choices which are not limited by tuition considerations, transportation costs, or school entrance requirements, the above system extends school choice in an egalitarian fashion to rich and poor families alike. And although even the most aggressive choice counseling centers will not be able to reach all low-income parents with the same quality of information that wealthier parents will seek out, there is substantial evidence that over time the gap between low- and high-income parents' information and choice involvement diminishes. Experience has shown that with every year a school choice program operates in an area, a greater percentage of low-income and poorly educated parents become active choosers.[70]

One further advantage of implementing a system of controlled choice is that it gives districts an opportunity to acknowledge older children's growing autonomy. While primary schools will in all likelihood be chosen by parents, perhaps in brief consultation with their children, the move to secondary school represents a new, more independent phase in students' lives. In recognition of this fact, school districts might require that students (as well as their parents) sign the secondary school choice request form. School choice advisors might also direct more of their information toward secondary school students as opposed to their parents. Overall, older students would be recognized as partially autonomous actors who deserve to participate in making choices about their future schooling. Similar increases in student-directed choice might be offered within each school, as well, in the form of a variety of graduation plans, opportunities to specialize in particular subject areas, student participation on the school's governing board or other administrative body, and so forth.

Diversity and commonality among liberal schools

The above subsection concluded that an ideal system of liberal education provision would allow parents and students controlled choice among a diverse range of schools. What was not clarified, however, was the amount or kind of variation that schools of choice should exhibit. School choice—even controlled choice—makes sense only if schools are different from one another in identifiable and valuable ways. Schools must be *identifiably* different because a choice between clones is no choice at all.[71] Furthermore, schools must be different in *valuable* ways because a choice among bad options—or even one good option and many bad options—is also not truly a choice: 'A choice between good and evil is not enough.'[72] In addition, as I noted above, children have a wide variety of needs and interests that cannot all be met by a single type of school—even if that school is a good one by many measures. Thus, an ideal liberal school system would provide families a variety of good schools (and no bad schools) from which to choose.

But the question remains as to what kinds or types of schools are valuable and not valuable from a liberal educational perspective. For example, what variations should children *not* have the opportunity to choose within a liberal controlled choice system? I have already delineated some bad variations in the abstract. Bad schools are ones which are not common, are not detached, and do not help children develop their capacities for autonomy. But what does this mean in practice? I suggested above that one thing it means is that schools should not reflect fundamental or socially divisive conceptions of the good. Such schools would violate both the conditions of detachment (by failing to provide an autonomy-promoting community that is separate from children's home communities) and the common school ideal (insofar as a conservative Southern Baptist school, for example would be unlikely to attract children from contrasting religious backgrounds). I admit that the concept of a 'fundamental' conception of the good is extraordinarily vague, and to say that such a conception is 'socially divisive' is not much help either. It is both impossible and inappropriate, however, to give these concepts more content in the absence of a particular social and political context. The significance to an individual or a community of a set of values or way of life varies enormously with the culture of the community or state in which it is set; thus, one can make the concept of a 'fundamental and socially divisive' conception of the good more concrete only within a culturally concrete context.

Religion in the United States, for example, both is a fundamental element of many people's lives and is socially divisive within the body politic. As individuals, Americans take religion seriously. Church attendance is high, and many Americans' religious convictions are 'comprehensive',[73] in that their religious convictions determine the entire shape and character of their lives. Furthermore, evangelical and fundamentalist Protestantism constitute the fastest-growing religious denominations in the

United States. At a time when church attendance, religious affiliation, and even belief in God are declining in other industrialized democracies, Americans' religiosity—and especially evangelical and fundamentalist religiosity—remains strong and in the case of fundamentalists may even be increasing.[74] On a political level in the US, as well, religion occupies a prominent and influential role.[75] Despite the constitutional separation between church and state, Americans' religious beliefs—again, especially those of fundamentalists and evangelicals, who are extremely well organized politically—exert a tremendous influence on politics at a local, statewide, and even national level. The anti-abortion movement, the Christian Coalition, and campaigns for school prayer are just three of the most obvious examples of the connections between religion and US politics. These religiously inspired political movements, however, are strongly opposed by other citizens on religious, political, moral, and other grounds. In James Fishkin's terms, religion represents a 'cleavage' within American society.[76] As a result of religion's place in the individual, social, and political lives of Americans, I suggest that it would be inappropriate for liberal schools in the United States to differentiate themselves on religious grounds. Because of religion's status as both a fundamental and a socially divisive conception of the good, religious schools would violate the liberal educative aims of commonality, autonomy, and citizenship.

Religiously affiliated schools in Great Britain, on the other hand, might until recently have been perfectly compatible with the liberal educational ideal. A variety of studies show that religion in the post-war period has until recently played a fairly insignificant role in the lives of most British families, and that it exerts little influence over the life of the country as a whole.[77] This is not to say that Britain is not a Christian country—it most definitely is, as British Muslims and Jews will be quick to point out. But until the recent growth of the Muslim population, Britain was not a religiously divided or religiously devoted country. Barely 15 to 20 per cent of Britons are affiliated with a church; church attendance is far lower;[78] and moral education in most Church of England or even Roman Catholic voluntary-aided schools seems to consist primarily of teaching children to be nice to each other.[79] Until recently at least, schools affiliated with religious organizations in Great Britain have not been socially or politically divisive (except in the case of some Muslim schools) or autonomy-inhibiting on an individual level;[80] thus, liberal controlled choice in Britain could have included religious schools. 'Until recently', however, is a key caveat—now that Britain has become more religiously diverse, and Muslim communities in particular have been requesting public funding for religious schools that are explicitly not autonomy-promoting, religious schools in Britain become suspect or even unacceptable from a liberal educational standpoint.

Religion is not the only form of the good that is 'fundamental' and 'socially divisive' in certain cultures and not in others. It simply serves as an example of the necessarily local nature of such judgements about the constitution of the detached school of choice. It is an important example, because many American liberal theorists, especially, wrongly regard church schools (or any association between the state and religion) as necessarily antithetical to liberalism. American theorists need to recognize the blinkered nature of this view, just as I argued in Chapter 4 that all theorists need to recognize the local character and limitations of different versions of citizenship education. I do believe that division of schools by race or ethnicity could never be socially or politically innocuous. But other sources of identification or value might be proper sources of school affiliation in some countries but not others. Schools that teach in only one of a state's multiple official languages, for example, may be acceptable in a country such as India or Switzerland but not in parts of Canada or South Africa, where one's linguistic identification is extremely important culturally and is socially divisive. Single-sex schools, military-affiliated schools, and schools with other distinctive orientations may also violate the terms of detachment, autonomy, or citizenship in countries in which these affiliations are associated with fundamental cultural, political, or social cleavages.

These examples suggest other limitations on variation among schools of choice, specifically in the areas of curriculum, pedagogy, and administration. I suggested above that schools can and should diversify in these areas. The problem is that curriculum, school structure and administration, and pedagogy all have an effect on children's development of the capacity for autonomy. Thus, there must be some limitations to the kind and level of diversity available in these areas. A school that adopts an old-fashioned pedagogy of lectures, recitations, and tests measuring recall and comprehension rather than analysis and synthesis, for example, will probably inhibit rather than encourage children's development of autonomy. Likewise, a curriculum that teaches 'scientific creationism' or colonial history from a completely one-sided and uncritical perspective will also not help children's development of autonomy. Finally, a school that is marked by constant discipline problems, inadequate facilities, out-of-date textbooks, huge classes, poorly trained teachers, and low morale among students, teachers, and parents—conditions which unfortunately afflict many inner-city schools in the United States as well as elsewhere—cannot reliably teach even basic academic and social skills to all of its students, and therefore cannot provide them the intellectual, social, and emotional foundations for the capacity for autonomy. Simply being a state-controlled, common, even possibly detached school is therefore not enough; schools must *teach* students as well, and teach them carefully and rigorously across the disciplines.

Does this mean that a liberal system of education would require a national curriculum, or a national pedagogic approach and/or administrative structure? I have to admit that I do not know; the answers to these questions depend on psychological and educational analyses of the development of autonomy, as well as on the particular politics of various countries, that go beyond the scope of this book. Substantial regulation of schools is clearly necessary, insofar as there exist many skills, habits, and areas of knowledge (partially discussed in Chapters 2 and 4) that all children need to master in order to be well educated and to develop their capacities for autonomy. Schools must be monitored in order to ensure that they foster these capacities. On the other hand, teachers who are well trained and then given autonomy themselves to shape their classrooms and the curriculum as they think best may end up serving children's needs better than teachers who are bound to teach a single, set curriculum. Local conditions and resources, individual students' strengths and weaknesses, student and teacher interests, and other factors can all combine to make a curriculum good for one classroom or school but not for another. Flexibility and responsiveness are almost always necessary (but not sufficient) keys to good education.

A possible compromise, one that sets high standards but does not dictate how teachers and students reach those standards, is to impose a set of national exams or other forms of assessment (for example, a portfolio of essays, projects, and other work). These are already common, of course, in many countries across the world and especially in almost all European countries. National standards in the United States are a different story; due to the invidious and incessant politicization of education in the United States, combined with its fiercely defended history of state and local educational control, thoughtful and acceptable national standards continue to face an uphill battle. In certain ways this is appropriate. As with any national curriculum, care must be taken that national assessments set high but reasonable standards for meaningful student achievement in all areas of skills and knowledge that serve the overall goal of education (i.e. students' development of their capacities for autonomy). Because politics, power, educational or intellectual fads, poor research, entrenched interests, and simple carelessness can readily distort implementation and assessment of educational goals, there is good reason to be extremely cautious about moving toward national assessments and/or curricula in countries that do not yet have them—and even in some countries that do.[81] But in the absence of a clear answer as to the need for a national curriculum to guide liberal education provision, national assessments may make a lot of sense *if* properly planned, developed, and implemented.[82]

5.3 GETTING THERE FROM HERE: CONCLUDING THOUGHTS

National standards and curricula are, of course, not the only issues that arise when one raises the question of how to achieve the implementation of the liberal educational ideal in imperfectly liberal, contemporary states. Rather, there are a number of legal, social, and educational institutions and practices that need to be reformed before the liberal educational ideal can achieve fruition. A number of reforms of schools' educational aims and curricula, financing formulas, school choice policies, private schools' roles and privileges, schools' relationship with parents, national versus local control over education, and so forth, have been introduced and discussed throughout this book. But the implementation of these reforms presupposes that the political, social, and cultural conditions already exist for implementing the liberal school ideal (of which the above are components). In this section, I examine what kind of political, social, cultural, legal, and educational reforms would need to take place simply to enable liberal education to get off the ground. In other words, I ask: how can we get there (to the realization of the liberal educational ideal) from here? In the discussion that follows, I will concentrate primarily on reforms that would need to be implemented in the United States and Britain in order to achieve a liberal system of education, in large part because American and British educational theory, practices, and research have provided the touchstone for much of my analysis thus far; the reader can easily extend these ideas, however, to other modern, industrialized democracies.

First, it is essential to remember that as section 3.1 discussed, we cannot merely rely on the state's or the government's good will to promote the aim of helping children develop their capacities for autonomy; rather, we must have institutions and structures in place that *force* the state to realize its obligations toward children. As I argued in Chapter 2, helping children to develop their capacities for autonomy through schooling is a fundamental matter of justice, equivalent to adults' right to freedom of speech or association. In contemporary liberal theory, matters of basic justice are typically provided for in the constitution—they are considered to be 'constitutional essentials'. Thus, one essential reform for ensuring the long-term implementation of the liberal educational ideal, as demanded by justice, is to embed children's rights to an autonomy-promoting education in the constitution. A Bill of Rights or other constitutional component should include a provision affirming children's right to a free and adequate education within a common school, and state that the aim of children's education within school is to help them develop their capacities for autonomy. A constitutional mandate might also be established which requires that inequality in the provision of education be to the advantage of the least privileged children (or some other similarly liberal formula). In these ways, children's right to an autonomy-promoting education will be embedded within the legal foundation of the liberal state, and thus begin to be protected and promoted.[83]

Second, the United States in particular may require further constitutional reforms and/or reinterpretation of judicial decisions in order to permit the implementation of liberally mandated educational aims. Two cases are particularly relevant here. The first case is *Pierce* v. *Society of Sisters* (1925), in which the United States Supreme Court explicitly upheld individuals' constitutional right to establish and send their children to private schools.[84] Justice McReynolds' majority opinion stated, 'The fundamental theory of liberty upon which all governments in this Union repose excludes any general power of the state to standardize its children by forcing them to accept instruction from public teachers only. The child is not the mere creature of the state; those who nurture him and direct his destiny have the right, coupled with the high duty, to recognize and prepare him for additional obligations.'[85] As a result, the Supreme Court declared that, 'Requiring all children between the ages of eight and sixteen years to attend the public schools unconstitutionally interferes with the liberty of parents and guardians to direct the upbringing and education of children under their control.'[86] Nothing in the opinion explicitly disallows extensive regulation of private schools by state authorities, and private as well as state schools are equally acceptable within liberal education policy, as I argued in section 2. *Pierce* can certainly be interpreted, however, as giving operators of private schools extensive leeway in determining curriculum, fees, admission policies, and so forth—all of which should come under government scrutiny and regulation according to the liberal educational ideal. A reversal or modification of precedent, therefore, would probably be required.

Other reversals of precedent would be needed in more specific cases, such as *Wisconsin* v. *Yoder* (1972). In this case, the United States Supreme Court granted to Amish families the right to withdraw their children from any education—state or private—at the age of 14, two years earlier than the state-mandated minimum school-leaving age of 16.[87] Although this case has rightly been interpreted not to apply to other groups in the quarter-century since it was decided, it still contravenes what I have argued is a fundamental right of children within any self-consistent liberal order: namely, their right to an education that helps them develop the capacity for autonomy. I say this not because schooling during those two years necessarily makes the difference between a child's possessing and not possessing the capacity for autonomy. Rather, the very grounds of the Amish Order's case was that if their children were forced to attend school from ages 14 to 16, they would develop a worldliness and intellectual sophistication that would make it difficult for them to sustain Amish beliefs and practices. Confronting the Amish arguments solely on their own terms, then, we see that they claim the right to withdraw their children from experiences that they predict will essentially increase their children's capacity for autonomy. As my arguments throughout this book have made clear, this parental 'right' is insupportable within liberal theory, and is not an acceptable ground on which to deny children their right to autonomy-focused schooling. Further constitutional reform and/or judicial reinterpretation of constitutional rights, therefore, is probably necessary for full implementation of the liberal educational ideal in the United States.

Third, cultural change regarding the purpose of education is needed in a broad range of countries, and both the US and Britain especially need to reform their cultures of private education. Private schools in the US and Britain draw about 10 per cent of the school-age population and are generally perceived as elite institutions that are presumptively better than local state schools. Thus, extensive state regulation of private schools, along with the mandate that private schools enter the controlled choice lottery and limit their fees to a level covered by government grants, will likely meet fierce opposition in these countries. In countries such as France, Germany, Japan, and Denmark, by contrast, private schooling is extremely rare, and to the extent that it exists at all, it is more often perceived either as being equivalent to state schooling or as providing remedial education for students who cannot keep up with the state school curriculum. Private schooling in these countries is thus perceived as being less prestigious than, or at best equally prestigious to, state schooling. State regulation of private schools, therefore, will be far more acceptable in these states (and in many countries around the world). A cultural reorientation is probably required for American and British citizens to accept the possibility of achieving high educational standards outside elite and expensive private schools.

Likewise, even broader reform is required in many countries' conception of the purpose of education. With the publication of every new international survey or analysis of national examination results (e.g. TIMMS, an international comparison of students' math and science achievement among many nations; GCSEs, which measure academic achievement at age 16 in Britain; and SATs, which purport to measure students' likelihood for success in college in the United States), it seems that politicians, journalists, parents, and even teachers are led to ask, 'How can we better compete?' or 'How can we better teach what our businesses need our students to know?' Instead, we should ask, 'What do we want our students to achieve?' and 'How can we better teach our students what they need and deserve to know?' The latter questions, insofar as they are student-centered and take into account the best interests of the child, are central to the generation and implementation of the liberal educational ideal; the former are not. On a local level, this means that we need to talk to each other and our children differently. Crucially, we should remind both students and each other that there is more to school than getting a good job and/or getting into a good college or university. From primary school onwards, we too often use these reasons—and only these reasons—to justify to children why they need to pay attention and get good grades in school. These are laudable goals, but they radically and pathetically understate the broader aim and life-changing nature of education, at least within the liberal educational ideal. The aim of liberal education is to teach children the skills, habits, knowledge, and dispositions for them to be thoughtful, mature, self-assured individuals who map their path in the world with care and confidence, take responsibility for their actions, fulfill their duties as citizens, question themselves and others when appropriate, listen to and learn from others, and ultimately lead their lives with dignity, integrity, and self-respect—i.e. to be autonomous in the fullest sense of the word as discussed in this book. This is what we should tell our children and our students (in age-appropriate terms they can understand, of course) when they ask why they have to go to school, follow directions, or do their homework; and it is for these purposes that those directly involved in education should shape schools, assign homework, develop curricula, give directions, and so forth, as I discuss below. Until we change students', parents', teachers', and citizens' attitudes in general about the purpose of education, we will never be able to achieve a liberal system of education on a broad scale.

I attribute such an important role to changing our cultural attitudes because, I assert, social change of the sort called for by the liberal educational ideal can never succeed on the basis of legal reform alone. We must change the constitution of both educators' and citizens' beliefs and values, in addition to changing the legal constitution of the state. This is because the legal imposition of an ideal is generally unsuccessful in the absence of a communal belief in the importance of the ideal. As I discussed in Chapter 4, for example, regardless of the number of laws or even constitutional provisions that forbid certain kinds of racial, religious, or gender-based discrimination, citizens will likely act in a non-discriminatory manner only if they have actually learned to be tolerant and mutually respectful, and to value these attributes. If the value of toleration is to be realized, Chapter 4 argued, it must be embedded within the social and cultural 'constitution' of a society, as well as within its legal or textual constitution. The same is true, I suggest, of the value of autonomy. One cannot successfully legislate (or constitutionally impose) education for autonomy unless the ideal is also embedded within the national culture.[88]

Regardless of whether or not it would be politically justified, therefore, *forcing* citizens and states via the imposition of constitutional and legislative mandates to educate for autonomy is not satisfactory, because unilateral legislation in favor of autonomy-driven education cannot succeed in the absence of an autonomy-valuing liberal culture, nor in the absence of teachers and school administrators who both want to and know how to educate for autonomy. A community which has been legally constituted for decades or centuries by a text mandating education for autonomy will likely by now also be culturally and socially constituted to favor children's development of autonomy and to favour autonomy-driven education. Teachers who have been taught in common, detached schools in such a way as to develop their own capacities for autonomy are also likely to replicate that in their own teaching, especially since research consistently shows that teachers generally teach the way they have been taught. Thus, the constitutional entrenchment of children's rights to an autonomy-promoting education may represent an ideal for liberal states. But to impose the liberal educational ideal upon a modern liberal state now would most likely be ineffective, at least in the short term and especially in the absence of other reforms, because of the lack of a social, cultural, and legal history of autonomy-driven education.

A fourth reform, therefore, that must be implemented in order to support the development of an educational and political culture that supports an autonomy-driven ideal of common schooling is a reform of teacher education. Teachers are one essential key to realizing a liberal system of education provision. As a result, pre-service teacher education and in-service teacher training must be improved, and the social standing of teachers must be increased. We must make sure that teachers have the skills to think critically and creatively, to read and write effectively, to understand and analyze current events, and so forth before we ask them to impart these skills to our children. We also must make sure that they understand, are committed to, and know how to implement the educational aims discussed throughout this book. In part, this means that we must educate teachers better before they enter the classroom. Possibly, all teachers should be required to gain a degree in an academic discipline, rather than in education itself, before training to become teachers. At the very least, teachers should be forced to meet much higher academic standards than they do currently (such as demonstrating that they can read and write well, have a good knowledge of their subject area, etc.) before being allowed into the classroom. Furthermore, all pre-service teachers should be required to analyze lesson plans, curricula, discipline plans, classroom organization, etc. to determine not just the daily objectives (e.g. 'describe the parts of a plant', 'analyze character development in *Macbeth*') but the broader educational aims implicit in them. Ideally, this should initially take place within a philosophy of education class, and then be continually reinforced throughout the teacher education process. In-service teacher training should also emphasize teachers' continued use of academic and intellectual skills, and continue to emphasize the relationship among curriculum, classroom management, organization, administration, objectives, and broader educational aims. Teachers should be encouraged to use a wide variety of assignments and assessments (such as essays, projects, demonstrations, portfolio presentations, etc.) to complement a more limited regime of textbook-based homework and pencil-and-paper tests; curricula should emphasize the building of both basic and higher-level skills and knowledge; and children should be given the opportunity frequently to see how what they are learning is important in their own lives and the lives of their community, nation, and world.

Higher standards and more rigorous training requirements will succeed, however, only if primary and secondary teachers come to be held in higher esteem than they currently are in the United States and Britain. In both countries, university students who decide to enter teaching, especially in the state schools, are on average less academically able and prepared than their counterparts who enter other professions. Although many reasons have been advanced for why this is so, it is evident that teachers' low social standing in the US and Britain is one major cause. Any individual who is capable of entering a profession other than teaching has a strong incentive to do so. He or she is virtually assured of greater respect from friends and acquaintances, greater autonomy on the job, a higher salary, and increased receipt of other symbols of prestige and respect. Teachers' social standing must therefore be increased dramatically if we wish to raise standards within the teaching profession in order to achieve the liberal educational ideal. Otherwise, increased standards will be an empty promise, with a severe teacher shortage being its only foreseeable result. The examples of France, Germany, Japan, and Canada should provide some inspiration for this move; all have cultures that value teaching on a level comparable with other professions, and all have a supply (even an oversupply, in Canada's case) of better-educated teaching forces as a result.

At the same time as we set higher standards for teachers entering and working in the profession, we must also honestly and openly confront the appalling conditions evident in many state schools—especially those in some American inner cities. One of the reasons that many theorists, policy makers, politicians, and parents favor decreasing rather than increasing the state's role in education—supporting school choice plans, for example, that use government money to pay for students to attend private schools without extending state regulatory requirements over those schools—is that state schools are widely perceived to have failed. Those of us who support state-regulated education cannot and should not turn our backs on these arguments. We should all agree, liberal and non-liberal alike, that it is a gross injustice for some students—predominantly poor, predominantly minority—to attend school for ten or twelve years and leave without even basic knowledge or skills, as occurs in frighteningly many schools, especially in the American inner cities. From liberal and non-liberal perspectives alike, this has the inexcusable effect of disabling students from getting a good job, supporting their families adequately, and contributing substantially to society. Furthermore, these outcomes are problematic for liberals also within the wider context insofar as without basic skills in reading, writing, and math, for example, students are ill equipped to achieve a whole range of goals that individuals set themselves in trying to direct their lives as a whole in a truly autonomous fashion. While I have argued throughout this book in favor of state-regulated (and usually state-run) schools that are common and open to all, therefore, I want to emphasize that I have never suggested that common, state schools are always adequate for achieving the liberal educational ideal. We cannot excuse schools that do a poor job of teaching reading, math, science, history, writing, art, etc. just because they are common and state-controlled. Children's development of higher-order skills is dependent upon their having a solid foundation of basic skills. The two work hand in hand.

By admitting that state control or regulation of schools is not sufficient for providing a good education, by extending student choice (and public funding) to private schools, and by encouraging a much greater degree of diversity among all schools, liberals should assuage some people's concerns that the liberal educational ideal is a blueprint for institutionalizing failure in the form of state schooling. In addition, even imperfect implementation of many aspects of the liberal ideal of education—controlled choice, educational desegregation (by class and residence as well as race and ethnicity), increased flexibility, improved teacher training, increased parent involvement, rigorous civic education, and institutionalized practices and incentives that encourage all schools to educate for autonomy—should help all schools to improve.

This is not to say that all doubters will be satisfied: far from it, since I have not tried to convince individuals of the desirability of liberalism itself. Rather, as I promised in the Introduction, I took liberalism as a given, and explored what principles and policies are necessary to realize it in theory and practice. This approach has two, interrelated implications. First, readers who were not liberals when they started reading this book will have been given few reasons to become liberals in the meantime. Liberalism is a socially activist and transformative philosophy (despite some political liberals' claims to the contrary), and this book has simply made its activism more apparent. Second, the number of self-identifying liberals may well go down, because of readers' discomfort with the educational implications expounded here. Some liberals might choose to abandon liberalism rather than accept the model of education that I have presented. The same may be true for non-liberals, insofar as they may decide that the liberal educational ideal represents the *reductio ad absurdum* of liberal principles. 'If this is what liberalism is about,' such readers may think, 'then I want no part of it.'

There are, none the less, a few ways in which the preceding arguments may be essential to securing the success of liberal education—and to helping *children*, for whose benefit the liberal educational ideal was developed in the first place, achieve success and realize their full capacities as well. First, the arguments I have made here should convince many even if not all citizens of the coherence and value of the autonomy-driven, liberal educational ideal. Second, following on from this, citizens who are convinced by my arguments should be driven to *act* upon the principles and policies I have articulated, rather than merely affirming them passively. It is only by acting upon our principles, and by encouraging children to adopt and to develop the habit of acting upon these principles as well, that we can ensure that liberal aims and practices will flourish as part of the national culture. In the case of liberal education, this means implementing the policies that have been analyzed, discussed, and advocated throughout this book. I hope that the discussion pursued in the above five chapters will help move us toward this end.

Third, the arguments I have presented should serve to convince both theorists and practitioners—philosophers of education and/or politics, educators at all levels, policy analysts and policymakers, and liberals and non-liberals alike—to take the association between education and politics seriously, and to re-examine some of their own intuitions, theories, and practices as a result. One of my underlying themes throughout this book has been the indivisible relationship between politics and education both in theory and in practice. In the case of liberalism in particular, I have repeatedly argued that liberal education must be formulated with liberal political principles in mind, and that liberal political principles must be (re)formulated with liberal education in mind. Neither liberal politics nor liberal education can be fully understood—or fully implemented—without the other. In the end, therefore, I hope that this book will do something to move philosophers and practitioners—of education, of liberalism, and of politics in general—'from here to there': from a naive conception of liberalism and education as only distantly related enterprises to a complex and sophisti-cated understanding of the two as intimately linked partners in a single enterprise; and more specifically, from an intuitive impression of liberal education as best realized through parents' uncontrolled choice over their children's education to a reflective understanding of liberal education as best realized through the ideal of controlled choice among a wide variety of detached, autonomy-driven schools. On the basis of this reform of our conceptions about education, politics, and schooling, I hope that the other reforms I have discussed above will be generated and nurtured.

NOTES

Notes to Introduction

1. See Eamonn Callan, *Creating Citizens* (Oxford: Oxford University Press, 1997); Harry Brighouse, 'Civic Education and Liberal Legitimacy', *Ethics*, 108 (1998), 727–53; William Galston, *Liberal Purposes* (Cambridge: Cambridge University Press, 1991), ch. 5; William Galston, 'Two Concepts of Liberalism', *Ethics*, 105/3 (Apr. 1995), 516–34; Amy Gutmann, 'Children, Paternalism, and Education,' *Philosophy and Public Affairs*, 9/4 (1980), 338–58; Amy Gutmann, 'Civic Education and Social Diversity', *Ethics*, 105/3 (Apr. 1995), 557–79; Stephen Macedo, 'Liberal Civic Education and Religious Fundamentalism: The Case of God v. John Rawls?', *Ethics*, 105/3 (Apr. 1995), 468–96; T. H. McLaughlin, 'Liberalism, Education, and the Common School', *Journal of Philosophy of Education*, 29/2 (1995), 239–55; Kenneth A. Strike, *Educational Policy and the Just Society* (Chicago: University of Illinois Press, 1982); John White, *Education and the Good Life: Beyond the National Curriculum* (London: Kogan Page, 1990). There are also many books and articles about *democratic* education, but as I discuss later in the Introduction and in Ch. 4, democratic and liberal principles are distinct, with distinct and sometimes even contrary implications for education.
2. See R. S. Peters, 'Criteria of Education', *Ethics and Education* (London: George Allen and Unwin, 1966); R. S. Peters, 'Aims of Education—A Conceptual Inquiry', *The Philosophy of Education* (Oxford: Oxford University Press, 1973), 11–57.
3. See Galston, 'Two Concepts of Liberalism'.
4. John Dewey, *Democracy and Education* (New York: Free Press, 1944); Amy Gutmann, *Democratic Education* (Princeton: Princeton University Press, 1987); James Tarrant, *Democracy and Education* (Aldershot: Gower Publishing Company, 1989); David M. Steiner, *Rethinking Democratic Education: The Politics of Reform* (Baltimore, Md.: Johns Hopkins University Press, 1994). See also Benjamin R. Barber, *An Aristocracy of Everyone: The Politics of Education and the Future of America* (New York: Ballantine Books, 1992).

Notes to Chapter 1

1. I cite Locke rather than Thomas Hobbes because Hobbes' contractarianism does not comply with all five legitimation conditions. Hobbesian contracts are able to be instituted by force, with agreement exacted through fear rather than through deliberative equality or reasoned unanimity. Hobbes considered contracts made under threat to be binding, a stance which runs counter to the legitimation conditions of contemporary liberalism. See Thomas Hobbes, *Leviathan* (Cambridge: Cambridge University Press, 1991; 1st pub. 1651), ch. 14, pp. 97–8.
2. John Locke, 'An Essay Concerning the True Original, Extent and End of Civil Government', (hereafter referred to as *Second Treatise*) in *Two Treatises of Government* (London: Everyman's Library, 1990; 1st pub. 1690), sect. 95.
3. Locke, *Second Treatise*, sect. 122.
4. Liberals, note, who are also concerned neither to restrict such agreements to men, nor to assume the metaphysical trappings of the state of nature.
5. Locke, *Second Treatise*, sect. 99. This emphasis on public legitimation, of course, sits uneasily with Locke's other famous doctrine, that of tacit consent (see sect. 119). Contemporary liberals have in response often collapsed the two, arguing in favor of a hypothetical legitimation process whose principles could (and should) be publicly embraced. See my discussion of Rawls later in the chapter.
6. Bruce Ackerman, *Social Justice in the Liberal State* (New Haven: Yale University Press, 1980), 3–15.
7. '[T]he notion of constrained conversation [between individuals] should serve as *the* organizing principle of liberal thought' (Ackerman, *Social Justice in the Liberal State*, 10).
8. See Ronald Dworkin, 'Liberalism', in *A Matter of Principle* (Oxford: Oxford University Press, 1985), 181–204.
9. See William Galston, *Liberal Purposes* (Cambridge: Cambridge University Press, 1991); David Gauthier, *Morals by Agreement* (Oxford: Oxford University Press, 1986). Many other contemporary liberal theorists could be surveyed, of course, for their adherence to the legitimation conditions laid out above, but most of them build upon the groundwork laid by Locke, Mill, Rawls, or Dworkin. See, e.g., Stephen Macedo, *Liberal Virtues* (Oxford: Oxford University Press, 1990); Will Kymlicka, *Liberalism, Community, and Culture* (Oxford: Oxford University Press, 1989).
10. John Rawls, *A Theory of Justice* (Cambridge, Mass.: Harvard University Press, 1971).
11. This is, of course, merely a representative sample of traditional liberal freedoms, not a systematic or exhaustive list.
12. I address the issue of liberal neutrality in sect. 2, below, and in Ch. 2.
13. Rawls, *A Theory of Justice*, (italics mine).

14. Rawls, *A Theory of Justice*, 86.
15. Joseph Raz, *The Morality of Freedom* (Oxford: Clarendon Press, 1986).
16. Interestingly, however, Raz also suggests that any given culture may have some shared values whose imposition neutralist liberals would oppose. See Raz, *The Morality of Freedom*, 128.
17. John Stuart Mill, *On Liberty* (Harmondsworth: Penguin Books, 1974; 1st pub. 1859).
18. 'If it were felt that the free development of individuality is one of the leading essentials of well-being; that it is not only a co-ordinate element with all that is designated by the terms civilization, instruction, education, culture, but is itself a necessary part and condition of all those things, there would be no danger that liberty should be undervalued' (Mill, *On Liberty*, 120).
19. There are theorists, as well, who take (A) and (B) seriously and thereby find themselves led to reject (C); but as I argued at the end of the last section, they would not be viewed (nor do they view themselves) as true liberals, since the substantive freedoms represented by (C) are central to liberalism's identity.
20. See John Rawls, 'Justice as Fairness: Political not Metaphysical', *Philosophy and Public Affairs*, 14 (1985), 223–51.
21. See John Rawls, *Political Liberalism* (New York: Columbia University Press, 1993).
22. It should be noted that in the half-decade following Rawls' publication of *Political Liberalism*, many different 'political liberalisms' have sprung up, often sporting different characteristics and aims than Rawls' original. I am not concerned about analyzing all of them here. Rather, in this section, I focus on what I consider (controversially, perhaps) to be the 'purest' form of political liberal theory: namely, a theory that asserts that (A), (B), and (C) can simultaneously be made compatible. Unlike comprehensive or perfectionist liberalism, Rawls and like-minded political liberals assert, political liberalism can justify liberal freedoms and institutions on grounds that all reasonable people will accept. As I argue later, by inserting the condition '*reasonable* people', Rawlsian political liberals violate their own agenda, either by wildly underestimating the extent of pluralism (and thus the number of 'unreasonable' people) in modern society, or by making acceptance of the value—and even some of the habits— of autonomy a precondition of participation in the legitimation process and/or of the justification of liberal freedoms and institutions. To prove that Rawls' form of political liberalism is similarly 'sectarian' to comprehensive liberalism, however, is not to prove that all versions are so constituted. In Ch. 4, therefore, I pick up the challenge of political liberalism once more in its more civic guise. For the purposes of this section, however, 'political liberalism' should be taken to refer to Rawls' theory as expressed in his book of the same name.
23. Rawls, *Political Liberalism*, 302; see also 19.
24. Rawls, *Political Liberalism*, 54. The other element of the first moral power is a commitment to moral reciprocity.
25. Rawls, *Political Liberalism*, 56–7.

26. As Eamonn Callan puts it, 'The idea of the burdens of judgement is introduced by Rawls both to explain the possibility of irreconcilable ethical disagreement among reasonable persons and to justify the mutual tolerance that public reason must promote whenever such disagreement threatens to become social conflict' (Eamonn Callan, 'Political Liberalism and Political Education', *The Review of Politics*, 58/1 (Winter 1996), 10). See also ch. 2 of Callan's latest book, *Creating Citizens* (Oxford: Oxford University Press, 1997), for a similarly motivated and extremely incisive critique of political liberalism's theoretical groundwork.
27. Rawls, *Political Liberalism*, 54.
28. Rawls, *Political Liberalism*, 60.
29. Callan's argument to this effect is most telling. See *Creating Citizens*, ch. 2.
30. Callan, 'Political Liberalism and Political Education', 12.
31. Rawls, *Political Liberalism*, 302.
32. Rawls, *Political Liberalism*, 308; Rawls, *A Theory of Justice*, 62, 90–5.
33. Rawls, *Political Liberalism*, 313.
34. Rawls, *Political Liberalism*, 310–12.
35. Will Kymlicka, *Multicultural Citizenship* (Oxford: Oxford University Press, 1995), 82.
36. Kymlicka, *Multicultural Citizenship*, 82.
37. I assume in this section that Rawls means 'revise' to indicate an ability to engage in internally motivated revision as opposed to simple reaction to adverse events. For if the revision is supposed to be self-generated in some way, then Rawls' definition of individuals' capacity for the good definitely seems to presuppose autonomy. If, on the other hand, the second stipulation merely means that individuals should not experience an utter breakdown of their personality if any event occurs (either inwardly generated or externally imposed) that forces them to revise their conception of the good, then autonomy may not be involved. This latter case is simply a condition of what it means to be fully human—that one doesn't have a breakdown in the face of change. While this is an essential distinction, I presume on the basis of further statements he makes in the text (see *Political Liberalism*, 30–1, 313–14) that he means the revision to imply what we would refer to as autonomous action.
38. Rawls, *Political Liberalism*, 300.
39. Rawls, *Political Liberalism*, 73–4.
40. Ronald Dworkin, 'In Defense of Equality', *Social Philosophy and Policy*, 1/1 (1983), 26; quoted in Kymlicka, *Liberalism, Community, and Culture*, 12.
41. Rawls, *Political Liberalism*, 313.
42. Rawls, *Political Liberalism*, 314.
43. I do not mean to claim that contemporary liberal theory is composed solely of 'political' and 'comprehensive' theories; nor does a discussion of two of Rawls' arguments constitute a complete evaluation of political liberalism. I do suggest, however, that insofar as the above analysis permits an evaluation of some central arguments made by core figures within contemporary liberal

theory, we can conclude that autonomy plays a central (and necessary) role within the mainstream of contemporary liberal thought.

44. I discuss in further detail the threat of state tyranny in relation to judging adults' possession of autonomy in sect. 2.2. See also sect. 3.1 on the 'liberalism of fear'.

45. Rawls, *Political Liberalism*, 32.

46. I borrow the notion of a liberal trilemma from James Fishkin, although I identify a different set of trilemmic elements from those he identifies. See James Fishkin, *Justice, Equal Opportunity, and the Family* (New Haven: Yale University Press, 1983), for an excellent analysis of a different trilemma lurking within liberalism: namely, that between justice, equal opportunity, and family integrity.

47. Eamonn Callan addresses the same challenge in *Autonomy and Schooling*: 'The word "autonomy" does not exhibit a highly stable pattern of use in either theoretical or ordinary discourse which we could simply describe, and then approve for philosophical purposes, with minor alterations at most. But neither does it provide us with a conceptual *tabula rasa* upon which we can inscribe whatever sense we choose. Clearly, it is an idea not without substance but still rather inchoate' (Eamonn Callan, *Autonomy and Schooling* (Montreal: McGill-Queen's University Press, 1988), 25).

48. Stanley Benn, *A Theory of Freedom* (Cambridge: Cambridge University Press, 1988), *passim*. While I will use much of Benn's terminology and many of his arguments in this section, I disagree with some of his assumptions and conclusions. Thus, I will make use of his ideas without adopting either the structure or the overall content of his argument. For instance, I will speak as if autarchic persons are the same as Benn's notion of 'natural persons', an equivalence with which he would disagree but which I believe is both valid and useful for my purposes. Also, Benn's principle of autarchy seems to veer strangely close at times to his principle of autonomy, even though the point of his using the former phrase is to distinguish it from the latter. So I will also attribute fewer powers to the autarchic person than he seems to at times. It is his distinction between autarchy and autonomy that interests me, along with his defense of the principles of equal respect and non-interference that result from a recognition of autarchy. I am not committed to his argumentative framework as a whole.

49. 'Fundamental to a person's autarchy is his consciousness of himself as the author of intentional changes in the world' (Benn, *A Theory of Freedom*, 177).

50. Benn, *A Theory of Freedom*, 91.

51. See Benn, *A Theory of Freedom*, 152–69.

52. Rawls suggests that persons be seen as having three respects in which they are free: (1) they have the 'moral power to have a conception of the good'; (2) 'they regard themselves as self-authenticating sources of valid claims'; and (3) they are 'capable of taking responsibility for their ends'. These three conditions seem very close (if not identical) to the conditions listed for autarchic agents. See Rawls, *Political Liberalism*, 30, 32, 33.

53. Read 'autarchic person' for my purposes (although not for Benn's).
54. Benn, *A Theory of Freedom*, 98. Benn introduces a second, related argument for equal respect as non-interference in a section rejecting that paternalistic interference which is designed to realize an agent's goals better than the agent himself can: 'But such paternalistic management would be a kind of theft, stealing from the author the plans for a world in the making of which he sought the expression and realization of his own nature and identity, leaving him without a part in what he meant to be his own creation' (Benn, *A Theory of Freedom*, 111).
55. Gerald Dworkin, *The Theory and Practice of Autonomy* (Cambridge: Cambridge University Press, 1988), 15–17.
56. For more on first-order and second-order desires, see Harry Frankfurt, 'Freedom of the Will and the Concept of a Person', in John Christman, (ed.), *The Inner Citadel: Essays on Individual Autonomy* (Oxford: Oxford University Press, 1989), 63–76.
57. Dworkin, *The Theory and Practice of Autonomy*, 17.
58. Dworkin, *The Theory and Practice of Autonomy*, 18.
59. See Dworkin, *The Theory and Practice of Autonomy*, 18–19, 29.
60. His mother's rule need not be 100% effective. Abner could justify his slavishness by proving that following his mother's orders was the most effective, albeit imperfect, way of achieving his autonomously adopted fundamental good.
61. Dworkin, *The Theory and Practice of Autonomy*, 15.
62. As Mill remarks: 'In this and most other civilized countries, for example, an engagement by which a person should sell himself, or allow himself to be sold, as a slave would be null and void. . . . [b]y selling himself for a slave, he abdicates his liberty; he forgoes any future use of it beyond that single act. He therefore defeats, in his own case, the very purpose which is the justification of allowing him to dispose of himself. . . . The principle of freedom cannot require that he should be free not to be free. It is not freedom to be allowed to alienate his freedom' (Mill, *On Liberty*, 173).
63. Benn, *A Theory of Freedom*, 228.
64. Dworkin, *The Theory and Practice of Autonomy*, 21.
65. Joel Feinberg, 'Autonomy', in Christman, (ed.), *The Inner Citadel*, 38.
66. Benn, *A Theory of Freedom*, 179.
67. Feinberg, 'Autonomy,' 33.
68. It is more correct to say that individuals must feel embedded within some coherent set of norms and practices, whether these norms come from a single or small set of cultures or not. As G. A. Cohen has helpfully pointed out to me, a person can enjoy identity coherence even if the elements forming his identity come from a wide variety of cultures and therefore lack cultural coherence. It remains true, however, that many people are not cosmopolitans in this sense—and that many people who are find support within a culture of similar cosmopolitans. As a result, I will confine my attention from here on to cultural coherence, rather than identity coherence in general, although the distinction will resurface in Chs. 3 and 5. A compelling argument does remain that we are

all products of 'many fragments' of many cultures, rather than being products of one culture. See Jeremy Waldron, 'Multiculturalism and Mélange', in Robert Fullinwider, (ed.), *Public Education in a Multicultural Society* (Cambridge: Cambridge University Press, 1996), 90–118.

69. Émile Durkheim, *The Division of Labor in Society*, trans. W. D. Halls (New York: Free Press, 1984); in this context see also Benn, *A Theory of Freedom*, 176.

70. T. H. McLaughlin, 'Parental Rights and the Religious Upbringing of Children', *Journal of Philosophy of Education*, 18/1 (1984), 82. But see in response Peter Gardner, 'Religious Upbringing and the Liberal Ideal of Religious Autonomy', *Journal of Philosophy of Education*, 22/1 (1988), 89–105, and McLaughlin's reply, 'Peter Gardner on Religious Upbringing and the Liberal Ideal of Religious Autonomy', *Journal of Philosophy of Education*, 24/1 (1990), 107–25. On this same idea of religious education being a partial means of developing an autonomous person, see Eamonn Callan, 'Faith, Worship, and Reason in Religious Upbringing', *Journal of Philosophy of Education* 22/2 (1988), 183–93.

71. I should emphasize that the practice of questioning oneself is, of course, central to the exercise of autonomy. Sister Susan is thus incapable of autonomy because psychologically almost no human being—Sister Susan presumably included—can question the very foundation of her identity and psychological existence (assuming that there is a single foundation, as is true in Sister Susan's case) without suffering trauma and/or breakdown. Thus it is Sister Susan's presumed inability to question herself deeply without risking psychological breakdown that accounts for her lack of autonomy.

72. A common critique of liberal autonomy, and especially of Rawlsian autonomy, is that individuals have to become somehow atomistic or divorced from all of their commitments in order to achieve autonomy. This charge seems completely fallacious. Although it is true that one must establish some measure of critical distance in order properly to reflect on an idea (desire, value, etc.), it is silly to think that one need abandon all of one's other ideas in order to do so. One works *from* the standpoint of one's other ideas; there is no good reason to think that if we question one belief or desire, we necessarily have to question them all at the same time. As Andrew Mason puts it, 'A person cannot (logically) at the same time call into question *all* of her beliefs and commitments but it may be possible for her to call *each* into question, one at a time' (Andrew Mason, 'Personal Autonomy and Identification with a Community', in David Milligan and William Watts Miller, (eds.), *Liberalism, Citizenship, and Autonomy* (Aldershot: Avebury, 1992), 181).

73. As David Miller rightly points out, we may even resolve to be satisfied with the inconsistency, judging that human experience sometimes demands conflicting outlooks, of which this inconsistency is an example. See David Miller, ' "Autonomous" v. "Autarchic' Persons" ' (review of Benn's *A Theory of Freedom*), *Government and Opposition*, 24 (1989), 244–8.

74. Michael Walzer's notion of 'connected criticism' is apposite here. As Walzer emphasizes in *The Company of Critics* (London: Peter Halban, 1989), even the most vitriolic cultural criticism must proceed from an acceptance of some cultural principles in order to succeed. Criticism must be *connected*, in that it can call into question one set of cultural commitments only in terms of other, more deeply held commitments. And likewise, critical solutions in the form of reshaped or new commitments must be shown at least to accord with, if not to derive from, these other, continuing deep commitments. Otherwise, neither the criticisms nor the solutions will be accepted by others within the society. This vision of cultural criticism and change seems helpful in reflecting on the process of an *individual's* self-criticism as well. While we can question ourselves, our projects, and our visions of the good, we cannot question everything at once. In this respect, many of our heteronomously adopted norms (cultural and otherwise) will function as at least temporary restraints on our efforts to reconceive the good—although no particular norm is privileged to escape re-examination. In this way, the process of enacting one's autonomy proceeds in a 'connected' way that mirrors the process of cultural or societal self-criticism.

75. Gabrielle Taylor, *Pride, Shame, Guilt* (Oxford: Clarendon Press, 1985), 128.

76. This does not mean that individuals who possess a plurality of constitutive beliefs and values will *necessarily* be open to others' assessments of themselves. As Marc Stears and Andrew Hurrell have both pointed out to me, an individual may have a plurality of constitutive values but nonetheless be a close-minded 'fundamentalist' in all areas of his life—devoted to football, the Church of England, and the Tory Party, and contemptuous of cricket, Catholics, and the Labour Party. It does seem evident, however, that somebody who has a plural conception of value will be more likely to respond to others' evaluations of themselves than somebody who does not have such a conception.

77. Raz, *The Morality of Freedom*, 250.

78. Steven Macedo, 'Community, Diversity, and Civic Education: Toward a Liberal Political Science of Group Life', *Social Philosophy and Policy*, 13/2 (1996), 254-5.

Notes to Chapter 2

1. This might not be the case if the exercise of autonomy were merely an instrumental good needed to satisfy an end or need that was generated only by the possession of autonomy itself. For example, it could be argued that if one has the capacity for autonomy, one will be unhappy if the capacity is frustrated and unhappiness is intrinsically bad, so people with the capacity for autonomy should be able to exercise it. But the argument for autonomy was never made in this way—nor should it have been. It is autonomy itself that is viewed as a good, not its exercise as a means to satisfying the burden of its possession.

2. Amy Gutmann, *Democratic Education* (Princeton: Princeton University Press, 1987), 30. See also Eamonn Callan, 'Tradition and Integrity in Moral Education', *American Journal of Education* 101 (1992), 23.

3. This is not to ignore Aristotle's important insight about habits—that often the best way to develop a capacity (for courage, temperance, or virtue, say) is to be forced to exercise it, awkwardly and with much coaching at first, and then more confidently as time goes on. But even Aristotle reminds us that instruction, which is separate from the act of being courageous or temperate, is also demanded for the successful acquisition of (a) virtue (Aristotle, *Nicomachean Ethics*, x. 9). For a further discussion of habits, see sects. 2–4 and 4.2.

4. For further justification of this point see Diana T. Meyers, *Self, Society, and Personal Choice* (New York: Columbia University Press, 1989), 193: 'Although the availability of a variety of options provides an incentive to master autonomy skills, children cannot gain autonomy competency simply by being flooded with options. A more direct attack on the problem is needed. The competency of autonomy must be handled in the same way that other desirable competencies are. It must be deliberately taught. Parents and teachers must encourage their charges to attend to their self-referential responses and must help them to find acceptable ways to act on these insights.'

5. This is not to say that no elements are shared between adults exercising and children developing their autonomy. Some provisions, such as adequate shelter, food, health care, and security, in addition to less tangible goods such as self-esteem, the capacity for reason, and imagination, are equally essential to the development as to the exercise of autonomy. There are many points of overlap. But it remains true that a much larger set of the conditions for the exercise of autonomy, as with shoe-tying, either are irrelevant to or actually conflict with its development.

6. A. I. Herzen, quoted in Anthony O'Hear, *Education, Society, and Human Nature* (London: Routledge and Kegan Paul, 1981), 46.

7. This description is obviously unrealistic insofar as the choices a person makes at one stage of his adult life inevitably shape and limit his future possible choices, even if his opportunities are in theory the same as they were before. Furthermore, the choices that *other* adults make about their exercise of freedom and autonomy will, in many cases, alter the choices available in practice to oneself. Autonomy-advancing cultures and communities do pose a threat to autonomy-fearing individuals, and especially to the maintenance of certain autonomy-fearing cultures and communities. Significantly, the threat can go the other way as well. Even if a state guarantees all the liberal freedoms discussed in Ch. 1, if a substantial segment of the population engages in self-censorship, choosing not to avail themselves of the freedoms of speech, press, or association, then all citizens will suffer reduced autonomy as a result of the desiccated political culture. Thus, my claims about the costlessness of adults' choices regarding the exercise of autonomy would need modification in practice. The point remains the same, however: there is a fundamental difference

in kind between *guaranteeing freedoms* for adults (to exercise autonomy) and *coercing* children (to develop their autonomy).

8. Nomi Maya Stolzenberg, ' "He Drew a Circle that Shut Me Out": Assimilation, Indoctrination, and the Paradox of a Liberal Education', *Harvard Law Review*, 106/3 (1993), 597 n. 26.

9. Stolzenberg, ' "He Drew a Circle that Shut Me Out" ', 633.

10. Howard Cohen, *Equal Rights for Children* (Totowa, NJ: Rowman and Littlefield, 1980), 43.

11. Cohen, *Equal Rights for Children*, 45 (italics his).

12. This is not to claim that paternalism$_a$ is always impermissible, or to deny that it poses controversial problems for the modern liberal state. There is a tremendous amount of debate about whether the state is justified in paternalistically$_a$ violating citizens' autonomy in order ultimately to protect it, and about what one does in clashes between individuals' short-term goals and their longer-term preservation of autonomy. It is certainly arguable that paternalistic mandatory seat belt or crash helmet laws, for instance, violate some individuals' autonomous pursuit of their conceptions of the good; whether these measures are unjustified as a result is a much more controversial question. But in any case, the *legitimacy* of paternalistic$_a$ legislation is irrelevant to the argument at hand. The issue is one of equal rights of children and adults against paternalism—not the legitimacy of paternalism altogether. If adults can rightfully be subject to paternalistic seat belt laws, then so can children; if seat belt laws are invalid for adults, the argument goes, then neither should they be imposed upon children. We can remain agnostic on the justifiability of specific examples of paternalism$_a$, yet still acknowledge that adults are granted rights and protected from most paternalism (such as being forced to live according to the ruler's vision of the moral life, or to go to church in order to gain salvation) on the basis of their capacity to exercise autonomy.

13. John Locke, 'An Essay Concerning the True Original, Extent and End of Civil Government' (hereinafter referred to as *Second Treatise*), in *Two Treatises of Government* (London: Everyman's Library, 1990; 1st pub. 1690), sect. 61. For an analysis of the scope of parental versus state authority, see the second half of this section and sect. 3.

14. J. S. Mill expresses a variation of this fear in *On Liberty*: 'If protection against themselves is confessedly due to children and persons under age, is not society equally bound to afford it to persons of mature years who are equally incapable of self-government?' (John Stuart Mill, *On Liberty* (Harmondsworth: Penguin Books, 1974; 1st pub. 1859), 147).

15. John Harris, 'The Political Status of Children', in Keith Graham, (ed.), *Contemporary Political Philosophy* (Cambridge: Cambridge University Press, 1982), 37.

16. For an interesting summary of and objection to this critique based on consequentialist grounds, see Laura M. Purdy, *In Their Best Interest? The Case against Equal Rights for Children* (Ithaca, NY: Cornell University Press, 1992), 21–54.

17. David Miller has pointed out to me that this might be overstating the case a bit,

since as I noted in sects. 1.2–1.3, state recognition of autarchy—which almost all adults possess—would guarantee the presence of a number of basic freedoms, including those of speech, movement, association, etc. If it is true that respect for autarchy adequately generates these freedoms, however, then liberals find themselves confronted by an important dilemma. Most children over the age of 5 or 6 years might be said to possess autarchy—yet children are routinely denied the sorts of freedoms I've suggested political regard for autarchy might generate. This might imply that children *should* be accorded many more rights and freedoms than they currently possess. The fear remains, however, that political recognition of children's autarchy (through granting political freedoms) would stunt the long-term goal of helping children develop their autonomy. We are back at square one, in a certain way, again grappling with the question: does any moral justification exist for treating children and adults differently in the political sphere?

18. John Kleinig, *Paternalism* (Manchester: Manchester University Press, 1983), 156.

19. Again, this is not to say that the *possession* of autonomy is age-sensitive, insofar as it is admitted that many adults currently do not possess autonomy. But given that we assume everyone possesses autonomy unless proven otherwise, and that 100% of young children (say, under 5 years old) have been proven otherwise, then the presumption of autonomy distribution by the liberal state is legitimately age-dependent.

20. See Cohen, *Equal Rights for Children*, 52–5 for a convincing argument against establishing a state board of competence to examine the young for autonomy competency on a case-by-case basis. See also Francis Schrag, 'From Childhood to Adulthood: Assigning Rights and Responsibilities', in Kenneth Strike and Keiran Egan, (eds.), *Ethics and Educational Policy* (London: Routledge and Kegan Paul, 1978), 61–78, for an interesting argument against evaluating children's 'maturity' as a means for giving them equal citizenship rights.

21. As Cohen points out in an application of the sorites paradox, if the average child aged 16 has sufficient autonomy to decide to leave school, then so must the average child aged 15 years and 11 months—and one can always keep subtracting a month. See Cohen, *Equal Rights for Children*, 49–51.

22. Harris, 'The Political Status of Children', 37, paraphrasing Shakespeare's *Richard III*.

23. Shelley Burtt asks virtually the same question—and ultimately arrives at virtually the opposite answer—in her thoughtful and provocative article, 'In Defense of *Yoder*: Parental Authority and the Public Schools', in Ian Shapiro and Russell Hardin, (eds.), *Nomos XXXVIII: Political Order* (New York: New York University Press, 1996), 412–37.

24. Amy Gutmann, 'Children, Paternalism, and Education', *Philosophy and Public Affairs*, 9/4 (1980), 341. This is not to deny that there are many consequentialist moral reasons, as well as parent-regarding reasons, for favoring parental control; these are addressed in the next section. It is rather that parents have no intrinsic pre-legitimation claims to control over the child. Insofar as Locke is right to reject the notion that children are the property of their parents (see

Locke, *Second Treatise*, sects. 54–8), and insofar as children are recognized as separate individuals who are more than mere extensions of their parents, there exists no obvious a priori reason to free parents from the burden of legitimation (of their right to coercive control over their children). This may prove to be an easy burden to fulfill, on grounds that will be discussed in section 3, but it is not trivial or unnecessary.

25. As Gutmann agrees: 'Nor is it a valid objection to say that the democratic state ... is simply imposing *its* values on children. Some values must be imposed in any case. What is at issue here is not *whose* values but *what* values ought to be imposed upon children' (Gutmann, 'Children, Paternalism, and Education', 351).

26. Gutmann again sums up this conclusion well: 'We *can* justify limitations upon parents' rights [to limit 'a child's future ability to exercise meaningful choice' (p. 350)] because our valuation of liberal freedom to pursue differing conceptions of the good is dependent upon that freedom being exercised by beings who have been raised under conditions conducive to choice' (Gutmann, 'Children, Paternalism, and Education', 351).

27. Joseph Raz, *The Morality of Freedom* (Oxford: Clarendon Press, 1986), 410.

28. Raz, *The Morality of Freedom*, 411.

29. I must append one caveat to this rosy picture of the trouble-free advancement of autonomy. There is a chance that the individual's newfound capacity for autonomy will lead her to reject the community in which she was raised, but will not give her the means to put a revised conception of the good in its place. Rather, she becomes directionless, overwhelmed by a seeming infinitude of choice and having no principles or settled values by which to sort through and choose one set of beliefs over another. Deprived both of a determinate set of values and of the linchpins of her former personality, such an individual ends up being stripped of two of the essential prerequisites of autonomous action. She falls into anomie instead of attaining autonomy. In such a case, the state's effort at developing her autonomy actually leaves her worse off than when she started. I address this problem in sects. 3.4 and 5.1.

30. See John Rawls, *Political Liberalism* (New York: Columbia University Press, 1993), 192-4, on the desirability of 'neutrality of aim' (although not, notably, neutrality of effect or influence, nor procedural neutrality).

31. This has parallels, I suggest, with Alan Montefiore's example of the father who remains 'neutral' in a dispute between his two children when he knows that the older, stronger child will win if he doesn't intervene (quoted in Raz, *The Morality of Freedom*, 113-14). It also has parallels with modern outrage over Bosnia—the belief that abdication of responsibility by Western countries under the guise of 'neutrality' during the early 1990s led to the otherwise potentially avoidable torture, death, and loss of territory of hundreds of thousands of Bosnian Muslims.

32. One author who feels no compunction about asserting radical state control over parents and their right to bear and rear children is Hugh LaFollette: see his 'Licensing Parents', *Philosophy and Public Affairs*, 9/2 (1980), 182–97. See

also Lawrence E. Frisch, 'On Licentious Licensing: A Reply to Hugh LaFollette', *Philosophy and Public Affairs*, 11/2 (1981), 173–80; and LaFollette's response in the same issue, 'A Response to Frisch', 181–3.

33. Gutmann, 'Children, Paternalism, and Education', 341.

34. My use of the terms 'parents' (in the plural) and 'family' in this section are not meant to indicate bias against single-parent-families or other non-nuclear family child-raising conditions. I adopt the term 'parents' solely for ease of exposition.

35. James G. Dwyer, 'Parents' Religion and Children's Welfare: Debunking the Doctrine of Parents' Rights', *California Law Review*, 82/6 (1994), 1375. Dwyer's article is an excellent and extremely tightly argued rejection of parents' rights; I borrow my distinction between parents' rights and privileges from him. Other theorists who take a similar approach include Yael Tamir, 'Whose Education Is it Anyway?', *Journal of Philosophy of Education*, 24/2 (1990), 161–70; John Wilson, 'Indoctrination and Rationality', in I. A. Snook, (ed.), *Concepts of Indoctrination* (London: Routledge and Kegan Paul, 1972), 17–24; Barbara Bennett Woodhouse, ' "Who Owns the Child?": *Meyer* and *Pierce* and the Child as Property', *William and Mary Law Review*, 33/4 (1992), 995–1122; and Richard Arneson and Ian Shapiro, 'Democratic Autonomy and Religious Freedom: A Critique of *Wisconsin* v. *Yoder*', in Shapiro and Hardin, (eds.), *Political Order*, 365–411.

36. Judith N. Shklar, 'The Liberalism of Fear', in Nancy Rosenblum, (ed.), *Liberalism and the Moral Life* (Cambridge, Mass.: Harvard University Press, 1989), 21–38.

37. Gutmann, 'Children, Paternalism, and Education', 344.

38. Locke, *Second Treatise*, sect. 58.

39. I would like to thank Daniel Markovits for bringing this argument to my attention. See also Eamonn Callan, *Creating Citizens* (Oxford: Oxford University Press, 1997), 142–3.

40. Charles Fried, *Right and Wrong* (Cambridge, Mass.: Harvard University Press, 1978), 152; quoted in Gutmann, *Democratic Education*, 29 n. 20. Gutmann also cites another proponent of this view, namely the Irish Constitution, Article 41, which 'recognizes the Family as the natural primary and fundamental unit group of Society, and as a moral institution, possessing inalienable and imprescriptible rights, antecedent and superior to all positive law' (Gutmann, *Democratic Education*, 29).

41. Stolzenberg cites five published opinions (Stolzenberg, ' "He Drew a Circle that Shut Me Out," ', 584): *Mozert* v. *Hawkins County Public Schools*, 579 F. Supp. 1051 (E. D. Tenn. 1984); *Mozert* v. *Hawkins County Public Schools*, 582 F. Supp. 201 (E. D. Tenn. 1984); *Mozert* v. *Hawkins County Public Schools*, 765 F. 2d 75 (6th Cir. 1985); *Mozert* v. *Hawkins County Public Schools*, 647 F. Supp. 1194 (E. D. Tenn. 1986); and *Mozert* v. *Hawkins County Board of Education*, 827 F. 2d 1058 (6th Cir. 1987), certiorari denied, 484 US 1066 (1988).

42. Various sources quoted in Stolzenberg, ' "He Drew a Circle that Shut Me Out," ', 595–6.

43. 'Lost' is a term of art in this case, as Harry Brighouse has pointed out, since in response to the court case: some parents removed their children from the state school and placed them in fundamentalist Christian schools instead; Hawkins County Public Schools dropped the offending curriculum; and the textbook publishers excised the disputed passages from future editions. See Harry Brighouse, 'Egalitarian Liberals and School Choice', *Politics and Society*, 24/4 (1996), 467.
44. Stolzenberg, ' "He Drew a Circle that Shut Me Out," ', 596.
45. Quoted in Stolzenberg, ' "He Drew a Circle that Shut Me Out," ', 631.
46. Kleinig, *Paternalism*, 145. One argument in support of parents' ownership of children is the bizarre but comparatively recent lawyer's brief to the US Supreme Court in 1925: 'In this day and under our civilization, the child of man is his parent's child and not the state's. Gone would be the most potent reason for women to be chaste and men to be continent, if it were otherwise' (brief by William D. Guthrie for appellee, *Pierce v. Society of Sisters*, 268 US 510 (1925) (no. 583), 66–7; cited in Woodhouse, ' "Who Owns the Child?" ', 1102). Aristotle provides another unambiguous note of historical support: 'There cannot be injustice in an unqualified sense towards that which is one's own; and a chattel, or a child until it is of a certain age and has attained independence, is as it were a part of oneself; and nobody chooses to injure himself (hence there can be no injustice toward oneself); and so neither can there be any conduct towards them that is politically just or unjust' (Aristotle, *Nicomachean Ethics*, 1134b; quoted in Woodhouse, ' "Who Owns the Child?" ', 1044).
47. Ferdinand Schoeman, 'Rights of Children, Rights of Parents, and the Moral Basis of the Family', *Ethics*, 91 (1980), 6.
48. Schoeman, 'Rights of Children', 8, 14.
49. Callan, *Creating Citizens*, 143; see also 142–5.
50. Kleinig, *Paternalism*, 145.
51. Kleinig, *Paternalism*, 147.
52. I take no stand at this point on how the provision by the state of liberal education is to be achieved—either directly through state schools or indirectly through state-regulated private schools. I address the specifics of school provision, administration, funding, and so forth in Ch. 5.
53. To those who object that this conception of autonomy is overly demanding and unrealistic, I would respond that while it is demanding, so that probably no individual ever does satisfy all of the demands of full autonomy, that should not prevent us from holding autonomy up as a (distant, utopian) goal. There is no point in weakening the ideal of autonomy simply because a thinner version would be easier to achieve, any more than we should accommodate human cowardice in assessing the meaning of courage. Gutmann makes a similar point regarding education for democracy and citizenship: 'Were the only goal of a democratic state to prepare its members for citizenship, its maxim would be, 'Mandate the maximum education.' Citizens would be forced to spend most of their lives preparing for citizenship rather than exercising it. . . . That is why

we encounter no paradox, only a serious problem, when we acknowledge that democratic states have the authority to make schooling compulsory for children but not for adults who fall below the democratic threshold of education. Since the threshold defines not a fully but an adequately educated citizen, this constraint on democratic authority may leave many adults less than adequately educated. A stricter constraint—mandating the maximum education—is ruled out by our recognition of the primacy of treating adults as sovereign citizens' (Gutmann, *Democratic Education*, 278–9).

54. Stolzenberg, ' "He Drew a Circle That Shut Me Out" ', 597.

55. This point is parallel to my argument for children's development of autonomy (and thus for education) in the first place; liberal freedoms have meaning and value only in a context in which people have the capacities actually to avail themselves of these freedoms—likewise with autonomy.

56. Eamonn Callan, *Autonomy and Schooling* (Montreal: McGill-Queen's University Press, 1988), 146.

Notes to Chapter 3

1. Judith Shklar, 'The Liberalism of Fear', in Nancy Rosenblum, (ed.), *Liberalism and the Moral Life* (Cambridge, Mass.: Harvard University Press, 1989), 21.

2. It is a sufficient and not a necessary condition because lives with which one does identify may also be bad. But the liberal state must remain agnostic about this; it may not judge the relative merits of competing conceptions of the good which are autonomously chosen. Thus, this section ignores other conditions of bad lives as lying outside the purview of the liberal state.

3. It is worth noting that this formulation is compatible with the weakly perfectionist liberal stance because it allows individuals to lead non-autonomous lives—the state simply cannot force individuals to lead such lives.

4. As Karl Popper agrees: 'A certain amount of state control in education . . . is necessary, if the young are to be protected from a neglect which would make them unable to defend their freedom, and the state should see that all educational facilities are open to everybody. But too much state control in educational matters is a fatal danger to freedom since it must lead to indoctrination' (Karl Popper, *The Open Society and Its Enemies*, vol. 1 (London: Routledge and Kegan Paul, 1952), 117).

5. Paradoxically, the act of positing *autonomy* as the aim of education may be especially dangerous. Autonomy has a dangerous propensity to 'drift' politically toward authoritarianism, as Isaiah Berlin outlines in *Four Essays on Liberty*: 'My thesis is that historically the notion of "positive" liberty—in answer to the question "Who is master?"—diverged from that of "negative" liberty, designed to answer "Over what area am I master?"; and that this gulf widened as the notion of the self suffered a metaphysical fission into, on the one hand, a "higher", or a "real", or an "ideal" self, set up to rule "lower", "empirical", "psychological" self or nature, on the other. . . . in the course of

this process, what began as a doctrine of freedom turned into a doctrine of authority and, at times, of oppression, and became the favourite weapon of despotism, a phenomenon all too familiar in our own day' (Isaiah Berlin, *Four Essays on Liberty* (Oxford: Oxford University Press, 1969), p. xliv). If liberal education is structured as sect. 2.4 suggests, then it would be quite easy for the state to veer over time to a more rigid and demanding notion of "autonomy" that would rightly fall afoul of Berlin's criticisms concerning positive liberty and tyranny. The point is not merely that the state has undue power to inter- pret the aims of education by its own lights, but that the drift toward tyranny is more likely precisely *because* it is justified in terms of autonomy—i.e. because citizens are less likely to be vigilant in judging acts (such as education) conducted under the name of freedom than under the banner of other educa- tional goals. Thus, it is not only the imbalance of power between the educative state and the parents that raises the specter of state tyranny, but also the fact that autonomy—which according to Berlin has historically been a byword for authoritarianism—is the justificatory aim.

6. Amy Gutmann, *Democratic Education* (Princeton: Princeton University Press, 1987), 69.
7. John Stuart Mill, *On Liberty* (Harmondsworth: Penguin, 1974; 1st pub. 1859), 177. John Locke responds similarly to William Penn's Frame of Government order to 'Erect and order all public schools', commenting that it imposes 'The surest check upon liberty of conscience, suppressing all displeasing opinions in the bud' (quoted in Maurice Cranston, *John Locke* (Oxford: Oxford University Press, 1985), 262).
8. Mill, *On Liberty*, 176.
9. Mill, *On Liberty*, 176.
10. Bonna Devora Haberman, 'What is the Content of Education in a Democratic Society?', *Journal of Philosophy of Education*, 28/2 (1994), 185.
11. William Galston uses this same reasoning to reject the positing of autonomy as such as the aim of the liberal state: 'To place an ideal of autonomous choice— let alone cosmopolitan bricolage—at the core of liberalism is in fact to narrow the range of possibilities available within liberal societies. In the guise of protecting the capacity for diversity, the autonomy principle in fact represents a kind of uniformity that exerts pressure on ways of life that do not embrace autonomy' (William Galston, 'Two Concepts of Liberalism', *Ethics*, 105/3 (Apr. 1995), 523).
12. Although this argument has treated pluralism solely as an instrumental good, it is in no way harmed—and is in fact strengthened—if pluralism is taken to be an intrinsic good as well. Likewise, the fact that I have focused on the instrumental benefits of pluralism (as promoting autonomy) does not mean that I reject, or even take a position on, the notion of pluralism as an intrinsic good.
13. See Joseph Raz, *The Morality of Freedom* (Oxford: Oxford University Press, 1986), esp. ch. 14.
14. 'The "pluralism" commonly identified with the state of families is superficial

because its internal variety serves as little more than an ornament for onlookers. Pluralism is an important political value insofar as social diversity enriches our lives by expanding our understanding of differing ways of life. To reap the benefits of social diversity, children must be exposed to ways of life different from their parents and—in the course of their exposure—must embrace certain values, such as mutual respect among persons, that make social diversity both possible and desirable' (Gutmann, *Democratic Education*, 33).

15. Lawrence A. Cremin, *Popular Education and its Discontents* (New York: Harper and Row, 1990), 64.

16. Cremin, *Popular Education and Its Discontents*, 59.

17. Cremin, *Popular Education and Its Discontents*, 61.

18. James S. Coleman, *Equality and Achievement in Education* (London: Westview Press, 1990), 128. The role of parent involvement in mediating children's education is addressed at much greater length in sect. 2 of this chapter.

19. Wisconsin Department of Public Instruction, *Families and Education: An Educator's Resource for Family Involvement* (Madison, Wisc.: Wisconsin Department of Public Instruction, 1991), 6. For just a small sampling of American studies demonstrating a causal link between parent involvement and student achievement, see the following: Association for Supervision and Curriculum Development, *Parent Involvement* (Alexandria, Va.: Association for Supervision and Curriculum Development, 1995); Joyce L. Epstein, 'Effects on Student Achievement of Teachers' Practices of Parental Involvement', in *Advances in Reading/Language Research*, vol. 5 (Greenwich, Conn.: JAI Press, 1991), 261–76; Paul G. Fehrmann, Timothy Z. Keith, and Thomas M. Reimers, 'Home Influence on School Learning: Direct and Indirect Effects of Parental Involvement on High School Grades', *Journal of Educational Research*, 80/6 (Aug. 1987), 330–7; Thomas Kallaghan *et al.*, *The Home Environment and School Learning: Promoting Parental Involvement in the Education of Children* (San Francisco: Jossey-Bass, Inc., 1993); Janine Bempechat, 'The Role of Parent Involvement in Children's Academic Achievement: A Review of the Literature', *Trends and Issues*, no. 14 (New York: ERIC Clearinghouse on Urban Education, June 1994); Anne T. Henderson, Carl L. Marburger, and Theodora Ooms, *Beyond the Bake Sale: An Educator's Guide to Working with Parents* (New York: National Committee for Citizens in Education, 1986); and Nancy Feyl Chavkin, (ed.), *Families and Schools in a Pluralistic Society* (Albany, NY: State University of New York Press, 1993).

Far fewer British studies exist, in part because 'parent involvement' has been understood in the recent past to mean parental choice about schools, as opposed to involvement in their children's actual learning. Such studies as do exist, however, include: Barbara Tizard *et al.*, *Young Children at School in the Inner City* (London: Lawrence Erlbaum, 1988); Central Advisory Committee for Education, *Children and their Primary Schools* (Plowden Report) (London: HMSO, 1967); Jack Tizard, W. N. Schofield, and J. Hewison, 'Symposium: Reading—Collaboration between Teachers and Parents in Assisting Children's

Reading', *British Journal of Educational Psychology*, 52/1 (1982), 1–15; Paul Widlake and Flora Macleod, *Raising Standards: Parental Involvement Programmes and the Language Performance of Children* (Coventry: Community Education Development Centre, 1984); Sandra Jowett and Mary Baginsky with Morag MacDonald MacNeil, *Building Bridges: Parental Involvement in Schools* (Windsor: NFER-Nelson, 1991); and Miriam E. David, *Parents, Gender, and Education Reform* (Cambridge: Polity Press, 1993).

20. James Coleman and Thomas Hoffer, *Public and Private High Schools: The Impact of Communities* (New York: Basic Books, 1987), 52.

21. Barry Rutherford, (ed.), *Creating Family/School Partnerships* (Columbus, Ohio: National Middle School Association, 1995), 54.

22. A representative sample of studies would include: Joyce Epstein and Susan Dauber's discussion of 'School Programs and Practices of Parent Involvement in Inner-city Elementary and Middle Schools', *Elementary School Journal*, 91/3 (1988), 289–305; Anne T. Henderson, (ed.), *The Evidence Continues to Grow: Parent Involvement Improves Student Achievement* (Columbia, Md: National Committee for Citizens in Education, 1987); David Armor *et al.*, *Analysis of the School Preferred Reading Program in Selected Los Angeles Minority Schools* (Santa Monica, Calif.: Rand Corporation, 1976); Council of Chief State School Officers, *A Guide for State Action: Early Childhood and Family Education* (Washington, DC: Council of Chief State School Officers, 1988); and James P. Comer, 'Educating Poor Minority Children', *Scientific American*, 259/5 (Nov. 1988), 2–8. Dozens if not hundreds of other studies exist which prove the same point.

23. Coleman and Hoffer, *Public and Private High Schools*; James Coleman, Thomas Hoffer, and Sally Kilgore, *High School Achievement: Public, Catholic and Other Private Schools Compared* (New York: Basic Books, 1982).

24. Her five levels of involvement are identified as: basic parental obligations, basic school obligations, parent involvement at school, parent involvement in learning at home, and parent involvement in decision-making, governance, and advocacy. More recently, she has added a sixth form of involvement at the level of community collaboration. See Joyce L. Epstein, 'School/Family/Community Partnerships: Caring for the Children We Share', *Phi Delta Kappan*, 76/9 (May 1995), 701–12; *School and Family Partnerships: Report No. 6* (Baltimore, Md.: Center on Families, Communities, Schools, and Children's Learning, Johns Hopkins University, 1992); 'How Do We Improve Programs of Parent Involvement?', *Educational Horizons*, 66/2 (1988), 58–9.

25. Anne T. Henderson, 'Parents Are a School's Best Friends', *Phi Delta Kappan*, 78 (Oct. 1988), 150.

26. Vivian R. Johnson, 'Parent Centers Send a Clear Message: Come Be a Partner In Educating Your Children', *Equity and Choice*, 10/2 (Winter 1994), 42–4; Leon Lynn, 'Building Parent Involvement', *Practitioner*, 20/5 (May 1994), 2.

27. Barbara Tizard, Jo Mortimore, and Bebb Burchell, 'Involving Parents from Minority Groups', in John Bastiani, (ed.), *Parents and Teachers 2: From Policy to Practice* (Windsor: NFER-Nelson, 1988), 77, 83.

28. Daphne Johnson and Joyce Ransom, 'Family and School—the Relationship Reassessed', in Bastiani (ed.), *Parents and Teachers 2*, 58–71; Hazel Joucks, 'Increasing Parent/Family Involvement: Ten Ideas That Work', *NASSP Bulletin* (April 1992), 19–23.

29. Margaret Finders and Cynthia Lewis, 'Why Some Parents Don't Come to School', *Educational Leadership*, 51 (May 1994), 53.

30. See Concha Delgado-Gaitan, 'Involving Parents in the Schools: A Process of Empowerment', *American Journal of Education*, 100/1 (Nov. 1991), 20–46; Tizard, Mortimore, and Burchell, 'Involving Parents from Minority Groups', 83.

31. As a result, they are also likely to be successful only when teachers are given the resources and support they need to contact parents regularly. Such support might include smaller classes, extra planning time built into the school day specifically for meeting with parents, compensation for frequent evening or weekend PTA or coaching duties, and even simply a telephone in or close to the classroom (a luxury afforded to few teachers) so that teachers can easily and quickly make phone calls to parents between classes.

32. Norm Fruchter, Anne Galletta, and J. Lynne White, 'New Directions in Parent Involvement', *Equity and Choice*, 9/3 (Spring 1993), 38–9.

33. Delgado-Gaitan, 'Involving Parents in the Schools', 21.

34. See Tizard, Mortimore, and Burchell, 'Involving Parents from Minority Groups'.

35. Norris M. Haynes and James P. Comer, 'The Yale School Development Program: Process, Outcomes, and Policy Implications', *Urban Education*, 28/2 (July 1993), 167.

36. 'Character education' has inspired a great deal of interest and writing in America, as well as less but still significant interest in Britain, where it is often linked with citizenship education. See Patricia White, *Civic Virtues and Public Schooling: Educating Citizens for a Democratic Society* (London: Teachers College Press, 1996); Thomas Lickona, *Educating for Character: How Our Schools Can Teach Respect and Responsibility* (New York: Bantam, 1992); Thomas Lickona, *What Is Good Character? And How Can We Develop It In Our Children?* (Bloomington, Ind.: Poynter Center, 1991).

37. To the extent that parents or children value additional educational experiences that are compatible with the liberal educational ideal, schools should be varied and flexible enough to be able to provide such experiences, and to be chosen by interested families. I discuss school choice and diversity in detail in sect. 5.2.

38. James Coleman, Thomas Hoffer, and Sally Kilgore, *Public and Private Schools* (Washington, DC: National Center for Education Statistics, 1981), and Coleman, Hoffer, and Kilgore, *High School Achievement*. Coleman and Hoffer refined their argument in *Public and Private High Schools: The Impact of Communities*, to which I primarily refer in the rest of this section. All studies controlled, of course, for student's initial ability, family background, etc.

39. See two special issues of the journal *Sociology of Education*: 55/2 and 3 (Apr./July 1982) and 58/2 (Apr. 1985). See especially Karl Alexander and

Aaron M. Pallas, 'School Sector and Cognitive Performance: When is a Little a Little?', *Sociology of Education*, 58/2 (Apr. 1985), 115–28, and J. Douglas Willms, 'Catholic-School Effects on Academic Achievement: New Evidence from the High School and Beyond Follow-up Study', 98–114 of same issue.

40. Coleman and Hoffer, *Public and Private High Schools*, 7.

41. Coleman and Hoffer also mention a fourth advantage of functional communities for schools, that being the reinforced authority that schools and teachers enjoy in such communities. 'The absence of value dominance in a school, as exists in a value-heterogeneous residential area once the functional community has vanished, means that standards and demands can no longer be imposed by teachers, as is true where there is a functional community or where the teachers' values are shared by students. Rather, the demands, the efforts put forth, and the sets of standards must arise as a negotiated compromise between teacher and students, a compromise that in some settings may be very different from that which would be imposed by the same teacher if that teacher had the authority, legitimate in the students' eyes, to do so' (Coleman and Hoffer, *Public and Private High Schools*, 62). Perpetuation of authority based on homogeneity of values and replication of traditional hierarchies, however, is not desirable within a liberal, autonomy-driven system of education.

42. Coleman and Hoffer, *Public and Private High Schools*, 7.

43. Coleman and Hoffer, *Public and Private High Schools*, 221 ff. and *passim*; Claire Smrekar, *The Impact of School Choice and Community* (Albany, NY: State University of New York, 1996), 3–4.

44. '[S]chool administrators can initiate events and activities designed specifically to bring together parents of children in the school. Many administrators know that, by creating collective strength among parents, they create a force that can be a nuisance; less often do they recognize that this collective strength can be a resource that both eases their task of governing a school and benefits the children who attend it' (Coleman, *Equality and Achievement in Education*, 323).

45. Coleman and Hoffer, *Public and Private High Schools*, 55. See also Delgado-Gaitan, 'Involving Parents in the Schools'.

46. Coleman and Hoffer, *Public and Private High Schools*, 8.

47. Coleman and Hoffer, *Public and Private High Schools*, 214.

48. Anthony S. Bryk, Valerie E. Lee, and Peter B. Holland, *Catholic Schools and the Common Good* (Cambridge, Mass.: Harvard University Press, 1993), especially chs. 5 and 11.

49. Bryk *et al.*, *Catholic Schools*, 132–3.

50. Bryk *et al.*, *Catholic Schools*, 133.

51. Bryk *et al.*, *Catholic Schools*, 133.

52. Bryk *et al.*, *Catholic Schools*, 134–5.

53. See Ivan Illich, *Deschooling Society* (London: Calder and Boyars, 1971); Ian Lister, (ed.), *Deschooling* (Cambridge: Cambridge University Press, 1974); Everett Reimer, *School is Dead* (Harmondsworth: Penguin Books, 1972).

54. Illich, *Deschooling Society*, 31.

55. Nell Keddie, 'Classroom Knowledge', in Michael F. D. Young, (ed.), *Knowledge and Control* (London: Collier-Macmillan Publishers, 1971), 133–60.
56. Keddie, 'Classroom Knowledge', 139.
57. Keddie, 'Classroom Knowledge', 150.
58. Keddie, 'Classroom Knowledge', 155–6. Keddie gives evidence for this claim earlier in the article, citing the following interview:

> 'A pupils are generally more sensitive to what they have been told *about* the course. Thus when I asked them what they thought of the course, typical responses were:
>
> > "It's very good; you can disagree with the teacher."
> > "You can link up subjects."
> > "You can think out things for yourself."
> > "It's good for learning how to work at university."
>
> It seems likely they had accepted definitions received from teachers, because when I asked these pupils to tell me about a time they had disagreed with the teacher or about a time when they had been able to link up between subjects, they could recall no instances of either. There appears to be a discrepancy between their definition and their experience of the course of which they were not aware' (Keddie, 'Classroom Knowledge', 150).

59. Eamonn Callan makes a similar point: 'Teaching presupposes that the student defer to the teacher's judgment with regard to the material being taught, and since learning is necessarily directed through teaching in the school, it follows that this attitude will be a pervasive feature of students' participation in any form of that institution. The necessity for this pervasive attitude lends some plausibility to the deschoolers' claims about the psychological impotence any form of schooling is liable to induce' (Eamonn Callan, *Autonomy and Schooling* (Montreal: McGill-Queen's University Press, 1988), 94).
60. The term 'hidden curriculum' was coined by Philip W. Jackson, *Life in Classrooms* (New York: Holt, Rinehart and Winston, 1968).
61. Keddie, 'Classroom Knowledge', 151.
62. See Jackson, *Life in Classrooms*, Samuel Bowles and Herbert Gintis, *Schooling in Capitalist America* (London: Routledge and Kegan Paul, 1976); Martin Cornoy and Henry M. Levin, *Schooling and Work in the Democratic State* (Stanford: Stanford University Press, 1985); Joel Spring, *Education and the Rise of the Corporate State* (Boston: Beacon Press, 1971).
63. Bowles and Gintis, *Schooling in Capitalist America*, 9.
64. Jackson, *Life in Classrooms*, 36. Powell, Farrar, and Cohen corroborate this idea with the following striking depiction of the 'unspecial': 'The allotted role of the unspecial often seems to be to call attention to the specialness of others. They made up, for example, an important part of the audience for Friday night football. Spectatorship was their lot, and most played the role happily. . . . One teacher even thought that spectatorship, in the stands and in the classroom, was sound preparation for life. Such students would play roles in life requiring a "passive position." While in school they were "already orienting themselves

to the environment in which they're going to be." It was sound pedagogy to know that "they respond better if you don't try to force them to take over" ' (Arthur G. Powell, Eleanor Farrar, and David K. Cohen, *The Shopping Mall High School* (Boston: Houghton Mifflin, 1985), 176).

65. Jackson, *Life in Classrooms*, 36. Or again: 'Yet the habits of obedience and docility engendered in the classroom have a high pay-off value in other settings. So far as their power structure is concerned classrooms are not too dissimilar from factories or offices, those ubiquitous organizations in which so much of our adult life is spent. Thus, school might really be called a preparation for life, but not in the usual sense in which educators employ that slogan' (Jackson, *Life in Classrooms*, 33).

66. Bowles and Gintis, *Schooling in Capitalist America*, 125.

67. Who these agents are is, of course, a pertinent question, but one that seems to go unanswered by Bowles and Gintis. While they offer compelling a posteriori examples of how school reform has tended to help capitalism, they are much less good at identifying who ensures that this happens—i.e. who the agents of schools' subservience to capitalism are. As a result, there is an air of conspiratorial fantasy surrounding their analysis (as is often the case with functionalism). I am doubtful about how seriously we must take such scenarios in developing our own theory of liberal education.

68. 'Returning to the situation in our schools, we can see that if students are to face the demands of classroom life with equanimity they must learn to be patient. This means that they must be able to disengage, at least temporarily, their feelings from their actions. It also means, of course, that they must be able to re-engage feelings and actions when conditions are appropriate. In other words, students must wait patiently for their turn to come, but when it does they must still be capable of zestful participation. They must accept the fact of not being called on during a group discussion, but they must continue to volunteer' (Jackson, *Life in Classrooms*, 18).

69. As David Paris comments, 'One should be cautious about ascribing too much—for good or ill—to the hidden curriculum. It is not clear exactly what it is, and it is odd that something hidden is often talked about as if it is well understood' (David C. Paris, 'Moral Education and the "Tie That Binds" in Liberal Political Theory', *American Political Science Review*, 85/3 (1991), 886). I might add that it is odd that something which is so well understood is often talked about as if it is hidden.

70. Illich, *Deschooling Society*, 81. His proposals might seem more plausible in an updated form encompassing use of the Internet and the World Wide Web. I suspect that Illich would reject this move, however, because computers and high technology are inaccessible to poor people. He rejects the use of television (1970s high technology) in favor of tape recorders on the same grounds.

71. 'There is in effect really no point in debating whether there should be moral education in the schools. What needs to be debated is what form this education should take since we believe that moral education, in fact, "comes with the territory" ' (David Purpel and Kevin Ryan, 'It Comes With The Territory', in

David Purpel and Kevin Ryan, (eds.), *Moral Education . . . It Comes With The Territory* (Berkeley, Calif.: McCutchan, 1976), 44).

72. White, *Civic Virtues and Public Schooling*; Betty Sichel, *Moral Education: Character, Community, and Ideals* (Philadelphia: Temple University Press, 1988).

73. Gutmann, *Democratic Education*, 53.

74. Colin Shrosbree, *Public Schools and Private Education* (Manchester: Manchester University Press, 1988), p. vi.

75. Gail R. Benjamin, *Japanese Lessons* (New York: New York University Press, 1997).

76. See Robert D. Morrow, 'The Challenge of Southeast Asian Parental Involvement,' *Principal* (Jan. 1991), 20–2.

77. I am grateful to Stuart White for impressing upon me the importance of this argument, and for convincing me to devote space to this problem.

78. William Galston, *Liberal Purposes* (Cambridge: Cambridge University Press, 1991), 255.

79. For clarity's sake, it should be noted that this argument is distinct from the commonly articulated (and stereotyped) communitarian argument that liberals do not *value* cultural coherence and membership. This argument acknowledges that liberalism does value cultural embeddedness, but suggests that liberal policies inadvertently fail to protect it.

80. Galston, *Liberal Purposes*, 255. See also Shelley Burtt, 'In Defense of *Yoder*: Parental Authority and the Public Schools', in Ian Shapiro and Russell Hardin, (eds.), *Nomos XXXVIII: Political Order* (New York: New York University Press, 1996), 426.

81. Jean Piaget, *Judgement and Reasoning in the Child*, trans. Marjorie Warden (New York: Harcourt, Brace, and Co., 1928); Jean Piaget, *The Psychology of Intelligence*, trans. Malcolm Piercy and D. E. Berlyne (London: Routledge and Kegan Paul, 1950), ch. 5; Victor Lee and Prajna Das Gupta, (eds.), *Children's Cognitive and Language Development* (Milton Keynes: The Open University and Oxford: Blackwell, 1995); Patricia H. Miller, *Theories of Developmental Psychology*, 3rd edn. (New York: W. H. Freeman, 1993).

82. Benjamin Barber, *An Aristocracy of Everyone: The Politics of Education and the Future of America* (New York: Ballantine Books, 1992), 142.

83. I am indebted to Joseph Raz for pointing this out to me.

84. Jeremy Waldron, 'Multiculturalism and Mélange', in Robert K. Fullinwider, (ed.), *Public Education in a Multicultural Society* (Cambridge: Cambridge University Press, 1996), 106.

85. 'Where social group differences exist, and some groups are privileged while others are oppressed, this propensity to universalize the particular reinforces that oppression. The standpoint of the privileged, their particular experience and standards, is constructed as normal and neutral. If some groups' experience differs from this neutral experience, or they do not measure up to those standards, their difference is constructed as deviance and inferiority' (Iris Marion Young, *Justice and the Politics of Difference* (Princeton: Princeton University Press, 1990), 116).

86. See Salman Rushdie, *Midnight's Children* (New York: Knopf, 1981) for a magnificent exploration of self-construction in a culturally divided India.

Notes to Chapter 4

1. See Stephen Macedo, 'Liberal Civic Education and Religious Fundamentalism: The Case of God v. John Rawls?', *Ethics*, 105/3 (Apr. 1995), 468–96; Amy Gutmann, 'Civic Education and Social Diversity', *Ethics*, 105/3 (Apr. 1995), 557–79; William Galston, 'Two Concepts of Liberalism', *Ethics*, 105/3 (Apr. 1995), 516–34; Eamonn Callan, *Creating Citizens* (Oxford: Oxford University Press, 1997). See also John Rawls, *Political Liberalism* (New York: Columbia University Press, 1993), 199.
2. Norman H. Nie, Jane Junn, and Kenneth Stehlik-Barry, *Education and Democratic Citizenship in America* (Chicago: University of Chicago Press, 1996), 2.
3. See Nie, Junn, and Stehlik-Barry, *Education and Democratic Citizenship in America*; Raymond E. Wolfinger and Steven J. Rosenstone, *Who Votes?* (New Haven: Yale University Press, 1980); Paul M. Sniderman, Richard A. Brody, and James H. Kuklinsky, 'Policy Reasoning and Political Values: The Problem of Racial Equality', *American Journal of Political Science*, 28 (1984), 75–94.
4. Gutmann, 'Civic Education and Social Diversity', 561. It may be too much to expect citizens to regard each others' ways of life positively themselves, given the fundamental conflicts in values and beliefs inherent among many ways of life. But citizens should learn to regard each other positively—i.e. to display mutual respect—insofar as they all act in ways that do not violate others' rights and freedoms.
5. Or attend the same state schools, for that matter, if choice of school is determined by choice of residence and residential segregation becomes the norm—as is currently the case in the United States and presumably would be likely in a state that was devoid of mutual respect. I discuss the fact of residential and educational segregation in detail in sect. 5.2.
6. Gutmann, 'Civic Education and Social Diversity', 573.
7. I am grateful to Harry Brighouse for this idea. See Harry Brighouse, 'Civic Education and Liberal Legitimacy', *Ethics*, 108 (1998), 734.
8. It is important that this does not translate simply into a 'wait and see' approach on the part of most citizens. Active involvement in politics comes too late if civic institutions are already being dismantled or if the barbarians (fascists, racists, authoritarians) are already beating down the door. Children should therefore be encouraged to be too sensitive to violations of justice, if anything, rather than not sensitive enough, so as to overcome the apathy, distraction, and procrastination inherent in many adults' responses to injustice or other civic challenges.
9. It should be noted that this conception of national citizenship is also compatible with a broader notion of, and education in, global citizenship. Teaching

children to be attentive to, and to engage in, political and civic action to prevent violations of human rights, dignity, and freedoms throughout the world is fully in concert with an autonomy-promoting education, including with a civic education focused on the preservation and maintenance of liberal institutions and freedoms. I will not pursue these issues of educating for global citizenship further here, however, because as I mentioned in the Introduction, the purview of this book is limited to education within modern, industrialized, liberal states. I purposefully remain agnostic about the appropriate relationship among these states, liberal principles, and the wider world because of the continuing controversy over the notions of global justice and the reach of liberal principles—controversy that is equally strong within liberal thought and outside of it.

10. Quentin Skinner calls this a 'paradox of political liberty'. See Quentin Skinner, 'The Paradoxes of Political Liberty', in David Miller, (ed.), *Liberty* (Oxford: Oxford University Press, 1991), 183–205. '[I]n those circumstances', Skinner notes, 'we can scarcely call it paradoxical—though we may certainly find it disturbing—if we are told what Rousseau tells us so forcefully in *The Social Contract*: that if anyone regards "what he owes to the common cause as a gratuitous contribution, the loss of which would be less painful for others than the payment is onerous for him", then he must be "forced to be free", coerced into enjoying a liberty he will otherwise allow to degenerate into servitude' (Skinner, 'The Paradoxes of Political Liberty', 191).

11. In the interests of emphasizing the role of the state school in establishing and maintaining the 'public square' and the public liberal democratic virtues, I choose in this chapter to use the American term 'public school' in place of the British 'state school' to designate state-maintained schools.

12. It is a bit misleading to refer to American school provision in national terms, as education is governed and provided almost entirely at the state and local level. Because the features of school provision that I want to examine, however, are fairly uniform across the country—both because constitutional restrictions such as the First Amendment place limits upon public school policy, and because larger states exercise significant indirect power over smaller states' education policy (through textbook selection, for example)—I will speak in this chapter as if the United States has an identifiable national educational policy.

13. French and American policies in particular toward private schools are both historically and normatively at odds with their public educational commitments. It is only because one million people marched in Paris on 24 June 1984 against the suggested closure of Catholic schools that they still exist; likewise, it is because public schools in the United States were anti-Catholic from their founding until the middle of this century (and thus violated their self-professed neutralist commitments) that the private and parochial school movement took hold in America. In neither case does the position of private schools intrinsically reflect each country's public educational aims, despite their giving dissenting families a private educational outlet. It does not make

sense, therefore, to try to integrate public and private education policies into a single, coherent model, because no such coherent, principled stance exists. (England's sympathetic attitude toward private schooling, on the other hand, is completely consistent with its approach to public education, as sect. 2 will show.)

14. This model of schooling also seems to be most like the one for which William Galston calls. See William Galston, *Liberal Purposes* (Cambridge: Cambridge University Press, 1991), 241–56.

15. It should be noted that Wales also exemplifies this philosophy, as school provision practices and the National Curriculum are virtually the same in England and Wales. (See Education Act 1944 (London: HMSO) and Education Reform Act 1988 (London: HMSO).) Both for ease of exposition and because Wales has the additional linguistic complication of balancing Welsh-language and English-language education, however, I use England, rather than England and Wales, as the touchstone for this model.

16. Lord Swann, *Education for All* (Swann Report) (London: HMSO, 1985), 499.

17. The fate of Muslim schooling in England is a complex one that itself symbolizes many of the conflicting pulls within liberalism discussed in this book. In a longer chapter, it would be illuminating to discuss Muslim schools' supposed violation of the principles of equal and democratic education, and the implications of this judgement for the place of Muslim families and citizens within the liberal polity in general.

18. See Education Reform Act 1988, sect. 30, subsec. (3): 'A local education authority shall, if so requested by the governors of an aided or special agreement school maintained by the authority, make arrangements with the governors in respect of the admission of pupils to the school for preserving the character of the school.'

19. Department for Education, *Statistics of Education: Schools* (London: HMSO, 1993), 140–2.

20. Again, I do not mean to suggest that all (or even a majority of) English schools fit this model in practice, nor that English society is as radically divided as this description might imply. As I explained above, what is of significance is not the empirical outcome of these models of schooling, but their theoretical limits; in other words, English education is structured so as to *permit* the effective privatization of nominally public schools, and thus also to permit the establishment of the divided pluralism I will describe below.

21. Margaret Thatcher, *The Downing Street Years* (London: HarperCollins, 1993), 570.

22. Education Act 1980 (London: HMSO), sect. 17.

23. Department for Education, *Our Children's Education: The Updated Parent's Charter* (London: HMSO, 1994), 7.

24. Education Act 1980, sects. 6–7.

25. 'Parent Power', *The Economist*, 25 Mar. 1995, 17.

26. Disillusion with the class-based homogeneity of selective grammar schools was one of the primary reasons for Labour's introduction of non-selective

'comprehensive' schools in the 1960s. As the 1967 Plowden Report made clear, 'Selection for secondary education ... has been criticized as being socially divisive both because it gives middle class children a better chance than manual workers' children to secure grammar school places, and because it gives better career openings to grammar school than to modern school pupils. The same arguments are also used against selection for primary school classes, or streaming' (Central Advisory Committee for Education, *Children and their Primary Schools* (Plowden Report) (London: HMSO, 1967), p. 288, para. 809). See also Department of Education and Science, *The Organization of Secondary Education*, Circular 10/65 (London: HMSO, 1965); J. Stuart Maclure, *Educational Documents* (London: Methuen and Co. Ltd, 1973); David Rubinstein and Brian Simon, *The Evolution of the Comprehensive School 1926–1966* (London: Routledge and Kegan Paul, 1969); Clyde Chitty, *Towards a New Education System: The Victory of the New Right?* (London: Falmer Press, 1989).

27. Ron Dearing, *The National Curriculum and Its Assessment: Final Report* (London: School Curriculum and Assessment Authority, 1994), paras. 2.2, 3.24, 4.28–29; Thatcher, *Downing Street Years*, 594.

28. For more on the structure of the National Curriculum, see Jim Sweetman, *Curriculum Confidential Two: The Complete Guide to the National Curriculum* (Tamworth: Bracken Press, 1992).

29. What little guidance is given is to be found in the National Curriculum Council's *Education for Citizenship: Curriculum Guidance 8* (London: National Curriculum Council, 1990).

30. It is possible, of course, to integrate citizenship education into the curriculum under a different name—through history and literature classes, social studies, and so forth. While some of this might go on in the National Curriculum as it stands, I suggest that for three reasons, it still does not satisfy the demands of civics education. First, students in English schools do not learn about the parliamentary system, the structures of state and local government, the passage of a bill through Parliament, etc. unless they specifically take an A-level course in British politics. This seems an unacceptable lacuna in any curriculum that is meant to restore public character to and inculcate civic virtues within an otherwise (potentially) privatized school system. Second and relatedly, civic concerns have thus far been addressed in the National Curriculum foundation subjects only within the history curriculum—a practice that may engineer the illusion of a common past, but which does not succeed in building a conception among students of a shared, public *present* or *future*. Finally, insofar as the National Curriculum itself provides for citizenship education as a separate, albeit cross-curricular, 'theme', the criticisms in the text of its lack of inclusion in the curriculum continue to hold true.

31. National Curriculum Council, *Curriculum Guidance 3* (London: National Curriculum Council, 1990).

32. It might be argued that such interactions can and do take place outside the school—in the neighborhood, or in mandatory national service programs

evident in countries like Israel and Switzerland—and thus that it is unnecessary for the *school* in particular to take responsibility for establishing a heterogeneous setting in which children are intentionally exposed to difference and taught to be tolerant. While it is true that schools are not the only social institutions to teach toleration and expose children to diversity, they nonetheless strike me as being one of the most important. Not only are they under direct state control—and can therefore explicitly adopt liberal aims as their own—but they also reach children when they are very young, as national service programs, integrated workplaces, and other institutions do not. Although this is not an analytic argument, I would suggest on pragmatic grounds at least that schools must play a central role in teaching toleration and bringing different groups together in one place.

33. Theodore R. Sizer, *Horace's School: Redesigning the American High School* (Boston: Houghton Mifflin Company, 1992), 69. On the subject and importance of habits, see also John Dewey, *Human Nature and Conduct* (New York: Random House, 1922), pt. I; Aristotle, *Nicomachean Ethics*, 1103a15–1104b3, 1179b20–1180a23.

34. It might be argued that religion is a special case in both countries—in the United States because of the First Amendment of the US Constitution; in France for historical reasons stemming from the French Revolution, anti-Catholicism, and the 'republican school' ideal promulgated by Jules Ferry in the 1870s. (See Mona Ozouf, *L'École, l'Église et la République* (Paris: Éditions Cana/Jean Offredo, 1982); Eugen Weber, *Peasants into Frenchmen* (London: Chatto and Windus, 1979).) Nonetheless, both the US and France pursue educational neutrality in relation to other cultural practices, 'lifestyle choices', and community mores as well.

35. The assumption that neutrality can mean equality even in theory has, of course, been sharply questioned for years by critics of liberalism and of liberal education. Nomi Maya Stolzenberg is especially suspicious of 'neutral' education, contending that from the perspective of fundamentalist Christian parents, schooling in the US that is neutral among all religious beliefs is patently unequal in relation to their own. (See sect. 2.1, above, and Nomi Maya Stolzenberg, ' "He Drew a Circle that Shut Me Out": Assimilation, Indoctrination, and the Paradox of a Liberal Education', *Harvard Law Review*, 106/3 (1993), 581–667.) In many ways the success of this anti-neutralist argument directly entails the failure of the public square as a theoretical possibility: if neutrality can never translate into equality, then the public square as a space equally open and accessible to all citizens is also a theoretical (as well as practical) impossibility. Insofar as this argument could very well put the lie to political liberalism as a coherent theory, it is an essential one to consider. Such criticisms fall outside the scope of this chapter, however, which attempts to apply aspects of political liberalism as opposed to treating political liberal principles as objects of study themselves. Thus, I shall not further address these criticisms explicitly—although they will continue to be explored indirectly, especially in sect. 4 on France, through discussion of other issues.

36. This is not to say that in *practice* American schools are always diverse. Because public schools depend on geographically defined catchment areas which are often highly segregated, many schools exhibit much less diversity than they should and/or are intended to do. But as in my description of the English model, I am interested in the theoretical, rather than empirical, implications of American public school provision. I discuss self-segregation and wealthy parents' exercise of de facto school choice in Ch. 5.

37. Consider Horace Bushnell's *Discourse on Common Schools* in 1853, for example: 'This great institution, too, of common schools, is not only a part of the state, but is imperiously wanted as such, for the common training of so many classes and conditions of people. There needs to be some place where, in early childhood, they may be brought together and made acquainted with each other; thus to wear away the sense of distance, otherwise certain to become an established animosity of orders; to form friendships; to be exercised together on a common footing of ingenuous rivalry. . . . Indeed, no child can be said to be well trained, especially no male child, who has not met the people as they are, above him or below, in the seatings, plays and studies of the common school. Without this he can never be a fully qualified citizen, or prepared to act his part wisely as a citizen.' Bushnell is equally forceful a page later: 'Indeed, I seriously doubt whether any system of popular government can stand the shock, for any length of time, of that fierce animosity, that is certain to be gendered, where the children are trained up wholly in their classes, and never brought together to feel, understand, appreciate and respect each other, on the common footing of merit and of native talent, in a common school' (Horace Bushnell, 'Common Schools: A Discourse on the Modifications Demanded by the Roman Catholics', in Rush Welter, (ed.), *American Writings on Popular Education: The Nineteenth Century* (New York: Bobbs–Merrill Company, Inc., 1971), 182, 183).

38. I say 'nominally' because the appearance of a single curriculum open to all often masks the reality of a number of separate, mutually exclusive—sometimes even mutually hostile—curricula in operation at any one school. For a provocative account of this process of curricular differentiation and accommodation within American secondary schools as a whole, see Arthur G. Powell, Eleanor Farrar, and David K. Cohen, *The Shopping Mall High School: Winners and Losers in the Educational Marketplace* (Boston: Houghton Mifflin, 1985).

39. *West Virginia State Board of Education* v. *Barnette* 319 US 624 (1943). The pledge of allegiance is recited as follows: 'I pledge allegiance to the flag of the United States of America and to the Republic for which it stands, one nation under God, indivisible, with liberty and justice for all' (quoted from memory).

40. This structural accommodation of the public school to the union of private demands possibly gives insight, as well, into the absence of a national education policy, a national curriculum, and national exams in the US. Since, I have argued, the public school under the American model is not a homogeneous entity imposed from above but is instead constructed 'from below' from the multiplicity of individual identities, it makes sense that public schooling is governed on a local as opposed to national level.

41. Although the specific terms and characteristic expressions of contemporary multicultural education are relatively new, it should be noted that multicultural education itself has strong historical antecedents. One example of this is the 'hyphenated' characterization of America. As no less a figure than John Dewey declared in 1916, 'Such terms as Irish-American or Hebrew-American or German-American are false terms, because they seem to assume something that is already in existence in America, to which the other factors may be hitched on. The fact is, the genuine American, the typical American, is himself a hyphenated character. It does not mean that he is part American and that some foreign ingredient is in his makeup. He is no American plus Pole or German. But the American is himself Pole German English French Spanish Italian Greek Irish Scandinavian Bohemian Jew—and so on. The point is to see to it that the hyphen connects instead of separates. And this means at least that our public schools shall teach each factor to respect every other, and shall take pains to enlighten us all as to the great past contributions of every strain in our composite make-up' (John Dewey, speech to the (American) National Education Association (1916): quoted in Nathan Glazer, 'Multicultural "School Wars" Date to 1840s', *Sacramento Bee*, 28 Nov. 1993, FO1.)

42. Peter Gardner gives the argument a sharp twist: 'In reply to the objection that cultivating dispositional tolerance involves an unacceptable predetermination of character, we could point out that all education can be seen in this light; to say we should not attempt to influence children's values is to propose abandoning education' (Peter Gardner, 'Tolerance and Education', in John Horton, (ed.), *Liberalism, Multiculturalism, and Toleration* (London: Macmillan, 1993), 94–5).

43. François Bayrou, *Circular* to teachers and heads of schools: reprinted as 'Le texte du ministre de l'éducation national', *Le Monde*, 21 Sept. 1994, 13. Bayrou's statement was immediately and universally referred to as the 'Bayrou *Circular*', which is how I shall refer to it hereafter. I would like to thank Cathie Lloyd for translating it for me.

44. It may well be objected at this point that my use of 'public school' is misleading, because even though it is true that all state schools are secular, the French government nonetheless heavily subsidizes the 'private' Roman Catholic school system. Insofar as it partially funds a system of separate, homogeneous schools, the French system might be seen as more analogous to the English than to the American system, and consequently as far less neutral or democracy-advancing than I have claimed. The situation is further complicated by the fact that Roman Catholic schools are the only denominational schools that the French state will financially support; Jewish, Muslim, and even Lutheran and Methodist schools have no rights to (and will be refused) governmental funding. I admit that these facts do throw into question the empirical status of the French model. I can only remind the reader that the purview of this chapter is restricted to (officially) public schools, and that these national models should in the end be taken as just that—just models. For more on relations between the French government and Roman Catholic schools, see Ozouf, *L'École, l'Église et la République*.

45. Jules Ferry, 'Discours à la Chambre des Députés', 23 Dec. 1880, in *Vive La République 1792–1992* (Paris: Archives Nationales, 1992), 155 (my translation).
46. Bayrou *Circular*.
47. There are many summaries of the initial incident. Some of the most informative include the following: 'Behind the Yashmak', *The Economist*, 28 Oct. 1989, 68; 'Muslim Pupils Will Take Off Scarves in Class', *Los Angeles Times*, 3 Dec. 1989, A15; 'Muslims Object to School Ban on Headscarves', *Independent*, 15 Jan. 1990, 6; Anna Elisabetta Galeotti, 'Citizenship and Equality: The Place for Toleration', *Political Theory*, 21 (1993), 585–605; and Norma Claire Moruzzi, 'A Problem with Headscarves: Contemporary Complexities of Political and Social Identity', *Political Theory*, 22 (1994), 653–72. An interesting summary and interpretation of the first five years of *l'affaire du foulard* can be found in 'La saga des foulards', *Le Monde*, 13 Oct. 1994, p. v.
48. Moruzzi, 'A Problem with Headscarves', 68.
49. 'France, Reversing Course, Fights Immigrants' Refusal to Be French', *New York Times*, 5 Dec. 1993, 1.
50. 'France Bans Muslim Scarf in Its Schools', *New York Times*, 11 Sept. 1994, 4; 'Chador Wear Spurs Battle in France', *Rocky Mountain News*, 1 Dec. 1994, edn. F, p. 48A.
51. 'Choice of School is State or Catholic', *Independent*, 8 Sept. 1993, 7.
52. Bayrou *Circular*.
53. 'Chador Wear Spurs Battle in France', 48A.
54. See 'Le Conseil d'État tolère sous conditions l'absence scolaire le jour du shabbat', *Le Monde*, 16–17 Apr. 1995, 9; 'Le tribunal de Strasbourg annule l'exclusion de dix-huit jeunes filles voilées', *Le Monde*, 5 May 1995, 12.
55. Philippe Bernard, 'Le Conseil d'État a confirmé l'exclusion de vingt-trois élèves musulmanes voilées', *Le Monde*, 29 Nov. 1996; Marcel Scotto, 'A Strasbourg, Beyhan et ses sœurs ont pu garder le foulard', *Le Monde*, 29 Nov. 1996, 12.
56. See Edward Mortimer, 'Tale of Two Cultures', *Financial Times*, 5 Mar. 1997, 24; Milton Viorst, 'The Muslims of France', *Foreign Affairs*, 75/5 (1996), 78–96; Michel Delberghe, 'Des senateurs se déclarent hostiles à une loi sur le foulard islamique', *Le Monde*, 28 Mar. 1997, 12; Riva Kastoryano, 'Le rétour du foulard islamique', *Le Monde*, 16 Dec. 1996, 14.
57. 'Within republican thought, the political and cultural communities are made interchangeable; national political membership implies acceptance of French cultural values and principles' (Miriam Feldblum, 'Paradoxes of Ethnic Politics: The Case of Franco-Maghrebis in France', *Ethnic and Racial Studies*, 16 (1993), 55). See also Rogers Brubacker, *Citizenship and Nationhood in France and Germany* (Cambridge, Mass.: Harvard University Press, 1992), 46, where he agrees, 'By inventing the national citizen and the legally homogeneous national citizenry, the Revolution simultaneously invented the foreigner. Henceforth citizen and foreigner would be correlative, mutually exclusive, exhaustive categories.'
58. Quoted in Moruzzi, 'A Problem with Headscarves', 65.

59. 'France Bans Muslim Scarf in Its Schools', 4.
60. Pierre Lellouche, quoted in 'France, Reversing Course, Fights Immigrants' Refusal to be French', 1.
61. See 'La saga des foulards', p. v.
62. Elisabeth Badinter, Régis Debray, Alain Finkelkraut, Elisabeth de Fontenary, and Catherine Kintzler, 'Profs, ne capitulons pas!', *Le Nouvel Observateur*, 2–8 Nov. 1989, 30–1; Jean Daniel, 'Le message codé du "foulard" ', *Le Nouvel Observateur*, 26 Oct.–1 Nov. 1989, 30–1.
63. Moruzzi, 'A Problem with Headscarves', 664.
64. This conclusion rings especially true since the Conseil d'État's decision on 14 Apr. 1995 to permit Jewish students to miss Saturday classes, under certain conditions, in order to observe Shabbat. So long as it neither impedes the students' studies nor interferes with the life and public order of the school, headmasters may, at their own discretion, release observant Jewish students from Saturday classes. Although the Conseil d'État's decision was accompanied by a companion judgement that Muslim headscarves are not necessarily 'in themselves' ostentatious, it nonetheless raises the question of whether it is really the principle of 'la laïcité' that remains at work in French education, or if it is more truthfully (and condemnably) anti-Muslim sentiment and fear that drives French public schooling. As one 14-year-old Jewish student comments in this regard, 'Of course I am in favor of permitting [Jewish students to take Saturdays off] when possible. But it is hard to swallow allowing Jews to skip Saturdays when Muslim girls are forbidden to wear the *foulard*' (' "Dieu pardonne, l'examen ne pardonne pas" ', *Le Monde*, 16–17 Apr. 1995, 9 (my translation)). See also 'Le Conseil d'État autorise sous conditions l'absence scolaire le jour du shabbat', *Le Monde*, 16–17 Apr. 1995, 1; 'Le Conseil d'État tolère sous conditions l'absence scolaire le jour du shabbat', 9.
65. See Weber, *Peasants into Frenchmen*.
66. Gutmann, 'Civic Education and Social Diversity', 558.
67. Harry Brighouse makes a similar point in his 'Is There Any Such Thing As Political Liberalism?', *Pacific Philosophical Quarterly*, 75 (1994), 318–32.

Notes to Chapter 5

1. These commitments and practices, of course, may be revised or even rejected over time by autonomous (and also non-autonomous) adults.
2. David Miller, *On Nationality* (Oxford: Oxford University Press, 1995), 145.
3. Miller, *On Nationality*, 142. See also Stephen Macedo, 'Community, Diversity, and Civic Education: Toward a Liberal Political Science of Group Life', *Social Philosophy and Policy*, 14 (1996), 240–68.
4. Ron Dearing, *Review of Qualifications for 16 to 19 Year-Olds* (London: School Curriculum and Assessment Authority, 1996), sect. 2.1.
5. Dearing, *Review of Qualifications for 16 to 19 Year-Olds*, *passim*; see especially sect. 2.3.
6. This may be untrue for some people in a society which provides an uncondi-

tional basic income (UBI). But even in such a state, most citizens will wish to supplement their UBI with paid employment, either because they find satisfaction through working or because they desire a way or quality of life that cannot be supported on the basic income alone. For more on the provision of an unconditional basic income, see Phillipe van Parijs, 'Why Surfers Should Be Fed: The Liberal Case for Unconditional Basic Income', *Philosophy and Public Affairs*, 20/2 (Spring 1991), 101–33, and *Real Freedom for All: What (If Anything) Can Justify Capitalism?* (Oxford: Oxford University Press, 1995).

7. Ray Marshall and Marc Tucker, *Thinking for a Living: Education and the Wealth of Nations* (New York: Basic Books, 1992), p. xiii and *passim*; Robert Reich, *The Work of Nations: Preparing Ourselves for 21st-century Capitalism* (New York: Alfred A. Knopf, 1991), ch. 17; Robert Reich, *Tales of a New America* (New York: Times Books, 1987), 130.

8. See Kenneth A. Strike, *Educational Policy and the Just Society* (Chicago: University of Illinois Press, 1982), ch. 8.

9. Francis Schrag, *Back to Basics* (San Francisco: Jossey-Bass, 1995), 95.

10. Amy Gutmann, *Democratic Education* (Princeton: Princeton University Press, 1987), 55–6.

11. John Dewey comments in a different context in *Democracy and Education* that 'all communication is educative. . . . Try the experiment of communicating, with fullness and accuracy, some experience to another . . . and you will find your own attitude toward your experience changing; otherwise you resort to expletives and ejaculations. The experience has to be formulated to be communicated' (John Dewey, *Democracy and Education* (New York: Free Press, 1944), 5). Harry Brighouse presents a similar argument in 'Egalitarian Liberals and School Choice', *Politics and Society*, 24/4 (1996), 477.

12. Ronald Dworkin, *Taking Rights Seriously* (London: Duckworth, 1977) and 'Do We Have a Right to Pornography?', in *A Matter of Principle* (Oxford: Oxford University Press, 1985), 359–60; John Rawls, *A Theory of Justice* (Cambridge, Mass.: Harvard University Press, 1971), 31.

13. This 'trumping' of democracy exemplifies the difference between liberal and democratic theories of education. Amy Gutmann's *Democratic Education*, for example, is an excellent statement of democratic educational ideals and policy; as a result, in line with her democratic commitments, in this case she favors elevating public deliberation about the aims of education over children's rights to an autonomy-promoting education. While this is compatible with democratic theory, it is incompatible with liberalism, which protects certain civil rights from alteration or truncation via democratic deliberation.

14. Whether the aim of educating for autonomy should be enshrined in the constitution or protected through some other means is discussed in sect. 3.

15. For more on the distinction between negative and positive liberty, see Isaiah Berlin, 'Two Concepts of Liberty', in *Four Essays on Liberty* (Oxford: Oxford University Press, 1969), 118–72. For a persuasive argument concerning the indistinguishability of negative and positive liberty, see Gerald C. MacCallum, Jr., 'Negative and Positive Freedom', in David Miller, (ed.), *Liberty* (Oxford: Oxford University Press, 1991), 100–22.

16. See George Sher, *Desert* (Princeton: Princeton University Press, 1987).
17. Ronald Dworkin, 'What is Equality? Part 1: Equality of Welfare', *Philosophy and Public Affairs*, 10/3 (1981), 189; G. A. Cohen, 'On the Currency of Egalitarian Justice', *Ethics*, 99/4 (1989), 906–44.
18. Ronald Dworkin, 'What is Equality? Part 2: Equality of Resources', *Philosophy and Public Affairs*, 10/4 (1981), 283–345.
19. James Fishkin, *Justice, Equal Opportunity, and the Family* (New Haven: Yale University Press, 1983), 4.
20. Except possibly inversely: poorer children may require/deserve better or more intensive schooling than their better-off counterparts, because the quality of their education outside of school is correspondingly worse. Economically privileged children tend to have access to books in the house, better-educated parents who provide more opportunities for social and linguistic development, after-school dance lessons and football camps, etc., that economically disadvantaged children often lack. Better schooling is one important way that this educational disparity can be bridged, although rarely overcome.
21. For more on the notion of 'common schools', see T. H. McLaughlin, 'Liberalism, Education, and the Common School', *Journal of Philosophy of Education*, 29/2 (1995), 239–55.
22. As Eamonn Callan points out, 'the difference between common and separate schools has to do with institutional ethos and what is taught to whom. To assume either that the common schools worth having are necessarily safe once the pattern of governance and funding historically associated with them persists or that the ideal must be abandoned under any alternative to that pattern is simply irrational. We still lack a good understanding of the educational consequences of different patterns of funding and governance for schools in varying social conditions' (Eamonn Callan, *Creating Citizens* (Oxford: Oxford University Press, 1997), 165). See also Herbert Gintis, 'The Political Economy of School Choice', *Teachers College Record*, 96/3 (1995), 492–511, for a provocative and thoughtful argument that all schools should be privately run but heavily regulated by the state.
23. Private schools are subject to these requirements because it is in every child's basic interest to have such an education. As Sanford Levinson rightly points out, if students who attend private schools were exempted from these requirements then the state would implicitly be acknowledging that it is not in all children's interests to develop their capacities for autonomy or attend a common school. If this were the case, then dissident state school students (and/or their families) could justifiably request exemptions from elements of the state school program with which they disagreed—exemptions against which this book has consistently argued: 'once the state tolerates, either out of constitutional necessity or political ideology, what might be termed counter-hegemonic schools, then it seems hard, if not impossible, for the very same state to say that it has a "compelling state interest" justifying the burden placed on religious students by disallowing them from opting out of certain aspects of the public school curriculum. If the interest is truly "compelling", then one

would think that the state would act aggressively to make sure that no child is denied its enjoyment' (Sanford Levinson, 'Some Reflections on Multiculturalism, "Equal Concern and Respect", and the Establishment Clause of the First Amendment', *University of Richmond Law Review*, 27 (1989), 1011).

24. Stephen Macedo has pointed out to me that differences may be visible 'on the ground' between state-regulated but sectarian-controlled schools and their state-regulated and state-controlled counterparts. Curricula may be taught in a different spirit, or some state regulations may either be implemented according to the letter but not the spirit of the law, or simply be ignored by private operators of a school if they think they will not be caught. On the other hand, these differences may not all favor state-run schools. It is quite possible that some state schools may achieve some aims less successfully than private schools because of public inefficiencies, and the principal or head of a state school may ignore certain state regulations as readily as a private school head. In relation to the latter, many American state schools in the South and elsewhere daily violate the United States Constitution as well as state and local laws by incorporating religion or religious practice into the school: for example, students or teachers recite grace before lunch in the cafeteria before students may eat; teachers invoke God or Jesus during class to correct misbehavior; coaches pray with the football team before each game; and invited speakers exhort students at school assemblies to follow God or rely on their faith as they reach for success in school. (These examples are all drawn from a state-controlled school district in which I have taught; most American readers, I imagine, will be familiar with similar, common examples.) Insofar as even state control does not guarantee the realization of all state educational aims and regulations within a school, therefore, there is no a priori reason to prohibit private control of schools and school services in the service of the liberal educational ideal.

25. See Charles Glenn, *The Myth of the Common School* (Amherst, Mass.: University of Massachusetts Press, 1988).

26. James S. Coleman, *Equality and Achievement in Education* (London: Westview Press, 1990), 213.

27. For an interesting discussion of New Zealand's embrace of school choice principles within a free market rhetoric, see Gerald Grace, 'Education is a Public Good: On the Need to Resist the Domination of Economic Science', in David Bridges and Terence H. McLaughlin, (eds.), *Education and the Market Place* (London: Falmer Press, 1994), 126–37. Jørgen Grønnegaard Christensen provides a good guide to Denmark's embrace of quasi-market principles in 'Institutional Reform and the Governance of Education', a paper presented at The Politics of Education Workshop, ECPR Joint Sessions of Workshops, 27 Apr.–2 May 1995, Bordeaux.

28. See Gilbert Capano, 'Higher Education Reforms in Italy Since 1980: From Centralisation to Autonomy?'; Ivar Bleiklie, 'The Politics of Higher Education Reform'; Leonardo Sánchez-Ferrer, 'Implementation of Educational Policies: The Case of Teaching Staff Reform at the Spanish Universities'. All three

papers were presented at The Politics of Education Workshop, ECPR Joint Sessions of Workshops, 27 Apr.–2 May 1995, Bordeaux. See also Chiara R. Nappi, 'A Tale of Two School Systems', *Dissent*, 43/2 (1996), 60–6.

29. Because of the differences in administration and funding of schools in different countries, as well as broader variation in political structures more generally, it is difficult to describe choice programs in general terms. I will generally adopt American language, in large part because most of the systematic research on school choice has been done in the United States. I thus refer to school districts, for example, rather than to LEAs (local education authorities). I do try, however, to make my descriptions and analysis as applicable to as many different political, educational, and administrative structures as possible.

30. Examples include Britain's former Assisted Places Scheme, which from 1981–98 paid to send a limited number of children from low-income families to independent schools, and Milwaukee, Wisconsin's vaunted state and private school choice program. Milwaukee is unusual in the US in attempting to extend state-funded school choice not only to secular private schools but also to private religious schools, which many people contend breaks the constitutionally imposed barrier between church and state. Such constitutional considerations lead most discussions of school choice in America to distinguish school choice among: state schools only, state and secular private schools, and state, secular private, and religious schools. As I discuss in my response to the 'diversity versus commonality' objection later in the chapter, this distinction has much more political import in the United States than in most European countries.

31. Vouchers were originally proposed by Milton Friedman in *Capitalism and Freedom* (Chicago: University of Chicago Press, 1962), ch. 6. The idea has undergone substantial change and refinement since then.

32. See n. 30 above, and Amy Stuart Wells and Stuart Biegel, 'Public Funds for Private Schools: Political and First Amendment Considerations', *American Journal of Education*, 101/3 (May 1993), 209–33.

33. Notably, however, this money often does not follow the student *back* if she switches schools in the middle of the year—a feature of vouchers that many principals and school heads complain causes severe hardship for schools which accept students throughout the year (e.g. schools with highly transient and often underprivileged populations), or for schools that lose children initially to the siren call of choice but whose parents decide midway through in favor of the original school.

34. See John E. Chubb and Terry M. Moe, *Politics, Markets, and America's Schools* (Washington, DC: Brookings Institution, 1990); Mary Anne Raywid, 'The Case for Student Choice', *Phi Delta Kappa Fastback*, no. 283 (1989), 9–19, 27–32, 36–45; John F. Witte, *Choice in American Education* (Charleston, WV: Policy and Planning Center, Appalachia Educational Laboratory and Madison, Wisc.: Institute of Public Affairs, 1990), 11–17.

35. See Paul E. Peterson, 'Monopoly and Competition in American Education', in William H. Clune and John F. Witte, (eds.), *Choice and Control in American*

Education. Volume 1: The Theory of Choice and Control in Education (London: Falmer Press, 1990), 47–78.

36. James S. Coleman, Kathryn S. Schiller, and Barbara Schneider, 'Parent Choice and Inequality', in Barbara Schneider and James S. Coleman, (eds.), *Parents, Their Children, and Schools* (Oxford: Westview Press, 1993), 147–74.

37. Almost all comprehensive analyses of school choice studies reach the conclusion that school choice provides few definite benefits. See, for example, Witte, *Choice in American Education*; Timothy Young and Evans Clinchy, *Choice in Public Education* (New York: Teachers College Press, 1992); Edith Rasell and Richard Rothstein, (eds.), *School Choice: Examining the Evidence* (Washington, DC: Economic Policy Institute, 1990); Gary A. Orfield, 'Do We Know Anything Worth Knowing About Educational Effects of Magnet Schools?', in William H. Clune and John F. Witte, (eds.), *Choice and Control in American Education. Volume 2: The Practice of Choice, Decentralization and School Restructuring* (London: Falmer Press, 1990), 119–23; Peter W. Cookson, Jr., *School Choice: The Struggle for the Soul of American Education* (New Haven: Yale University Press, 1994); Bruce Fuller and Richard F. Elmore, (eds.), *Who Chooses? Who Loses? Culture, Institutions, and the Unequal Effects of School Choice* (New York: Teachers College Press, 1996); Sharon Gewirtz, Stephen J. Ball, and Richard Bowe, *Markets, Choice and Equity in Education* (Buckingham: Open University Press, 1995).

38. Young and Clinchy, *Choice in Public Education*, 28.

39. Young and Clinchy, *Choice in Public Education*, 31.

40. Young and Clinchy, *Choice in Public Education*, 29.

41. Young and Clinchy, *Choice in Public Education*, 28–30; Richard Rothstein, 'Introduction', in Rasell and Rothstein, (eds.), *School Choice*, 19–20. See also Seymour Fliegel, 'Creative Non-compliance', in Clune and Witte, (eds.), *Choice and Control*, vol. 2, pp. 199–222.

42. Richard Rothstein, 'Introduction', 20.

43. As respected educational policy analysts Richard F. Elmore and Bruce Fuller conclude, 'Greater choice in public education is unlikely, by itself, to increase either the variety of programs available to students or the overall performance of schools. Coupled with strong educational improvement measures, however, choice may increase variety and performance' (Richard F. Elmore and Bruce Fuller, 'Empirical Research on Educational Choice', in Fuller and Elmore, (eds.), *Who Chooses? Who Loses?*, 193).

44. John F. Witte, 'The Milwaukee Parental Choice Program', in Rasell and Rothstein, (eds.), *School Choice*, 70.

45. Young and Clinchy, *Choice in Public Education*, 26–8. See also Witte, *Choice in American Education*, 25–7.

46. Richard Rothstein, 'Introduction', 20. It should be noted that a forthcoming study indicates that District 4's scores are up again as of 1998 (at 80% higher than New York City averages) and claims that this increase is due to parental choice; until the study is published, however, its validity is hard to assess. See Mark Walsh, 'Study Credits Choice With Raising Test Scores', *Education Week*, 17/25 (4 Mar. 1998), 14.

47. Witte, 'The Milwaukee Parental Choice Program', 79; Ellen B. Goldring, 'Parental Involvement and School Choice: Israel and the United States', in Ron Glatter, Philip A. Woods, and Carl Bagley, (eds.), *Choice and Diversity in Schooling: Perspectives and Prospects* (London: Routledge, 1997), 93–4.
48. Amy Stuart Wells, 'The Sociology of School Choice', in Rasell and Rothstein, (eds.), *School Choice*, 29–48; J. Douglas Willms and Frank H. Echols, 'The Scottish Experience of Parental School Choice', in Rasell and Rothstein, (eds.), *School Choice*, 54; Richard F. Elmore, 'Choice as an Instrument of Public Policy: Evidence from Education and Health Care', in Clune and Witte (eds.), *Choice and Control*, vol. 1, pp. 306–7; Philip A. Woods, Carl Bagley, and Ron Glatter, *School Choice and Competition: Markets in the Public Interest?* (London: Routledge, 1998), 124–32.
49. Wells, 'The Sociology of School Choice'; Amy Stuart Wells, 'African-American Students' View of School Choice', in Fuller and Elmore, (eds.), *Who Chooses? Who Loses?*, 35–6, 44.
50. See Mary Erina Driscoll, 'Choice, Achievement, and School Community', in Rasell and Rothstein, (eds.), *School Choice*, 147–72; Claire Smrekar, *The Impact of School Choice and Community* (Albany, NY: State University of New York, 1996); Witte, 'The Milwaukee Parental Choice Program', 84, 95–9.
51. See Chubb and Moe, *Politics, Markets, and America's Schools*.
52. Tony Edwards and Geoff Whitty, 'Specialisation and Selection in Secondary Education', *Oxford Review of Education*, 23/1 (1997), 5–15; John Fitz, David Halpin, and Sally Power, ' "Between a Rock and a Hard Place": Diversity, Institutional Identity, and Grant-maintained Schools', *Oxford Review of Education*, 23/1 (1997), 17–30; David Halpin, Sally Power, and John Fitz, 'Opting Into the Past? Grant-maintained Schools and the Reinvention of Tradition', in Glatter, Woods, and Bagley, (eds.), *Choice and Diversity in Schooling*, 59–70; Ron Glatter, Philip A. Woods, and Carl Bagley, 'Diversity, Differentiation and Hierarchy: School Choice and Parental Preferences', in Glatter, Woods, and Bagley, (eds.), *Choice and Diversity in Schooling*, 7–28; Tony Edwards and Geoff Whitty, 'Marketing Quality: Traditional and Modern Versions of Educational Excellence', in Glatter, Woods, and Bagley, (eds.), *Choice and Diversity in Schooling*, 28–43.
53. Edwards and Whitty, 'Specialisation and Selection', 9.
54. Edwards and Whitty, 'Specialisation and Selection', 7.
55. Fitz, Halpin, and Power, 'Between a Rock and a Hard Place', 21–3.
56. Timothy Kenyon, 'Conservative Education Policy: Its Ideological Contradictions', *Government and Opposition*, 30/2 (Spring 1995), 211–13; Richard Pring, seminar on Philosophy of Education, University of Oxford (Hilary Term 1994).
57. Elmore, 'Choice in Public Education', 87.
58. For a good rebuttal of the use of the term 'consumer' in discussions of educational aims and curricula, see John White, 'Education and the Limits of the Market', in Bridges and McLaughlin, (eds.), *Education and the Market Place*, 117–25. See also David Bridges, 'Parents: Customers or Partners?', in Bridges

and McLaughlin, (eds.), *Education and the Market Place*, 74–7; Colin Wringe, 'Markets, Values and Education', in Bridges and McLaughlin, (eds.), *Education and the Market Place*, 114.

59. Witte, 'The Milwaukee Parental Choice Program', 70; Wells, 'The Sociology of School Choice'; Young and Clinchy, *Choice in Public Education*; Donald Moore and Suzanne Davenport, *The New Improved Sorting Machine* (Madison, Wisc.: National Center for Effective Secondary Schools, 1989).

60. Richard F. Elmore, 'Choice in Public Education', in William Lowe Boyd and Charles Taylor Kerchner, (eds.), *The Politics of Excellence and Choice in Education*, Politics of Education Association Yearbook 1987 (London: Falmer Press, 1987), 83. See also John Witte, 'Who Benefits from the Milwaukee Choice Program?' in Fuller and Elmore, (eds.), *Who Chooses? Who Loses?*, 118–37; Wells, 'African-American Students' View of School Choice', 35–8.

61. Young and Clinchy, *Choice in Public Education*, 24–5. See also Moore and Davenport, *The New Improved Sorting Machine*; Robert L. Crain, 'New York City's Career Magnet High Schools: Lessons About Creating Equity Within Choice Programs', in Rasell and Rothstein, (eds.), *School Choice*, 259–68.

62. Gewirtz, Ball, and Bowe, *Markets, Choice and Equity in Education*; Sally Tomlinson, 'Diversity, Choice, and Ethnicity: The Effects of Educational Markets on Ethnic Minorities', *Oxford Review of Education*, 23/1 (1997), 63–76; Diane Reay and Stephen J. Ball, ' "Spoilt for Choice": The Working Classes and Educational Markets', *Oxford Review of Education*, 23/1 (1997), 89–101.

63. Jeannie Oakes, *Keeping Track: How Schools Structure Inequality* (New Haven: Yale University Press, 1985); Jomills Henry Braddock II, *Tracking: Implications for Student Race-Ethnic Subgroups* (Baltimore, Md.: Johns Hopkins University, Center for Research on Effective Schooling for Disadvantaged Students, 1990); Jomills Henry Braddock II and Marvin P. Dawkins, 'Ability Grouping, Aspirations, and Attainments: Evidence from the National Educational Longitudinal Study of 1988', *Journal of Negro Education*, 62/3 (1993), 324–36; Carnegie Council on Adolescent Development, *Turning Points* (New York: Carnegie Council on Adolescent Development, 1989).

64. Oakes, *Keeping Track*; Anne Wheelock, *Crossing the Tracks: How 'Untracking' Can Save America's Schools* (New York: New Books, 1992); Robert Slavin, 'Ability Grouping and Student Achievement in Elementary Schools: A Best-evidence Synthesis', *Review of Educational Research*, 57 (1987), 347–50; Robert Slavin, 'Ability Grouping and Student Achievement in Secondary Schools: A Best-evidence Synthesis', *Review of Educational Research*, 60 (1990), 471–99; C. L. Kulik and J. Kulik, 'Effects of Ability Grouping on Secondary School Students: A Meta-analysis of Evaluation Findings', *American Educational Research Journal*, 19 (1982), 415–28; J. A. Kulik and C. L. Kulik, 'Effects of Ability Grouping on Student Achievement', *Equity and Excellence*, 23 (1990), 22–30; A. C. Kerckhoff, 'Effects of Ability Grouping in British Secondary Schools', *American Sociological Review*, 51 (1986), 842–58.

65. John Witte, 'The Milwaukee Parental Choice Program', 90–3.

66. Smrekar, *The Impact of School Choice and Community*.

67. As with almost every term used in the school choice debate, 'controlled choice' does not have a single meaning upon which all people would agree, and some controlled choice programs do not exhibit all of the characteristics listed below. The most successful controlled choice program, however, which is located in Cambridge, Massachusetts, and is viewed by many researchers across the US as the most promising, efficient, and equitable way to implement school choice, does incorporate the provisions listed in the text. For more on both the Cambridge, Massachusetts, program and the concept of controlled choice, see: Amy Stuart Wells, 'Public School Choice: Issues and Concerns for Urban Educators', ERIC/CUE Digest No. 63 (New York: ERIC Clearinghouse on Urban Education, n.d.) (ED 322275); Michael J. Alves and Charles V. Willie, 'Controlled Choice Assignments: A New Approach to School Desegregation', *Urban Review*, 19/2 (1987), 67–86; Young and Clinchy, *Choice in Public Education*, 25–6, 30–2, 37–8; Cookson, *School Choice*, 56–64, 93–4; William H. Clune, 'Introduction', in Clune and Witte, (eds.), *Choice and Control*, vol. 2, p. 5. See also Peter W. Cookson, Jr., 'School Choice and the Creation of Community', in Rina Shapira and Peter W. Cookson, Jr., (eds.), *Autonomy and Choice in Context: An International Perspective* (Oxford: Pergamon/Elsevier Science Ltd., 1997), 280–3, for a detailed description of two other admirable controlled-choice cities (Fall River, Massachusetts, and White Plains, New York) modeled on the Cambridge plan.

68. The latter discriminates between active and passive choosers, and is open to political pressure from well-connected parents, neither of which is compatible with liberal political ideals. See David Bennett, 'Choice and Desegregation', in Clune and Witte, (eds.), *Choice and Control*, vol. 2, pp. 128–9.

69. As I discuss later in the chapter, the characteristics of a 'common' school will vary from state to state and even community to community, depending on what divisions (racial, ethnic, class, religious, etc.) are significant in the community. See the next subsection ('Diversity and commonality among liberal schools').

70. Young and Clinchy, *Choice in Public Education*, 27; Bennett, 'Choice and Desegregation', 138.

71. See Joseph Raz, *The Morality of Freedom* (Oxford: Clarendon Press, 1986), 375.

72. Raz, *The Morality of Freedom*, 379.

73. Rawls, *Political Liberalism* (New York: Columbia University Press, 1993), 13.

74. Barry A. Kosmin and Seymour P. Lachman, *One Nation Under God: Religion in Contemporary American Society* (New York: Harmony Books, 1993), 8–9, 282.

75. Kosmin and Lachman, *One Nation Under God*, 155–208.

76. James Fishkin, *The Dialogue of Justice: Toward a Self-reflective Society* (New Haven: Yale University Press, 1992), 130; cited in Eamonn Callan, *Creating Citizens* (Oxford: Oxford University Press, 1997), 163–4.

77. Rosalie Osmond, *Changing Perspectives: Christian Culture and Morals in England Today* (London: Darton, Longman and Todd, 1993); Peter Brierley, *'Christian' England: What the English Church Census Reveals* (London: MARC Europe, 1991); Grace Davie, *Religion in Britain Since 1945: Believing without Belonging* (Oxford: Blackwell, 1994).

78. Kosmin and Lachman, *One Nation Under God*, 9; Steve Bruce, *Religion in Modern Britain* (Oxford: Oxford University Press, 1995), 35–40; John Wolffe, ' "And There's Another Country . . .": Religion, the State, and British Identities', in Gerald Parsons, (ed.), *The Growth of Religious Diversity: Britain from 1945*, vol. 2 (London: Routledge, 1994), 88.

79. Studies show that 'there is likely to be no measurable effect on attitudes towards Christianity among children attending Church of England schools (indeed in some cases any effect that did exist was found to be negative), although the effects of Catholic education were usually more positive' (Davie, *Religion in Britain Since 1945*, 134). A study of Cornish mothers and children further confirmed that 'hostility' actually arose if teachers or other school officials seemed to be too active in trying to influence children's religious beliefs (Davie, *Religion in Britain Since 1945*, 135). For additional evidence of the non-doctrinal nature of religious education, conceived instead as an 'ethical core . . . of tolerance, neighbourliness and kindness', see Gerald Parsons, 'There and Back Again? Religion and the 1944 and 1988 Education Acts', in Parsons, (ed.), *The Growth of Religious Diversity*, vol. 2, 169 ff.

80. See Parsons' review and analysis of 'Agreed Syllabuses' for religious education in 'There and Back Again?'

81. For a thoughtful, related set of criticisms of England and Wales' National Curriculum, developed for the first time as a result of the 1988 Education Act, see Philip O'Hear and John White, *A National Curriculum for All: Laying the Foundations for Success*, Education and Training Paper No. 6 (London: IPPR, 1992), and John White, *Education and the Good Life: Beyond the National Curriculum* (London: Kogan Page, 1990).

82. Diane Ravitch insightfully analyzes the value and potential pitfalls of establishing US national standards in her book *National Standards in American Education: A Citizen's Guide* (Washington, DC: Brookings Institution, 1995).

83. Such a reform faces an additional challenge in Britain, which has no formal, codified constitution. This fact attests to the imperfect character of Britain as a liberal state, however, rather than to the inappropriateness or irrelevance of embedding basic rights—including children's rights to an autonomy-promoting education—in a constitution.

84. *Pierce* v. *Society of Sisters* 268 US 510 (1925). See Barbara Bennett Woodhouse, ' "Who Owns the Child?": *Meyer* and *Pierce* and the Child as Property', *William and Mary Law Review*, 33/4 (Summer 1992), 995–1122, for a marvelous, revisionist discussion of this case and its implications for the relationship among children, families, and the state.

85. *Pierce*, at 535.

86. *Pierce*, at 510.

87. *Wisconsin* v. *Yoder* 406 US 205 (1972).

88. Aristotle's dual use of the word 'constitution' in the *Politics* is apposite here: the psychological or social 'constitution' of a liberal state must be in accord with its legal, textual 'constitution' in order for it to function effectively and to realize the principles expressed in the latter document.

BIBLIOGRAPHY

ACKERMAN, BRUCE, *Social Justice in the Liberal State*, New Haven: Yale University Press, 1980.

ALEXANDER, KARL and AARON M. PALLAS, 'School Sector and Cognitive Performance: When is a Little a Little?', *Sociology of Education*, 58/2 (April 1985): 115–28.

ALVES, MICHAEL J., and CHARLES V. WILLIE, 'Controlled Choice Assignments: A New Approach to School Desegregation', *The Urban Review*, 19/2 (1987): 67–86.

ARISTOTLE, *Nicomachean Ethics*, rev. trans. J. Barnes, Princeton: Princeton University Press, 1984.

ARMOR, DAVID, *et al.*, *Analysis of the School Preferred Reading Program in Selected Los Angeles Minority Schools*, Santa Monica, Calif.: Rand Corporation, 1976.

ARNESON, RICHARD J. and IAN SHAPIRO, 'Democratic Autonomy and Religious Freedom: A Critique of *Wisconsin v. Yoder*', in Ian Shapiro and Russell Hardin (eds.), *Nomos XXXVIII: Political Order*, New York: New York University Press, 1996: 365–411.

ASSOCIATION FOR SUPERVISION AND CURRICULUM DEVELOPMENT, *Parent Involvement*, Alexandria, Va.: Association for Supervision and Curriculum Development, 1995.

BADINTER, ELISABETH, RÉGIS DEBRAY, ALAIN FINKELKRAUT, ELISABETH DE FONTENARY, and CATHERINE KINTZLER, 'Profs, ne capitulons pas!', *Le Nouvel Observateur*, 2–8 Nov. 1989: 30–1.

BARBER, BENJAMIN, *An Aristocracy of Everyone: The Politics of Education and the Future of America*, New York: Ballantine Books, 1992.

BASTIANI, JOHN (ed.), *Parents and Teachers 2: From Policy to Practice*. Windsor: NFER-Nelson, 1988.

BAYROU, FRANÇOIS, 'Le texte du ministre de l'éducation nationale', *Le Monde*, 21 Sept. 1994: 13.

'Behind the Yashmak', *The Economist*, 28 Oct. 1989: 68.

BEMPECHAT, JANINE, 'The Role of Parent Involvement in Children's Academic Achievement: A Review of the Literature', *Trends and Issues*, no. 14, New York: ERIC Clearinghouse on Urban Education, June 1994.

BENJAMIN, GAIL, *Japanese Lessons*, New York: New York University Press, 1997.

BENN, STANLEY, *A Theory of Freedom*, Cambridge: Cambridge University Press, 1988.

BENNETT, DAVID, 'Choice and Desegregation', in William H. Clune and John F. Witte (eds.), *Choice and Control in American Education. Volume 2: The Practice of Choice, Decentralization and School Restructuring*, London: Falmer Press, 1990: 125–52.

BERLIN, ISAIAH, *Four Essays on Liberty*, Oxford: Oxford University Press, 1969.

BERNARD, PHILIPPE, 'Le Conseil d'État a confirmé l'exclusion de vingt-trois élèves musulmanes voilées', *Le Monde*, 29 Nov. 1996, 12.

BLEIKLIE, IVAR, 'The Politics of Higher Education Reform', paper presented at the Politics of Education Workshop, ECPR Joint Sessions of Workshops, Bordeaux, 27 Apr.–2 May 1995.

BOWLES, SAMUEL, and HERBERT GINTIS, *Schooling in Capitalist America*, London: Routledge and Kegan Paul, 1976.

BOYD, WILLIAM LOWE, and CHARLES TAYLOR KERCHNER (eds.), *The Politics of Excellence and Choice in Education* (Politics of Education Association Yearbook 1987), London: Falmer Press, 1987.

BRADDOCK, JOMILLS HENRY, II, *Tracking: Implications for Student Race-Ethnic Subgroups*, Baltimore, Md: Johns Hopkins University, Center for Research on Effective Schooling for Disadvantaged Students, 1990.

—— and MARVIN P. DAWKINS, 'Ability Grouping, Aspirations, and Attainments: Evidence from the National Educational Longitudinal Study of 1988', *Journal of Negro Education*, 62/3 (1993): 324–36.

BRIDGES, DAVID, 'Parents: Customers or Partners?', in David Bridges and Terence H. McLaughlin (eds.), *Education and the Market Place*, London: Falmer Press, 1994: 65–79.

—— and TERENCE H. MCLAUGHLIN (eds.), *Education and the Market Place*, London: Falmer Press, 1994.

BRIERLEY, PETER, *'Christian' England: What the English Church Census Reveals*, London: MARC Europe, 1991.

BRIGHOUSE, HARRY, 'Civic Education and Liberal Legitimacy', *Ethics*, 108 (1998): 727–53.

—— 'Egalitarian Liberals and School Choice', *Politics and Society*, 24/4 (1996): 457–86.

—— 'Is There Any Such Thing As Political Liberalism?', *Pacific Philosophical Quarterly*, 75 (1994): 318–32.

BRUBACKER, ROGERS, *Citizenship and Nationhood in France and Germany*, Cambridge, Mass.: Harvard University Press, 1992.

BRUCE, STEVE, *Religion in Modern Britain*, Oxford: Oxford University Press, 1995.

BRYK, ANTHONY S., VALERIE E. LEE, and PETER B. HOLLAND, *Catholic Schools and the Common Good*, Cambridge, Mass.: Harvard University Press, 1993.

BURTT, SHELLEY, 'In Defense of *Yoder*: Parental Authority and the Public Schools', in Ian Shapiro and Russell Hardin (eds.), *Nomos XXXVIII: Political Order*, New York: New York University Press, 1996: 412–37.

BUSHNELL, HORACE, 'Common Schools: A Discourse on the Modifications Demanded by the Roman Catholics', in Rush Welter (ed.), *American Writings on*

Popular Education: The Nineteenth Century, New York: Bobbs-Merrill Company, Inc., 1971, 174–99.

CALLAN, EAMONN, *Autonomy and Schooling*, Montreal: McGill-Queen's University Press, 1988.

—— *Creating Citizens*, Oxford: Oxford University Press, 1997.

—— 'Faith, Worship, and Reason in Religious Upbringing', *Journal of Philosophy of Education*, 22/2 (1988): 183–93.

—— 'Political Liberalism and Political Education', *Review of Politics*, 58/1 (Winter 1996): 5–33.

—— 'Tradition and Integrity in Moral Education', *American Journal of Education*, 101 (1992): 1–28.

CAPANO, GILBERT, 'Higher Education Reforms in Italy Since 1980: From Centralisation to Autonomy?', paper presented at the Politics of Education Workshop, ECPR Joint Sessions of Workshops, Bordeaux, 27 Apr.–2 May 1995.

CARNEGIE COUNCIL ON ADOLESCENT DEVELOPMENT, *Turning Points*, New York: Carnegie Council on Adolescent Development, 1989.

CENTRAL ADVISORY COMMITTEE FOR EDUCATION, *Children and their Primary Schools* (Plowden Report), London: HMSO, 1967.

'Chador Wear Spurs Battle in France', *Rocky Mountain News*, 1 Dec. 1994: edn. F, 48A.

CHAVKIN, NANCY FEYL (ed.), *Families and Schools in a Pluralistic Society*, Albany, NY: State University of New York Press, 1993.

CHITTY, CLYDE, *Towards a New Education System: The Victory of the New Right?*, London: Falmer Press, 1989.

'Choice of School is State or Catholic', *Independent*, 8 Sept. 1993: 7.

CHRISTENSEN, JØRGEN GRØNNEGAARD, 'Institutional Reform and the Governance of Education', paper presented the Politics of Education Workshop, ECPR Joint Sessions of Workshops, Bordeaux, 27 Apr.–2 May 1995.

CHRISTMAN, JOHN (ed.), *The Inner Citadel: Essays on Individual Autonomy*, Oxford: Oxford University Press, 1989.

CHUBB, JOHN E. and TERRY M. MOE, *Politics, Markets, and America's Schools*, Washington, DC: Brookings Institution, 1990.

CLUNE, WILLIAM H., 'Introduction', in William H. Clune and John F. Witte (eds.), *Choice and Control in American Education. Volume 2: The Practice of Choice, Decentralization and School Restructuring*, London: Falmer Press, 1990.

—— and JOHN F. WITTE (eds.), *Choice and Control in American Education*, 2 vols., London: Falmer Press, 1990.

COHEN, G. A., 'On the Currency of Egalitarian Justice', *Ethics*, 99/4 (1989): 906–44.

COHEN, HOWARD, *Equal Rights for Children*, Totowa, NJ: Rowman and Littlefield, 1980.

COLEMAN, JAMES S., *Equality and Achievement in Education*, London: Westview Press, 1990.

—— and THOMAS HOFFER, *Public and Private High Schools: The Impact of Communities*, New York: Basic Books, 1987.

—— —— and SALLY KILGORE, *High School Achievement: Public, Catholic and Other Private Schools Compared*, New York: Basic Books, 1982.

—— —— —— *Public and Private Schools*, Washington, DC: National Center for Education Statistics, 1981.

—— KATHRYN S. SCHILLER, and BARBARA SCHNEIDER, 'Parent Choice and Inequality', in Barbara Schneider and James S. Coleman (eds.), *Parents, Their Children, and Schools*, Oxford: Westview Press, 1993: 147–74.

COMER, JAMES P., 'Educating Poor Minority Children', *Scientific American*, 259/5 (Nov. 1988): 2–8.

'Le Conseil d'État autorise sous conditions l'absence scolaire le jour du shabbat', *Le Monde*, 16–17 Apr. 1995: 1.

'Le Conseil d'État tolère sous conditions l'absence scolaire le jour du shabbat', *Le Monde*, 16–17 Apr. 1995: 9.

COOKSON, PETER W., JR., 'School Choice and the Creation of Community', in Rina Shapira and Peter W. Cookson, Jr. (eds.), *Autonomy and Choice in Context: An International Perspective*, Oxford: Pergamon/Elsevier Science Ltd., 1997: 271–96.

—— *School Choice: The Struggle for the Soul of American Education*, New Haven: Yale University Press, 1994.

CORNOY, MARTIN, and HENRY M. LEVIN., *Schooling and Work in the Democratic State*, Stanford: Stanford University Press, 1985.

COUNCIL OF CHIEF STATE SCHOOL OFFICERS, *A Guide for State Action: Early Childhood and Family Education*, Washington, DC: Council of Chief State School Officers, 1988.

CRAIN, ROBERT L., 'New York City's Career Magnet High Schools: Lessons About Creating Equity Within Choice Programs', in Edith Rasell and Richard Rothstein (eds.), *School Choice: Examining the Evidence*, Washington, DC: Economic Policy Institute, 1990: 259–68.

CRANSTON, MAURICE, *John Locke*, Oxford: Oxford University Press, 1985.

CREMIN, LAWRENCE A., *Popular Education and Its Discontents*, New York: Harper and Row, 1990.

DANIEL, JEAN, 'Le message codé du "foulard" ', *Le Nouvel Observateur*, 26 Oct.–1 Nov. 1989: 30–1.

DAVID, MIRIAM E., *Parents, Gender, and Education Reform*, Cambridge: Polity Press, 1993.

DAVIE, GRACE, *Religion in Britain Since 1945: Believing without Belonging*, Oxford: Blackwell, 1994.

DEARING, RON, *The National Curriculum and Its Assessment: Final Report*, London: School Curriculum and Assessment Authority, 1994.

—— *Review of Qualifications for 16 to 19 Year-Olds*, London: School Curriculum and Assessment Authority, 1996.

DELBERGHE, MICHEL, 'Des senateurs se déclarent hostiles à une loi sur le foulard islamique', *Le Monde*, 28 Mar. 1997, 12.

DELGADO-GAITAN, CONCHA, 'Involving Parents in the Schools: A Process of Empowerment', *American Journal of Education*, 100/1 (Nov. 1991): 20–46.

DEPARTMENT FOR EDUCATION, *Our Children's Education: The Updated Parent's Charter*, London: HMSO, 1994.

—— *Statistics of Education: Schools*, London: HMSO, 1993.

DEPARTMENT OF EDUCATION AND SCIENCE, *The Organization of Secondary Education* (Circular 10/65), London: HMSO, 1965.

DEWEY, JOHN, *Democracy and Education*, New York: Free Press, 1944.

—— *Human Nature and Conduct*, New York: Random House, 1922.

' "Dieu pardonne, l'examen ne pardonne pas" ', *Le Monde*, 16–17 Apr. 1995: 9.

DRISCOLL, MARY ERINA, 'Choice, Achievement, and School Community', in Edith Rasell and Richard Rothstein (eds.), *School Choice: Examining the Evidence*, Washington, DC: Economic Policy Institute, 1990: 147–72.

DURKHEIM, ÉMILE, *The Division of Labor in Society*, trans. W. D. Halls, New York: Free Press, 1984 (1st pub. 1933).

DWORKIN, GERALD, *The Theory and Practice of Autonomy*. Cambridge: Cambridge University Press, 1988.

DWORKIN, RONALD, 'Do We Have a Right to Pornography?', *A Matter of Principle*, Oxford: Oxford University Press, 1985: 335–72.

—— 'In Defense of Equality', *Social Philosophy and Policy*, 1/1 (1983): 24–40.

—— 'Liberalism', in *A Matter of Principle*, Oxford: Oxford University Press, 1985: 181–204.

—— *Taking Rights Seriously*, London: Duckworth, 1977.

—— 'What is Equality? Part 1: Equality of Welfare', *Philosophy and Public Affairs*, 10/3 (1981): 185–246.

—— 'What is Equality? Part 2: Equality of Resources', *Philosophy and Public Affairs*, 10/4 (1981): 283–345.

DWYER, JAMES G., 'Parents' Religion and Children's Welfare: Debunking the Doctrine of Parents' Rights', *California Law Review*, 82/6 (1994): 1371–1450.

Education Act 1944, London: HMSO, 1944.

Education Act 1980, London: HMSO, 1980.

Education Reform Act 1988, London: HMSO, 1988.

EDWARDS, TONY, and GEOFF WHITTY, 'Marketing Quality: Traditional and Modern Versions of Educational Excellence', in Ron Glatter, Philip A. Woods, and Carl Bagley (eds.), *Choice and Diversity in Schooling: Perspectives and Prospects*, London: Routledge, 1997: 28–43.

—— —— 'Specialisation and Selection in Secondary Education', *Oxford Review of Education*, 23/1 (1997): 5–15.

ELMORE, RICHARD F., 'Choice as an Instrument of Public Policy: Evidence from Education and Health Care', in William H. Clune and John F. Witte (eds.), *Choice and Control in American Education. Volume 1: The Theory of Choice and Control in Education*, London: Falmer Press, 1990: 285–317.

—— 'Choice in Public Education', in William Lowe Boyd and Charles Taylor Kerchner (eds.), *The Politics of Excellence and Choice in Education* (Politics of Education Association Yearbook 1987), London: Falmer Press, 1987: 79–98.

—— and BRUCE FULLER, 'Empirical Research on Educational Choice', in Bruce

Fuller and Richard F. Elmore (eds.), *Who Chooses? Who Loses? Culture, Institutions, and the Unequal Effects of School Choice*, New York: Teachers College Press, 1996: 187–201.

EPSTEIN, JOYCE L., 'Effects on Student Achievement of Teachers' Practices of Parental Involvement', in *Advances in Reading/Language Research*, vol. 5, Greenwich, Conn.: JAI Press, 1991: 261–76.

—— 'How Do We Improve Programs of Parent Involvement?', *Educational Horizons*, 66/2 (1988): 58–9.

—— *School and Family Partnerships: Report No. 6*, Baltimore, Md.: Center on Families, Communities, Schools, and Children's Learning, Johns Hopkins University, 1992.

—— 'School/Family/Community Partnerships: Caring for the Children We Share', *Phi Delta Kappan*, 76/9 (May 1995): 701–12.

—— and SUSAN DAUBER, 'School Programs and Practices of Parent Involvement in Inner-city Elementary and Middle Schools', *Elementary School Journal*, 91/3 (1988): 289–305.

FEHRMANN, PAUL G., TIMOTHY Z. KEITH, and THOMAS M. REIMERS, 'Home Influence on School Learning: Direct and Indirect Effects of Parental Involvement on High School Grades', *Journal of Educational Research*, 80/6 (Aug. 1987): 330–7.

FEINBERG, JOEL, 'Autonomy', in John Christman (ed.), *The Inner Citadel: Essays on Individual Autonomy*, Oxford: Oxford University Press, 1989: 27–53.

FELDBLUM, MIRIAM, 'Paradoxes of Ethnic Politics: The Case of Franco-Maghrebis in France', *Ethnic and Racial Studies*, 16 (1993): 52–74.

FERRY, JULES, 'Discours à la Chambre des Députés', in *Vive La République 1792–1992*, Paris: Archives Nationales, 1992: 155.

FINDERS, MARGARET, and CYNTHIA LEWIS, 'Why Some Parents Don't Come to School', *Educational Leadership*, 51 (May 1994): 50–4.

FISHKIN, JAMES, *Justice, Equal Opportunity, and the Family*, New Haven: Yale University Press, 1983.

FITZ, JOHN, DAVID HALPIN, and SALLY POWER, ' "Between a Rock and a Hard Place": Diversity, Institutional Identity, and Grant-maintained Schools', *Oxford Review of Education*, 23/1 (1997): 17–30.

FLIEGEL, SEYMOUR, 'Creative Non-compliance', in William H. Clune and John F. Witte (eds.), *Choice and Control in American Education. Volume 2: The Practice of Choice, Decentralization and School Restructuring*. London: Falmer Press, 1990: 199–222.

'France Bans Muslim Scarf in Its Schools', *New York Times*, 11 Sept. 1994: 4.

'France, Reversing Course, Fights Immigrants' Refusal to Be French', *New York Times*, 5 Dec. 1993: 1.

FRANKFURT, HARRY, 'Freedom of the Will and the Concept of a Person', in John Christman (ed.), *The Inner Citadel: Essays on Individual Autonomy*, Oxford: Oxford University Press, 1989: 63–76.

FRIED, CHARLES, *Right and Wrong*, Cambridge, Mass.: Harvard University Press, 1978.

FRIEDMAN, MILTON, *Capitalism and Freedom*, Chicago: University of Chicago Press, 1962.

FRISCH, LAWRENCE E., 'On Licentious Licensing: A Reply to Hugh LaFollette', *Philosophy and Public Affairs*, 11/2 (1981): 173–80.

FRUCHTER, NORM, ANNE GALLETTA, and J. LYNNE WHITE, 'New Directions in Parent Involvement', *Equity and Choice*, 9/3 (Spring 1993): 33–43.

FULLER, BRUCE, and RICHARD F. ELMORE (eds.), *Who Chooses? Who Loses? Culture, Institutions, and the Unequal Effects of School Choice*, New York: Teachers College Press, 1996.

FULLER, TIMOTHY (ed.), *Michael Oakeshott on Education: The Voice of Liberal Learning*, New Haven: Yale University Press, 1989.

FULLINWIDER, ROBERT K. (ed.), *Public Education in a Multicultural Society*, Cambridge: Cambridge University Press, 1996.

GALEOTTI, ANNA ELISABETTA, 'Citizenship and Equality: The Place for Toleration', *Political Theory*, 21 (1993): 585–605.

GALSTON, WILLIAM, *Liberal Purposes*, Cambridge: Cambridge University Press, 1991.

—— 'Two Concepts of Liberalism', *Ethics*, 105/3 (Apr. 1995): 516–34.

GARDNER, PETER, 'Religious Upbringing and the Liberal Ideal of Religious Autonomy', *Journal of Philosophy of Education*, 22/1 (1988): 89–105.

—— 'Tolerance and Education', in John Horton (ed.), *Liberalism, Multiculturalism, and Toleration*, London: Macmillan, 1993: 83–103.

GAUTHIER, DAVID, *Morals by Agreement*, Oxford: Oxford University Press, 1986.

GEWIRTZ, SHARON, STEPHEN J. BALL, and RICHARD BOWE, *Markets, Choice and Equity in Education*, Buckingham: Open University Press, 1995.

GINTIS, HERBERT, 'The Political Economy of School Choice', *Teachers College Record*, 96/3 (1995): 492–511.

GLATTER, RON, PHILIP A. WOODS, and CARL BAGLEY (eds.), *Choice and Diversity in Schooling: Perspectives and Prospects*, London: Routledge, 1997.

—— —— —— 'Diversity, Differentiation and Hierarchy: School Choice and Parental Preferences', in Ron Glatter, Philip A. Woods, and Carl Bagley (eds.), *Choice and Diversity in Schooling: Perspectives and Prospects*, London: Routledge, 1997: 7–28.

GLAZER, NATHAN, 'Multicultural "School Wars" Date to 1840s', *Sacramento Bee*, 28 Nov. 1993: FO1.

GLENN, CHARLES, *The Myth of the Common School*, Amherst, Mass.: University of Massachusetts Press, 1988.

GOLDRING, ELLEN B., 'Parental Involvement and School Choice: Israel and the United States', in Ron Glatter, Philip A. Woods, and Carl Bagley (eds.), *Choice and Diversity in Schooling: Perspectives and Prospects*, London: Routledge, 1997: 86–101.

GRACE, GERALD, 'Education is a Public Good: On the Need to Resist the Domination of Economic Science', in David Bridges and Terence H. McLaughlin (eds.), *Education and the Market Place*, London: Falmer Press, 1994: 126–37.

GRAHAM, KEITH (ed.), *Contemporary Political Philosophy*, Cambridge: Cambridge University Press, 1982.

GUTMANN, AMY, 'Children, Paternalism, and Education', *Philosophy and Public Affairs*, 9/4 (1980): 338–58.

—— 'Civic Education and Social Diversity', *Ethics*, 105/3 (Apr. 1995): 557–79.

—— *Democratic Education*, Princeton: Princeton University Press, 1987.

HABERMAN, BONNA DEVORA, 'What is the Content of Education in a Democratic Society?', *Journal of Philosophy of Education*, 28/2 (1994): 183–9.

HALPIN, DAVID, SALLY POWER, and JOHN FITZ, 'Opting Into the Past? Grant-maintained Schools and the Reinvention of Tradition', in Ron Glatter, Philip A. Woods, and Carl Bagley (eds.), *Choice and Diversity in Schooling: Perspectives and Prospects*, London: Routledge, 1997: 59–70.

HARRIS, JOHN, 'The Political Status of Children', in Keith Graham (ed.), *Contemporary Political Philosophy*, Cambridge: Cambridge University Press, 1982: 35–55.

HAYNES, NORRIS M., and JAMES P. COMER, 'The Yale School Development Program: Process, Outcomes, and Policy Implications', *Urban Education*, 28/2 (July 1993): 166–99.

HENDERSON, ANNE T. (ed.), *The Evidence Continues to Grow: Parent Involvement Improves Student Achievement*, Columbia, Md.: National Committee for Citizens in Education, 1987.

—— 'Parents Are a School's Best Friends', *Phi Delta Kappan*, 78 (Oct. 1988): 148–53.

—— CARL L. MARBURGER, and THEODORA OOMS, *Beyond the Bake Sale: An Educator's Guide to Working with Parents*, Columbia, Md.: National Committee for Citizens in Education, 1986.

HOBBES, THOMAS, *Leviathan*, Cambridge: Cambridge University Press, 1991 (1st pub. 1651).

HORTON, JOHN (ed.), *Liberalism, Multiculturalism, and Toleration*, London: Macmillan, 1993.

ILLICH, IVAN, *Deschooling Society*, London: Calder and Boyars, 1971.

JACKSON, PHILIP W., *Life in Classrooms*, New York: Holt, Rinehart and Winston, 1968.

JOHNSON, DAPHNE, and JOYCE RANSOM, 'Family and School—the Relationship Reassessed', in John Bastiani (ed.), *Parents and Teachers 2: From Policy to Practice*, Windsor: NFER-Nelson, 1988: 58–71.

JOHNSON, VIVIAN R., 'Parent Centers Send a Clear Message: Come Be a Partner In Educating Your Children', *Equity and Choice*, 10/2 (Winter 1994): 42–4.

JOUCKS, HAZEL, 'Increasing Parent/Family Involvement: Ten Ideas That Work', *NASSP Bulletin*, vol. 76, no. 543 (April 1992): 19–23.

JOWETT, SANDRA, and MARY BAGINSKY, with MORAG MACDONALD MACNEIL, *Building Bridges: Parental Involvement in Schools*, Windsor: NFER-Nelson, 1991.

KALLAGHAN, THOMAS, et al., *The Home Environment and School Learning: Promoting Parental Involvement in the Education of Children*, San Francisco: Jossey-Bass, Inc., 1993.

KASTORYANO, RIVA, 'Le retour du foulard islamique', *Le Monde*, 16 Dec. 1996: 14.

KEDDIE, NELL, 'Classroom Knowledge', in Michael F. D. Young (ed.), *Knowledge and Control*, London: Collier-Macmillan Publishers, 1971: 133–60.

KENYON, TIMOTHY, 'Conservative Education Policy: Its Ideological Contradictions', *Government and Opposition*, 30/2 (Spring 1995): 198–220.

KERCKHOFF, A. C., 'Effects of Ability Grouping in British Secondary Schools', *American Sociological Review*, 51 (1986): 842–58.

KILPATRICK, WILLIAM HEARD, 'Indoctrination and Respect for Persons', in I. A. Snook (ed.), *Concepts of Indoctrination*, London: Routledge and Kegan Paul, 1972: 47–54.

KLEINIG, JOHN, *Paternalism*, Manchester: Manchester University Press, 1983.

KOSMIN, BARRY A., and SEYMOUR P. LACHMAN, *One Nation Under God: Religion in Contemporary American Society*, New York: Harmony Books, 1993.

KULIK, C. L., and J. KULIK, 'Effects of Ability Grouping on Secondary School Students: A Meta-analysis of Evaluation Findings', *American Educational Research Journal*, 19 (1982): 415–28.

KULIK, J. A. and C. L. KULIK, 'Effects of Ability Grouping on Student Achievement', *Equity and Excellence*, 23 (1990): 22–30.

KYMLICKA, WILL, *Liberalism, Community, and Culture*, Oxford: Oxford University Press, 1989.

—— *Multicultural Citizenship*, Oxford: Oxford University Press, 1995.

LAFOLLETTE, HUGH, 'Licensing Parents', *Philosophy and Public Affairs*, 9/2 (1980): 182–97.

—— 'A Response to Frisch', *Philosophy and Public Affairs*, 11/2 (1981): 181–3.

LEE, VICTOR, and PRAJNA DAS GUPTA (eds.), *Children's Cognitive and Language Development*, Milton Keynes: The Open University and Oxford: Blackwell, 1995.

LEVINSON, SANFORD, 'Some Reflections on Multiculturalism, "Equal Concern and Respect", and the Establishment Clause of the First Amendment', *University of Richmond Law Review*, 27 (1989): 989–1021.

LICKONA, THOMAS, *Educating for Character: How Our Schools Can Teach Respect and Responsibility*, New York: Bantam, 1992.

—— *What Is Good Character? And How Can We Develop It In Our Children?*, Bloomington, Ind.: Poynter Center, 1991.

LISTER, IAN (ed.), *Deschooling*, Cambridge: Cambridge University Press, 1974.

LOCKE, JOHN, 'An Essay Concerning the True Original, Extent and End of Civil Government', in *Two Treatises of Government*, London: Everyman's Library, 1990: 117–242 (1st pub. 1690). Referred to in the text as *Second Treatise*.

LORD SWANN, *Education for All*, London: HMSO, 1985.

LYNN, LEON, 'Building Parent Involvement', *Practitioner*, 20/5 (May 1994): 1–4.

MACCALLUM, GERALD C., JR., 'Negative and Positive Freedom', in David Miller (ed.), *Liberty*, Oxford: Oxford University Press, 1991: 100–22.

MACEDO, STEPHEN, 'Community, Diversity, and Civic Education: Toward a Liberal Political Science of Group Life', *Social Philosophy and Policy*, 13/2 (1996): 240–68.

—— 'Liberal Civic Education and Religious Fundamentalism: The Case of God v. John Rawls?', *Ethics*, 105/3 (Apr. 1995): 468–96.

—— *Liberal Virtues*, Oxford: Oxford University Press, 1990.

MACLURE, J. STUART, *Educational Documents*, London: Methuen and Co. Ltd, 1973.

MARSHALL, RAY, and MARC TUCKER, *Thinking for a Living: Education and the Wealth of Nations*, New York: Basic Books, 1992.

MASON, ANDREW, 'Personal Autonomy and Identification with a Community', in David Milligan and William Watts Miller (eds.), *Liberalism, Citizenship, and Autonomy*, Aldershot: Avebury, 1992: 171–86.

MCLAUGHLIN, T. H., 'Liberalism, Education, and the Common School', *Journal of Philosophy of Education*, 29/2 (1995): 239–55.

—— 'Parental Rights and the Religious Upbringing of Children', *Journal of Philosophy of Education*, 18/1 (1984): 75–82.

—— 'Peter Gardner on Religious Upbringing and the Liberal Ideal of Religious Autonomy', *Journal of Philosophy of Education*, 24/1 (1990): 107–25.

MEYERS, DIANA T., *Self, Society, and Personal Choice*, New York: Columbia University Press, 1989.

MILL, JOHN STUART, *On Liberty*, Harmondsworth: Penguin Books, 1974 (1st pub. 1859).

MILLER, DAVID, ' "Autonomous" v. "Autarchic" Persons', review of Stanley I. Benn, *A Theory of Freedom*, *Government and Opposition*, 24 (1989): 244–8.

—— (ed.), *Liberty*, Oxford: Oxford University Press, 1991.

—— *On Nationality*, Oxford: Oxford University Press, 1995.

MILLER, PATRICIA H., *Theories of Developmental Psychology*, 3rd edn., New York: W. H. Freeman, 1993.

MILLIGAN, DAVID, and WILLIAM WATTS MILLER (eds.), *Liberalism, Citizenship, and Autonomy*, Aldershot: Avebury, 1992.

MOORE, DONALD, and SUZANNE DAVENPORT, *The New Improved Sorting Machine*, Madison, Wisc.: National Center for Effective Secondary Schools, 1989.

MORROW, ROBERT D., 'The Challenge of Southeast Asian Parental Involvement', *Principal*, 70/3 (1991): 20–2.

MORTIMER, EDWARD, 'A Tale of Two Cultures', *Financial Times*, 5 Mar. 1997: 24.

MORUZZI, NORMA CLAIRE, 'A Problem with Headscarves: Contemporary Complexities of Political and Social Identity', *Political Theory*, 22 (1994): 653–72.

'Muslim Pupils Will Take Off Scarves In Class', *Los Angeles Times*, 3 Dec. 1989: A15.

'Muslims Object to School Ban on Headscarves', *Independent*, 15 Jan. 1990: 6.

NAPPI, CHIARA, 'A Tale of Two Systems', *Dissent*, 43/2 (1996): 60–6.

NATIONAL CURRICULUM COUNCIL, *Curriculum Guidance 3*, London: National Curriculum Council, 1990.

—— *Education for Citizenship: Curriculum Guidance 8*, London: National Curriculum Council, 1990.

NIE, NORMAN H., JANE JUNN, and KENNETH STEHLIK-BARRY, *Education and Democratic Citizenship in America*, Chicago: University of Chicago Press, 1996.

OAKES, JEANNIE, *Keeping Track: How Schools Structure Inequality*, New Haven: Yale University Press, 1985.

O'HEAR, ANTHONY, *Education, Society, and Human Nature*, London: Routledge and Kegan Paul, 1981.

O'HEAR, PHILIP, and JOHN WHITE, *A National Curriculum for All: Laying the Foundations for Success* (Education and Training Paper No. 6), London: IPPR, 1992.

ORFIELD, GARY A., 'Do We Know Anything Worth Knowing About Educational Effects of Magnet Schools?', in William H. Clune and John F. Witte (eds.), *Choice and Control in American Education. Volume 2: The Practice of Choice, Decentralization and School Restructuring*, London: Falmer Press, 1990: 119–23.

OSMOND, ROSALIE, *Changing Perspectives: Christian Culture and Morals in England Today*, London: Darton, Longman and Todd, 1993.

OZOUF, MONA, *L'École, l'Église et la République*, Paris: Éditions Cana/Jean Offredo, 1982.

'Parent Power', *Economist*, 25 Mar. 1995: 17.

PARIJS, PHILLIPE VAN, *Real Freedom for All: What (If Anything) Can Justify Capitalism?*, Oxford: Oxford University Press, 1995.

—— 'Why Surfers Should Be Fed: The Liberal Case for Unconditional Basic Income', *Philosophy and Public Affairs*, 20/2 (Spring 1991): 101–33.

PARIS, DAVID C., 'Moral Education and the "Tie That Binds" in Liberal Political Theory', *American Political Science Review*, 85/3 (1991): 875–901.

PARSONS, GERALD (ed.), *The Growth of Religious Diversity: Britain from 1945*, vol. 2, London: Routledge, 1994.

—— 'There and Back Again? Religion and the 1944 and 1988 Education Acts', in Gerald Parsons (ed.), *The Growth of Religious Diversity: Britain from 1945*, vol. 2, London: Routledge, 1994: 161–98.

PETERS, R. S., *Ethics and Education*, London: George Allen and Unwin, 1966.

—— *The Philosophy of Education*, Oxford: Oxford University Press, 1973.

PETERSON, PAUL E., 'Monopoly and Competition in American Education', in William H. Clune and John F. Witte (eds.), *Choice and Control in American Education. Volume 1: The Theory of Choice and Control in Education*, London: Falmer Press, 1990: 47–78.

PIAGET, JEAN, *Judgement and Reasoning in the Child*, trans. Marjorie Warden, New York: Harcourt, Brace, and Co., 1928.

—— *The Psychology of Intelligence*, trans. Malcolm Piercy and D. E. Berlyne, London: Routledge and Kegan Paul, 1950.

Pierce v. Society of Sisters 268 US 510 (1925).

POPPER, KARL, *The Open Society and Its Enemies*, vol. 1, London: Routledge and Kegan Paul, 1952.

POWELL, ARTHUR G., ELEANOR FARRAR, and DAVID K. COHEN, *The Shopping Mall High School: Winners and Losers in the Educational Marketplace*, Boston: Houghton Mifflin, 1985.

PURDY, LAURA M., *In Their Best Interest? The Case against Equal Rights for Children*, Ithaca, NY: Cornell University Press, 1992.

PURPEL, DAVID, and KEVIN RYAN, 'It Comes With The Territory', in David Purpel and Kevin Ryan (eds.), *Moral Education . . . It Comes With The Territory*, Berkeley, Calif.: McCutchan, 1976: 44–54.

——— —— (eds.), *Moral Education . . . It Comes With The Territory*, Berkeley, Calif.: McCutchan, 1976.

RASELL, EDITH, and RICHARD ROTHSTEIN (eds.), *School Choice: Examining the Evidence*, Washington, DC: Economic Policy Institute, 1990.

RAVITCH, DIANE, *National Standards in American Education: A Citizen's Guide*, Washington, DC: Brookings Institution, 1995.

RAWLS, JOHN, 'Justice as Fairness: Political not Metaphysical', *Philosophy and Public Affairs*, 14 (1985): 223–51.

—— *Political Liberalism*, New York: Columbia University Press, 1993.

—— *A Theory of Justice*, Cambridge, Mass.: Harvard University Press, 1971.

RAYWID, MARY ANNE, 'The Case for Student Choice', *Phi Delta Kappa Fastback*, no. 283 (1989): 9–19, 27–32, 36–45.

RAZ, JOSEPH, *The Morality of Freedom*, Oxford: Clarendon Press, 1986.

REAY, DIANE and STEPHEN J. BALL, ' "Spoilt for Choice": The Working Classes and Educational Markets', *Oxford Review of Education*, 23/1 (1997): 89–101.

REICH, ROBERT, *Tales of a New America*, New York: Times Books, 1987.

—— *The Work of Nations: Preparing Ourselves for 21st-century Capitalism*, New York: Alfred A. Knopf, 1991.

REIMER, EVERETT, *School is Dead*, Harmondsworth: Penguin Books, 1972.

ROSENBLUM, NANCY (ed.), *Liberalism and the Moral Life*, Cambridge, Mass.: Harvard University Press, 1989.

ROTHSTEIN, RICHARD, 'Introduction', in Edith Rasell and Richard Rothstein (eds.), *School Choice: Examining the Evidence*, Washington, DC: Economic Policy Institute, 1990: 1–25.

ROUSSEAU, JEAN-JACQUES, *Émile*, trans. Barbara Foxley, New York: Dent, 1963 (1st pub. 1762).

RUBINSTEIN, DAVID, and BRIAN SIMON, *The Evolution of the Comprehensive School 1926–1966*, London: Routledge and Kegan Paul, 1969.

RUSHDIE, SALMAN, *Midnight's Children*, New York: Knopf, 1981.

RUTHERFORD, BARRY (ed.), *Creating Family/School Partnerships*, Columbus, Ohio: National Middle School Association, 1995.

'La saga des foulards', *Le Monde*, 13 Oct. 1994: p. v.

SÁNCHEZ-FERRER, LEONARDO, 'Implementation of Educational Policies: The Case of Teaching Staff Reform at the Spanish Universities', paper presented at the Politics of Education Workshop, ECPR Joint Sessions of Workshops, Bordeaux, 27 Apr.–2 May 1995.

SCHNEIDER, BARBARA, and JAMES S. COLEMAN (eds.), *Parents, Their Children, and Schools*, Oxford: Westview Press, 1993.

SCHOEMAN, FERDINAND, 'Rights of Children, Rights of Parents, and the Moral Basis of the Family', *Ethics*, 91/1 (1980): 6–19.

SCHRAG, FRANCIS, *Back to Basics*, San Francisco: Jossey-Bass, 1995.

—— 'From Childhood to Adulthood: Assigning Rights and Responsibilities', in

Kenneth A. Strike and Kieran Egan (eds.), *Ethics and Educational Policy*, London: Routledge and Kegan Paul, 1978: 61–78.

SCOTTO, MARCEL, 'À Strasbourg, Beyhan et ses sœurs ont pu garder le foulard', *Le Monde*, 29 Nov. 1996: 12.

SHAPIRA, RINA and PETER W. COOKSON, JR. (eds.), *Autonomy and Choice in Context: An International Perspective*, Oxford: Pergamon/Elsevier Science Ltd., 1997.

SHAPIRO, IAN and RUSSELL HARDIN (eds.), *Nomos XXXVIII: Political Order*, New York: New York University Press, 1996.

SHER, GEORGE, *Desert*, Princeton: Princeton University Press, 1987.

SHKLAR, JUDITH N., 'The Liberalism of Fear', in Nancy Rosenblum (ed.), *Liberalism and the Moral Life*, Cambridge, Mass.: Harvard University Press, 1989: 21–38.

SHROSBREE, COLIN, *Public Schools and Private Education*, Manchester: Manchester University Press, 1988.

SICHEL, BETTY, *Moral Education: Character, Community, and Ideals*, Philadelphia: Temple University Press, 1988.

SIZER, THEODORE R., *Horace's School: Redesigning the American High School*, Boston: Houghton Mifflin Company, 1992.

SKINNER, QUENTIN, 'The Paradoxes of Political Liberty', in David Miller (ed.), *Liberty*, Oxford: Oxford University Press, 1991: 183–205.

SLAVIN, ROBERT, 'Ability Grouping and Student Achievement in Elementary Schools: A Best-evidence Synthesis', *Review of Educational Research*, 57 (1987): 347–50.

—— 'Ability Grouping and Student Achievement in Secondary Schools: A Best-evidence Synthesis', *Review of Educational Research*, 60 (1990): 471–99.

SMREKAR, CLAIRE, *The Impact of School Choice and Community*, Albany, NY: State University of New York Press, 1996.

SNIDERMAN, PAUL M., RICHARD A. BRODY, and JAMES H. KUKLINSKY, 'Policy Reasoning and Political Values: The Problem of Racial Equality', *American Journal of Political Science*, 28 (1984): 75–94.

SNOOK, I. A. (ed.), *Concepts of Indoctrination*, London: Routledge and Kegan Paul, 1972.

SPRING, JOEL, *Education and the Rise of the Corporate State*, Boston: Beacon Press, 1971.

STEINER, DAVID M., *Rethinking Democratic Education: The Politics of Reform*, Baltimore, Md.: Johns Hopkins University Press, 1994.

STOLZENBERG, NOMI MAYA, ' "He Drew a Circle That Shut Me Out": Assimilation, Indoctrination, and the Paradox of a Liberal Education', *Harvard Law Review*, 106/3 (1993): 581–667.

STRIKE, KENNETH A., *Educational Policy and the Just Society*, Chicago: University of Illinois Press, 1982.

—— and KIERAN EGAN (eds.), *Ethics and Educational Policy*, London: Routledge and Kegan Paul, 1978.

SWEETMAN, JIM, *Curriculum Confidential Two: The Complete Guide to the National Curriculum*, Tamworth, Staffs.: Bracken Press, 1992.

TAMIR, YAEL, 'Whose Education Is It Anyway?', *Journal of Philosophy of Education*, 24/2 (1990): 161–70.

TARRANT, JAMES, *Democracy and Education*, Aldershot: Gower Publishing Company, 1989.

TAYLOR, GABRIELLE, *Pride, Shame, Guilt*, Oxford: Clarendon Press, 1985.

THATCHER, MARGARET, *The Downing Street Years*, London: HarperCollins, 1993.

TIZARD, BARBARA, *et al.*, *Young Children at School in the Inner City*, London: Lawrence Erlbaum, 1988.

—— JO MORTIMORE, and BEBB BURCHELL, 'Involving Parents from Minority Groups', in John Bastiani (ed.), *Parents and Teachers 2: From Policy to Practice*, Windsor: NFER-Nelson, 1988: 72–83.

TIZARD, JACK, W. N. SCHOFIELD, and J. HEWISON, 'Symposium: Reading—Collaboration between Teachers and Parents in Assisting Children's Reading', *British Journal of Educational Psychology*, 52/1 (1982): 1–15.

TOMLINSON, SALLY, 'Diversity, Choice, and Ethnicity: The Effects of Educational Markets on Ethnic Minorities', *Oxford Review of Education*, 23/1 (1997): 63–76.

'Le tribunal de Strasbourg annule l'exclusion de dix-huit jeunes filles voilées', *Le Monde*, 5 May 1995: 12.

VIORST, MILTON, 'The Muslims of France', *Foreign Affairs*, 75/5 (1996): 78–96.

Vive La République 1792–1992, Paris: Archives Nationales, 1992.

WALDRON, JEREMY, 'Multiculturalism and Mélange', in Robert K. Fullinwider (ed.), *Public Education in a Multicultural Society*, Cambridge: Cambridge University Press, 1996: 90–118.

WALSH, MARK, 'Study Credits Choice With Raising Test Scores', *Education Week*, 17/25 (4 Mar. 1998): 14.

WALZER, MICHAEL, *The Company of Critics*, London: Peter Halban, 1989.

WEBER, EUGEN, *Peasants into Frenchmen*, London: Chatto and Windus, 1979.

WELLS, AMY STUART, 'African-American Students' View of School Choice', in Bruce Fuller and Richard F. Elmore (eds.), *Who Chooses? Who Loses? Culture, Institutions, and the Unequal Effects of School Choice*, New York: Teachers College Press, 1996: 25–49.

—— 'Public School Choice: Issues and Concerns for Urban Educators' (ERIC/CUE Digest no. 63), New York: ERIC Clearinghouse on Urban Education, n.d.

—— 'The Sociology of School Choice', in Edith Rasell and Richard Rothstein (eds.), *School Choice: Examining the Evidence*, Washington, DC: Economic Policy Institute, 1990: 29–48.

—— and STUART BIEGEL, 'Public Funds for Private Schools: Political and First Amendment Considerations', *American Journal of Education*, 101/3 (May 1993): 209–33.

WELTER, RUSH (ed.), *American Writings on Popular Education: The Nineteenth Century*, New York: Bobbs-Merrill, 1971.

West Virginia State Board of Education v. *Barnette* 319 US 624 (1943).

WHEELOCK, ANNE, *Crossing the Tracks: How 'Untracking' Can Save America's Schools*, New York: New Books, 1992.

WHITE, JOHN, *Education and the Good Life: Beyond the National Curriculum*, London: Kogan Page, 1990.

—— 'Education and the Limits of the Market', in David Bridges and Terence H. McLaughlin (eds.), *Education and the Market Place*, London: Falmer Press, 1994: 117–25.

WHITE, PATRICIA, *Civic Virtues and Public Schooling: Educating Citizens for a Democratic Society*, London: Teachers College Press, 1996.

WIDLAKE, PAUL, and FLORA MACLEOD, *Raising Standards: Parental Involvement Programmes and the Language Performance of Children*, Coventry: Community Education Development Centre, 1984.

WILLMS, J. DOUGLAS, 'Catholic-School Effects on Academic Achievement: New Evidence from the High School and Beyond Follow-up Study', *Sociology of Education*, 58/2 (Apr. 1985): 98–114.

—— and FRANK H. ECHOLS, 'The Scottish Experience of Parental School Choice', in Edith Rasell and Richard Rothstein (eds.), *School Choice: Examining the Evidence*, Washington, DC: Economic Policy Institute, 1990: 49–68.

WILSON, JOHN, 'Indoctrination and Rationality', in I. A. Snook (ed.), *Concepts of Indoctrination*, London: Routledge and Kegan Paul, 1972: 17–24.

WISCONSIN DEPARTMENT OF PUBLIC INSTRUCTION, *Families and Education: An Educator's Resource for Family Involvement*, Madison, Wisc.: Wisconsin Department of Public Instruction, 1991.

Wisconsin v. *Yoder* 406 US 205 (1972).

WITTE, JOHN F., *Choice in American Education*, Charleston, WV: Policy and Planning Center, Appalachia Educational Laboratory and Madison, Wisc.: Institute of Public Affairs, 1990.

—— 'The Milwaukee Parental Choice Program', in Edith Rasell and Richard Rothstein (eds.), *School Choice: Examining the Evidence*, Washington, DC: Economic Policy Institute, 1990: 69–109.

—— 'Who Benefits from the Milwaukee Choice Program?', in Bruce Fuller and Richard F. Elmore (eds.), *Who Chooses? Who Loses? Culture, Institutions, and the Unequal Effects of School Choice*, New York: Teachers College Press, 1996: 118–37.

WOLFFE, JOHN, ' "And There's Another Country . . .": Religion, the State, and British Identities', in Gerald Parsons (ed.), *The Growth of Religious Diversity: Britain from 1945*, vol. 2, London: Routledge, 1994: 85–121.

WOLFINGER, RAYMOND E., and STEVEN J. ROSENSTONE, *Who Votes?*, New Haven: Yale University Press, 1980.

WOODHOUSE, BARBARA BENNETT, ' "Who Owns the Child?": *Meyer* and *Pierce* and the Child as Property', *William and Mary Law Review*, 33/4 (1992): 995–1122.

WOODS, PHILIP A., CARL BAGLEY, and RON GLATTER, *School Choice and Competition: Markets in the Public Interest?*, London: Routledge, 1998: 124–32.

WRINGE, COLIN, 'Markets, Values and Education', in David Bridges and Terence H. McLaughlin (eds.), *Education and the Market Place*, London: Falmer Press, 1994: 105–16.

Young, Iris Marion, *Justice and the Politics of Difference*, Princeton: Princeton University Press, 1990.

Young, Michael F. D. (ed.), *Knowledge and Control*, London: Collier-Macmillan Publishers, 1971.

Young, Timothy, and Evans Clinchy, *Choice in Public Education*, New York: Teachers College Press, 1992.

INDEX